Voice of the Marketplace

NUMBER THIRTEEN
Kenneth E. Montague Series
in Oil and Business History
Joseph A. Pratt, General Editor

Voice of the Marketplace

A HISTORY OF THE NATIONAL PETROLEUM COUNCIL

by Joseph A. Pratt, William H. Becker,
& William M. McClenahan, Jr.

Introduction by Daniel Yergin

Texas A&M University Press : College Station

Library of Congress Cataloging-in-Publication Data

Pratt, Joseph A.
    Voice of the marketplace : a history of the National Petroleum
Council / by Joseph A. Pratt, William H. Becker, William M.
McClenahan, Jr.
        p. cm. — (Kenneth E. Montague series in oil and business
history ; no. 13)
    Includes index.
    ISBN 1-58544-185-6 (cloth : alk. paper)
    1. National Petroleum Council—History.   2. Petroleum
industry and trade—Goverment policy—United States—
History.   3. Gas industry—Government policy—United States—
History.   4. Energy policy—United States History.
5. Environmental policy—United States—History.   6. Energy
advisory committees—United States—History.   7. Executive
Advisory bodies—United States—History   8. National security—
United States.   I. Becker, William H.   II. McClenahan,
William M.   III. Title.   IV. Series.
HD9566.P68   2002
338.2'728'097309045—dc21   2001006995

Contents

Acknowledgments

The authors would like to thank Marshall Nichols, Executive Director of the National Petroleum Council; John Guy, Deputy Executive Director; and their staff for help in completing this history. John and Marshall shared their own experiences. They also made available the records of the National Petroleum Council while introducing the authors to numerous participants in NPC studies. Especially useful were the interviews with Collis Chandler, James Winfrey, Bill Finger, Larry Smith, Bill White, James Schlesinger, Larry Fuller, Dennis Hendrix, and Joe B. Foster. Bruce Beaubouef shared with us his research on the history of the Strategic Petroleum Reserve.

INTRODUCTION

Good Advice on Vital Issues

The National Petroleum Council (NPC) was established in the middle of the twentieth century in order to ensure that there would be sufficient energy to meet the future needs of America's economy and its national security. The experience of World War II was much in the minds of the NPC's founders. They wanted to continue the industry-government cooperation that had contributed to victory during the war.

A half-century later, at the beginning of the twenty-first century, the U.S. government once again asked the council to focus on important issues of oil, natural gas, and war. But the cold war that dominated much of its work was over, and the specter of economic disruption seemed to have receded. Instead, in this pervasive information age a new focus emerged on the threat of cyberwar—the new vulnerabilities that are emerging and what such war might do to the vast energy infrastructure on which the nation depends. The context has changed, but the basic objective remains—to ensure the supplies of oil and gas our economy requires. The study began in 1999. The final report, *Securing Oil and Natural Gas Infrastructures in the New Economy,* issued in June 2001, set out to explore the new critical infrastructure protection challenges. It developed a series of timely recommendations. Three months later, terrorists used hijacked passenger planes to attack the World Trade Center in New York City and the Pentagon. Infrastructure security, including that of the energy industry, was turned into a central and urgent national issue overnight. The council's study provided the framework to help address these questions.

This arc underlines the strategic importance of oil and natural gas to the position of the United States in the world community and their bedrock importance to the modern American economy. It helps us understand the unique role of the National Petroleum Council, which is the subject of this important new book, for the history of the NPC embodies a half-century of the American oil and gas industry and its place in our national life. During this time we have seen the industry make an extraordinary contribution to the growth and standard of living of our country and to its security, and it has demonstrated a continuing commitment to technological progress, to environmental quality, and to serving the public. At the same time the oil and gas industry has been caught up in controversy and conflict, muddle and confusion.

This volume brings into sharp focus the forces and themes that have shaped the contemporary industry, as well as the issues that will be critical to its future. This is an important contribution. Often what seems "new" in fact has a long lineage, and understanding that lineage can improve our understanding and capability to deal with current issues and anticipate new demands.

THE NATIONAL SECURITY IMPERATIVE

To those who founded the National Petroleum Council, the strategic importance of oil needed no argument. While World War II had not been an "oil war," oil was a critical dimension. One of the most powerful discoveries for me in writing *The Prize* was to find what was often lost to the footnotes—how central oil had been to the war's origins, conduct, and outcome. Indeed, it had been a war for mobility.

In the Pacific the specific objective of Japanese expansion was the oil supplies of East Asia. When the Japanese invaded Vietnam in the summer of 1941, the United States put an oil embargo in place. Some months later came the attack on Pearl Harbor. Ironically enough, if on that fateful Sunday morning in December, 1941, the Japanese planes had come back for a third run and had destroyed the U.S. Navy's oil tanks, the Pacific War—in the considered judgment of Adm. Chester Nimitz—might well have gone on two years longer. Thereafter, once the war began, much U.S. strategy was aimed at cutting Japan's oil lines and immobilizing its fleet and aircraft.

In Europe when Hitler invaded the Soviet Union, one of his major objectives was the oil fields at Baku, around the Caspian Sea. Again and again German mobility was compromised by lack of oil. General Rommel's offensive in North Africa was halted by lack of oil. ("Shortage of petrol," the general wrote in his diary. "It's enough to make one weep.") When finally Germany's jet fighters were ready to take to the air, they had to be dragged out onto the runways by oxen.

For their part, the Germans tried to use U-boats to sink tankers and thus cut the Allied oil line across the Atlantic that linked the new world with the old. They came close, but they failed. As it turned out, the U.S. oil industry was one of the mainsprings of Allied victory.

There was tremendous cooperation and unity between the government and business. The government's Petroleum Administration for War worked closely with the Petroleum Industry War Council, composed of leaders from the American oil industry. This team did an outstanding job. It mobilized supply and developed an unprecedented cooperative spirit. It brought technology to bear rapidly, with great positive effect. Crude oil output in the United States increased by 30 percent. Among the most brilliant technological innovations was the rapid development and deployment of 100-octane aviation gasoline, which proved to be critical in the Battle of Britain and thereafter.

Altogether, of the 7 billion barrels of oil that the Allies used in World War II, 6 billion were produced in the United States. Out of all of this came powerful lessons in the capability and significance of the industry and in the importance of cooperation between government and industry.

These considerations were much in the minds of U.S. officials when in May, 1946, President Harry Truman instructed Interior Secretary Julius Krug to establish the National Petroleum Council as successor to the Petroleum Industry War Council. The president's objective was to continue "close and harmonious relations between government and industry." The role of the new council would be to "consult and advise" with the Interior Department secretary. The focus shifted to the secretary of energy when that department was established in 1977, but the role remains the same—to "consult and advise."

The council's first meeting was held on June 21, 1946. The chairman summed up the purpose of the new organization rather simply. It was, he said, to "get back on the beam," by which he meant continuing the kind of cooperation that had proved so critical and productive during World War II.

"LEARN AS YOU GO ALONG"

The NPC membership, appointed by the secretary, represents the diverse sectors of the oil, natural gas, and related industries. With time it has come to draw on a wider community—from service and technology industries, from consumer and environmental groups, and from consulting, finance, university and research groups. The NPC's essential function is to provide informed advice to the secretary of energy. The council provides a forum for continuing dialogue on issues critical to the industry and the country. In serving its role it undertakes studies that draw upon the expertise, knowledge, and data—and people—from companies and other institutions. Over its first half-century the NPC has conducted more than two hundred studies.

As the council entered its second half-century, council chairman H. Laurance Fuller asked his predecessor, Ray Hunt, to lead a fiftieth anniversary committee. That committee determined that it would be timely and valuable to examine the council's work in historical perspective in order to assess its contribution, identify key issues, highlight trends, and draw lessons for the future. Such a study would help decision-makers in both government and industry, as well as the public and specialists, to understand how the council's process has worked and would prove beneficial to anyone concerned with energy policy making in the future, whether in government or the private sector. It would provide both a context and a framework for those in government confronting—or anticipating—future crises and critical issues.

The council's work also serves as a useful model for cooperation between government and industry and for helping government to be more informed. In short, the work of the council can be seen—and rightly so—as a process of national learning. Often events and developments outrun thinking and understanding—as well as regulation and existing legislation. One of the council's main missions is to close that gap. It is an iterative process. As one secretary of the interior told the council, "You kind of learn as you go along." Thus this history should be conceived as a council study in the same tradition—in this case learning about the council's learning process.

At the heart of this process is the mobilization of the knowledge and experience of experts from within the petroleum industry. The procedure begins with an official request for a study from the secretary of energy. The council's Agenda Committee considers the matter and makes its recommendation to the council as a whole, which then accepts or rejects the request. If approved, the NPC chair, with advice of the council's Appointment Committee and approval of the secretary of energy, appoints a representative group of council members to a temporary working committee. This group creates an organizational structure within which to conduct the study.

This study committee draws on experts from within the membership of the council and has the power to create subcommittees as needed to complete its study. These subcommittees and the task groups they create call on the expertise of technical specialists from within the petroleum industry, as well as experts drawn from other industries, universities, and consulting firms. On important studies the knowledge of hundreds of specialists can be brought together quickly and efficiently through this committee system. Findings are debated within the subcommittees and in the study committee as a whole, giving these experts a chance to come together and build a consensus on the critical issues raised in their study.

To ensure accountability to the public, the Department of Energy (DOE) appoints a representative to each study committee. Most meetings of the NPC and its committees are open to the public, and action is taken by a majority of members in attendance. Verbatim transcripts of all council and committee meetings and detailed minutes of subcommittee and task group meetings are available for public inspection.

Once the data have been collected and analyzed, the study committee completes a draft report that is presented to the council as a whole for consideration. If approved, the draft is formally transmitted to the secretary of energy as a report of the NPC. These data-rich reports generally are presented in a straightforward style accessible to general readers. They offer useful information about vital issues and concrete recommendations for public-policy makers. All reports are available to the public and are widely distributed.

Compiled from data drawn from deep within the energy industries, these reports are the primary "products" of the NPC, whose essential mission is "good advice." Its reports avoid, in the authors' words, "aggressive lobbying." They are not advocacy. Instead, "like Joe Friday," the reports are "concerned with 'just the facts,'" and the reports have allowed "their hard-won facts to speak for themselves." Throughout the course of my participation on the NPC, I have seen this dedication to fundamental research, careful analysis, and the elucidation and clarification of complex issues.

In selecting Professors Pratt, Becker, and McClenahan to write its history, the council made a wise choice. As distinguished historians of the petroleum industry, business-government relations, and regulation, they bring to the task expertise, objectivity, and independent judgment.

In carrying out this study the authors worked with Marshall Nichols, the council's executive director; John Guy, deputy executive director; the staff of the NPC; and present and past participants in the work of the council. Their history came to focus on a number of key questions:

• What has been the impact of the NPC in the context of the times that its advice was sought?
• How has it contributed to the security and the well-being of the United States?

- How good has its process been at identifying and elucidating—and anticipating—critical issues?
- To what degree has it contributed to a clearer analysis of America's energy position and to risks?
- How productive—and how stressed—has been the relation between business and government, and how can those relations be improved in the future?

In considering the course of the council's work, one is struck by the dramatic growth of scale. In 1946, when the council was founded, U.S. oil consumption was 4.9 million barrels per day (MMB/D). Total world production was about 8 MMB/D, of which the United States was responsible for more than 60 percent. Not only did the U.S. industry meet the entire domestic demand, but it was also the leading exporter. Today world production is about 75 MMB/D, and the United States is responsible for just 11 percent. U.S. consumption is 19.5 MMB/D. Domestic U.S. production is 8.1 MMB/D, and net imports meet more than 55 percent of domestic demand. While world production has become much more diversified, the Middle East continues to hold 65 percent of proven reserves.

Natural gas consumption in 1946 was less than 4 trillion cubic feet (TCF). Today it is more than 20 TCF, 90 percent of which is met by domestic production, and it is the fuel of choice for new electric power generation. The offshore oil and natural gas industry had not even been born in 1946. Today nearly 30 percent of U.S. oil production and 25 percent of natural gas come from the Gulf of Mexico, whose deep waters constitute one of the industry's great new frontiers.

That much has changed is clear by glancing at the headlines from the day in May, 1946, when the council first convened: "Stalin Orders Stricter Discipline in Army to Increase Its Might"; "Big Four Divided over German Reparations." There was some technological forecasting: "Preview of Television Given: 8000 to 10,0000 Sets by Year-End Seen." Controversy over the judiciary was not new: "Two Senators Offer Plan to Oust Four Justices off the Supreme Court." And inflation was a concern: "Cost of Dining Out Rising." Tuna-fish sandwiches went from 30¢ to 35¢, shrimp cocktails from 35¢ to 50¢, and beef stew from 75¢ to $1.05. Alas, I could not find a price for premium bottled water. (Today a gallon of nationally advertised bottled water sells for $7, as compared to a recent price of $1.25 for a gallon of gasoline.)

In May, 1946, the first cold war crisis, which happened to be about Iran and oil, was in the process of being resolved, and the secretary of the navy had just informed the secretary of state that oil was "a hot subject." What was not in the headlines that month was that the first tanker of Kuwaiti oil was being loaded for shipment out of the Persian Gulf, pointing to what would be continuing controversy over the levels of imported oil. Imports would be a continuing, contentious, and divisive issue for the council, for the entire industry, and for the U.S. government. The cold war was only just beginning.

The cold war is now over. Much of the world is moving away, as Joseph Stanislaw and I observe in *The Commanding Heights,* from state control toward greater confidence in markets and toward borders much more open to trade and foreign investment. Around the world the seemingly ever-more-intense governmental control over oil and natural gas began to reverse in the 1980s. The growing movement toward deregulation and privatization has shifted decision making back to the marketplace, creating unthought-of opportunities and unleashing competitive dynamics that could not have been easily anticipated. Very recently, movement can be observed in the opposite direction. As already noted, the recent NPC study on cyberwarfare also pointed to a new focus on the security of the industry's infrastructure—a concern that loomed very large after the September 11 attacks. This is likely to be one of the council's preoccupations in the years ahead, for it is very well-suited to serve as an ongoing working group to address these issues.

THE CONTINUING THEMES

As the authors demonstrate, certain themes have dominated the work of the council. As befits its origins, the first and most obvious theme centers on national security, emergency preparedness, and crisis management. The luxury of time is usually not available in a crisis. Therefore, the prepositioning of knowledge and the establishment of channels of communications are critical to meeting sudden emergencies. This has consistently been the case with oil. The first test for the NPC was the Korean War. Subsequent crises have all involved the Middle East—the 1956 Suez Crisis, the 1967 Six-Day War, the 1973 Yom Kippur War, the 1979 Iranian Revolution, the 1990–91 Gulf Crisis. Each has portended a sudden disruption in supply. The council did a great deal to lay the basis for the establishment of the Strategic Petroleum Reserve. The success in preventing panic in the oil market during the Gulf Crisis can be attributed in part to the learning process that the council had helped to advance.

For many years natural gas was a highly regulated industry. But as deregulation proceeded, the NPC began to focus on the potential for natural gas. In 1992 one of its landmark studies, *The Potential for Natural Gas,* captured the shift from a "shortage" view of natural gas to one that saw it as a clean, abundant resource that could meet new energy needs in an environmental age. This was particularly timely as technological and commercial innovation reopened to gas an electric power industry that had been shut off by the regulatory-enforced "shortages" of the 1970s. The process of this study, as much as its results, changed the outlook and perspective of many in the industry. A follow-on study, *Meeting the Challenges of the Nation's Growing Natural Gas Demand,* in 1999 further explored the changing circumstances in both supply and demand. It is striking to consider that, while natural gas was prohibited from new electric power generation not so many years ago, today some 90 percent of new generation in the United States is slated to be based on natural gas.

A third major theme in the book is the impact of environmentalism. Environmental considerations arise at every stage of the oil and gas industry— from production and transmission through manufacturing and consumption. The authors demonstrate that the passage of the Clean Air Act in 1970 was a turning point for the industry. The environmental advance by this industry, in cooperation with others, such as the auto industry, has been enormous. A new car today puts out only 5 percent of the pollution of a new car in 1970.

The integration of environmental considerations into the operations of the industry has been a continuing focus for NPC studies. One of the council's contributions has been to bring forward the practical, real-world considerations of implementation in order to help ensure that environmental objectives are met in an efficient and timely manner, allowing maximum scope for innovation and technological progress and minimizing unnecessary burdens and costs. The industry has demonstrated again and again that it can meet new objectives and also that it can do its job best if the rules are rational, fact-based, and consistent. A theme running through the many studies is a preference for overarching objectives that encourage ingenuity over a highly prescriptive, command-and-control approach. As a *Future Issues* study expressed the matter in 1995, government policy would do well to move from its traditional "command control" approach toward a "more flexible, goal-based regulation" that "provides incentives to solve problems more innovatively and cost-effectively."

The industry suffers from stereotypes that go back to the nineteenth century. In fact, in many aspects it is a high-tech industry. It has one of the highest concentrations of advanced scientific and technological degrees of any industry in the country and is the number one industry in terms of providing further education to its personnel. It continues to push its technological frontiers. Just as it applies these talents to solving the problems of energy supply for consumers, so it applies these talents—as evidenced in the work of the council—to addressing the emerging environmental questions.

This narrative is practical. It provides a way to learn from history in order to improve decision making for the future. Energy is an important part of our economy in its own right. It is also central to critical issues for the future—whether they be enhancing the environment, protecting our economy, ensuring national security, or adapting to the advent of cyberspace. In short, getting things right is worth a lot. The record shows that the National Petroleum Council not only provides access to wide-ranging expertise and knowledge but also delivers what the authors call "the view of the marketplace." By bringing thinking and understanding forward it counteracts tendencies toward suspicion and miscommunication and confrontation—all of which have been abundant during the council's first half-century.

When government fails to understand how markets work, or tries to circumvent their workings, or ignores burdens and costs, the results are usually poor. The damage to one of the nation's leading industries can be lasting. This is something that continually needs to be remembered in our nation's regulatory processes. The council's process in its first half-century has served the interests of the American people. One of the lasting lessons of this book is that there is a lot to be said for what the council is all about—good advice, delivered in a timely way. The story of the council demonstrates one effective—and now time-tested—way to get such advice. Events and evident risks continue to underscore why the council will be needed in the future.

Daniel Yergin
Washington, D.C.

Voice of the Marketplace

CHAPTER 1

The Organization of the National Petroleum Council

THE NATIONAL PETROLEUM COUNCIL (NPC) emerged out of close cooperation between the petroleum industry and the federal government during World War II. To extend this cooperation after the war, in 1946 President Harry Truman requested the secretary of the interior to create an advisory committee to advise, inform, and make recommendations to the Department of the Interior (DOI) on petroleum-related issues. The NPC emerged as a federally chartered but industry-financed organization. Staffed by prominent representatives from all phases of the petroleum business, the NPC could reach deep within the industry for information on vital issues. In the years since 1946 the council has responded to requests from the DOI—and the Department of Energy (DOE) after its creation in 1977—by preparing timely, authoritative reports for the executive branch (see appendix A). These reports have consistently presented the voice of the marketplace, providing government officials with useful information about existing conditions in the petroleum industry and the potential impacts of government policies on the supply and demand for energy.[1]

More than a half-century has passed since the creation of the National Petroleum Council. In that time the council has proved its staying power amid astonishing changes in the petroleum industry. Skyrocketing world demand has pushed the industry around the world in search of new supplies.

Technological advances have allowed this search to move into harsh environments previously considered off limits. The rise of the Organization of Petroleum Exporting Countries (OPEC) has brought fundamental changes in international pricing, and the growth of national oil companies has introduced new competition. Far-reaching regulatory initiatives, ranging from strict environmental standards to the regulation and then the deregulation of natural gas, have transformed the legal rules within which the industry operates. The fall of communism has opened vast new opportunities and risks for the international petroleum industry, as has the rise of the internet and e-business. But through all of these changes the National Petroleum Council has remained a reliable source of authoritative information about its industry.

The council's resilience flowed from a series of good choices made by its founders and reinforced by later leaders, who created a unique advisory committee. The decision to make the council self-financing proved particularly important, since it helped ensure the NPC's independence. Instead of relying on government financing, the NPC paid its own way by using voluntary contributions from members to cover operating costs. Much more important were contributions of time by the industry specialists who undertook the council's studies while being paid by their companies. This approach to mobilizing the resources and personnel of the industry has enabled the NPC to complete more than two hundred reports. It also has assured the council an independent voice on often-controversial issues of great import to the petroleum industry and the nation.

The council has been one of the few organizations capable of encompassing the varied viewpoints within a diverse, highly competitive industry. The sharpest historical division within the petroleum industry has been between the "majors" and the "independents," and the NPC has worked hard to close this gap by including representatives of both groups on major studies and by regularly rotating the organization's chairmanship between the two camps. The petroleum industry also has long been divided into a competitive oil industry and a regulated natural gas industry, and the NPC has included representatives from both. In recent decades the council has adapted to the changes brought by the deregulation of natural gas by expanding its representation of this sector of the industry and by naming in 1996 its first chairman from the gas side, Dennis R. Hendrix. In recent decades the council has added members from various industry "stakeholders"—that is, groups such as consumers and environmentalists that are directly affected by the operations of the petroleum industry. The diversity of its membership has made the NPC an unusual forum for the study of energy-related issues.

The study process has tapped this diversity to examine conditions using data drawn from deep within the industry. After a letter from the DOI or the DOE requesting a study has been approved by the NPC's Agenda Committee and then by the council as a whole, a study group begins its work under the direction of a general committee drawn from the NPC's membership and including representatives from government. Studies usually require the creation of subcommittees and task groups composed of industry specialists who bring their expertise to bear on specified sections of the report. After the collection of data, task group reports are drafted and revised by industry participants before being consolidated into a proposed final report for approval by the council as a whole. This sort of organization and study process has allowed the NPC to complete timely, yet detailed reports on conditions within the industry.

In this way the NPC has been able to reflect the marketplace and give voice to the industry. Its reports are not theoretical treatments of the market, but rather reports from the front, showing how real world markets are being shaped by competition, regulation, technological change, and international pressures. For more than fifty years these reports have collected, interpreted, and conveyed to government policy makers accurate data on conditions affecting the supply and demand for energy.

From its earliest years the council has published the results of its studies in authoritative, data-rich reports presented in a dispassionate, detached tone (see appendixes B and C for titles of reports). Although the council has self-consciously avoided overt lobbying, its critics have characterized its work as the self-pleading of the oil industry. Indeed, the council's reports generally have reflected the worldview and values of its membership. This could hardly be otherwise, since reports are informed by an intimate knowledge of the inner workings of market forces. Even so, serving as a barrier to self-pleading has been the knowledge that the council's legitimacy in the eyes of government officials depends on its hard-won reputation for objectivity.

The NPC has been shaped by its dynamic relationship with the Department of the Interior and then, after 1977, the Department of Energy. The two federal departments to which the NPC has been linked determined the issues brought before the council. Military and economic security, the availability of an adequate supply of domestic energy, and the smooth operations of the oil and gas industries have remained dominant concerns of the DOI and the DOE. The NPC has had only indirect ties to other federal agencies focused on different aspects of oil and gas policy—notably, the State Department on diplomatic issues, the Environmental Protection Agency on pollution-related issues raised by the use of hydrocarbons, and the Federal Power Commission and, after 1977, the Federal Energy Regulatory Commission on the supply and price of natural gas. Although NPC reports have at times proved useful to other federal agencies, their timing, focus, and tone have generally reflected the concerns of the DOI and the DOE.

These two departments have not, of course, been immune to broad changes in the political environment, and their requests to the NPC have reflected the rise of new concerns within the body politic. The emphasis on preparedness in the early reports of the council came at a time when American society faced the threat of both conventional and nuclear wars at the height of the cold war. Beginning in the late 1960s the environmental movement shaped numerous requests by the DOI to the NPC; energy shortages spawned demands for a study discovering ways to insulate the United States from disruptions of imported oil supplies; and the deregulation of natural gas gave rise to the need for better information about the emerging market in this industry. In all of these cases the council contributed to the national debate on vital policy issues by responding to DOI and DOE requests for studies on matters of pressing political concern to the society at large.

One political concern that has remained constant has been antitrust, which has posed a continuing problem for an advisory committee reliant on industrywide cooperation in preparing its reports. The NPC's operations and reports have also been influenced by the antitrust climate created by the Department of Justice, several key congressional committees, and the recurring political skepticism about "Big Oil." From the moment of its creation the NPC has worked under the spotlight of public scrutiny, and its work has gone forward within rules shaped by the American tradition of strong antitrust laws. Overall, however, the careful consideration of implications of antitrust in the definitions of issues covered by reports has minimized problems. The NPC also has sought legitimacy by conducting its affairs openly, making thorough minutes of meetings available to the public, and avoiding lobbying. But in presenting the voice of industry and the market to government, the council inevitably has faced recurring antitrust challenges, and at times it has had to adjust its operating procedures accordingly.

ESTABLISHING THE NATIONAL PETROLEUM COUNCIL

The NPC was born out of the positive cooperative relationship the government and industry had forged through the Petroleum Administration for

War (PAW) and the Petroleum Industry War Council (PIWC) during World War II. The PIWC was a broad-based group of sixty-six petroleum executives working through numerous subcommittees, which linked the industry to the government through the PAW.[2]

President Truman wanted to retain some of the benefits of that relationship after the war. In a letter to Secretary of the Interior Julius A. Krug officially terminating the PAW, the president directed Krug to take steps "to assure coordination in peacetime of the Federal Government's many interests in petroleum, petroleum products and associated hydrocarbons." Truman observed that he had "been impressed with the great contribution of government-industry cooperation to the success of the war petroleum program, and [felt] that the values of such close and harmonious relations between Government and industry should be continued." He went on to suggest to Krug that he "establish an industry organization to consult and advise with you." In regard to the government, Truman instructed the secretary to take "the initiative in obtaining coordination and unification of Federal policy and administration with respect to the functions and activities relating to petroleum carried on by the various departments and agencies." He wanted the secretary of the interior to "serve as the channel of communication between the Federal Government and the petroleum industry, as the liaison agency of the Federal Government in its relations with appropriate State bodies concerned with oil and gas."[3]

The president specifically requested that the secretary keep on Ralph K. Davies, deputy petroleum administrator during the war, to help wind up the business of the PAW and to assist in organizing and launching the new cooperative arrangement with industry. Davies was a highly regarded industry executive who had been a vice president of Standard Oil of California before going to Washington during the war.[4]

Krug moved quickly. On May 6, 1946, three days after Truman's letter, the secretary established an Oil and Gas Division (OGD) in the Department of the Interior. He appointed Davies acting director of the DOI's new OGD and gave the new division responsibility for the "conservation of oil and gas resources . . . and the achievement of petroleum security." To meet these broad goals the new division was to coordinate the oil and gas policies of other federal departments and agencies; serve as the communications channel between the government and the petroleum industry; act as liaison between the federal government and state oil and gas authorities; and coordinate federal technology policies in regard to petroleum and "synthetic hydrocarbon fuels."[5]

The secretary also charged the OGD with responsibility for obtaining information about the industry and acting as a repository for statistics and technical data. The division was to follow technological developments and to keep timely information about the availability of petroleum products to meet current and future needs, something that the American Petroleum Institute (API) had done after World War I. It was this data-gathering responsibility that ultimately convinced some skeptics in Congress to support an industry advisory committee working closely with the Department of the Interior. In congressional testimony Davies made the point that the industry would provide the data and technical information at no cost to the government.[6] Many in the industry agreed that a private organization knowledgeable about the industry could provide such data faster, better, and cheaper than a government agency could.

Antitrust posed a formidable barrier, however, to the creation of an effective advisory committee. Several antitrust cases in the late 1930s remained in the minds of oilmen as they contemplated the continuation of wartime cooperation in the postwar era. The so-called Madison cases of 1936 remained a sharp, unpleasant memory for executives of small and large companies. Late in 1936 a federal grand jury in Madison, Wisconsin, had handed down criminal indictments against twenty-four companies and fifty-six executives. These oilmen had been involved from 1933 to 1935 in legal, cooperative activities fostered by the National Recovery Administration (NRA), a government-sponsored effort to revive the economy. After the Supreme Court declared the NRA unconstitutional in 1935, President Franklin D. Roosevelt and Secretary of the Interior Harold Ickes encouraged oilmen to continue their cooperative efforts. The subsequent trials for violation of the antitrust laws produced criminal convictions for sixteen individuals and thirty companies, as Ickes refused to confirm in court that government had encouraged continued cooperation. These convictions generated enormous ill will; many in the industry referred to them as the "Madison Crucifixion."[7]

A few years after the Madison cases, the Justice Department brought suit against the largest petroleum companies for "shared monopoly" in the so-called Mother Hubbard case. The American Petroleum Institute, twenty-two of the industry's largest companies, and their top executives found themselves accused of creating a monopolistic combination to restrain trade. When war broke out, the government suspended prosecution, but industry fears remained that such cases might return in peacetime.[8]

The promoters of postwar cooperation with government had a hard sell because of industry apprehensions about antitrust. Even those who had escaped previous prosecution were not about to commit themselves to cooperate with the government without explicit understandings with the government about antitrust. Seeking to clear the air on this issue, Interior Secretary Krug in May, 1946, wrote to Atty. Gen. Tom C. Clark for an opinion on the proposed National Petroleum Council.

Clark's prompt reply set guidelines that clearly shaped the NPC's basic mode of operations. The attorney general observed that consultation between industry and government certainly did not violate the antitrust laws. But he wrote that membership on the National Petroleum Council or its committees "cannot be regarded as conferring on the participants any immunity from the antitrust laws." An industry advisory committee, he went on, should confine itself to advice. It should not determine government policies, nor should it be asked to administer government programs. As for how the members of the industry were to work together, he stated that "the authority to consult and advise should not be considered as implying that members of such committees are authorized to get together and reach an agreed position in anticipation of such consultation." He concluded by saying that all groups within the industry should be included in the council's committee work. In other words, comprehensiveness would promote legitimacy.[9]

Thus, the NPC was to play no role in formulating or implementing policy. This was to be a departure from the industry's participation in the Petroleum Industry War Council—a companion to the PAW—which had a role in devising policy during the war. In contrast, the NPC was not to be proactive; Clark emphasized that the council should respond to requests from the DOI, not the other way around. On September 11, 1946, the acting attorney general, James P. McGraney, reinforced the point, noting that anything undertaken before the formal approval by the secretary of the interior or the director of the Oil and Gas Division fell outside the concept of consultation.[10]

The organization of an effective advisory committee was tricky business, given the nation's strong antitrust tradition. Cooperation was essential to collect and analyze data needed by the government, but such cooperation had to be carefully organized to avoid being construed as violating the antitrust laws—for example, in the process of sharing information on price. From the beginning, then, the NPC began walking the fine line separating legal cooperation in the national interest from illegal activities under the nation's antitrust statutes.

With Clark's interpretations on the record, Krug and Davies assembled a list of potential members for the NPC in late May and early June, 1946. In making the list Davies sought to give the new organization added legitimacy by ensuring that "each branch of the industry [was] to be represented, [and] each area in the country [was] to be represented."[11] Secretary Krug appointed eighty-five men to the NPC from the list. Of this number, fifty-five had served on the PIWC and twenty-two were high-level executives from the major integrated oil companies. Others included top managers from independent companies, trade association officials, and a few men drawn from the natural gas transmission industry.[12] These men became the original members of the National Petroleum Council, which was officially established on June 18, 1946 (see appendix D).

Three days after its establishment the NPC held its first meeting. Attending the June 21, 1946, meeting in Washington were fifty-three of its eighty-five members. Davies presided, and he frankly addressed the skepticism he had encountered in both government and the industry about forming the National Petroleum Council. Secretary Krug, the next speaker, sought to allay industry fears by assuring the audience that the NPC and the OGD were not the first steps of an effort to introduce government control over the oil and gas industry. Echoing Davies, he said that improving the working relationship between government and industry was the best way to ensure adequate supplies of oil and gas in the present and in the future.[13]

Krug emphasized the practical aspects of the NPC. In effect, he described a "new way" for business and government to work together. He told the assembled delegates that the council was not going to be merely a paper organization with an impressive list of names on stationery. Its members were going to have to work, but the end result would be worth their efforts. "Together," he concluded, "we can further the public interest, and whether we disagree or not, at least we will know what we are talking about. We will not have, as we had for a long period before the war, two separate armed bands making their own separate plans, concocting their own strategy, frequently with the public being caught in the middle."[14]

After Davies and Krug had their say, the assembled members of the NPC turned to the election of a chairman. They selected Walter S. Hallanan, president of Plymouth Oil Company in Charleston, West Virginia, an independent company he founded in 1923. Hallanan had started his career in journalism. Later he served as West Virginia's tax commissioner, and in 1928 he won a seat in the state senate. Throughout his career he had been active in Republican politics at the state and national levels.[15] Service on the Petroleum Industry War Council during World War II had introduced him to national petroleum policy. That experience began an involvement in developing a cooperative relationship between business and government that lasted for the rest of his life. Until a few months before his death in 1962 he served as chairman of the NPC.[16]

As his first act as chairman Hallanan appointed an organizational committee to define the NPC's responsibilities and procedures.[17] He asked this committee to make a report at the next meeting of the NPC, scheduled for September. The organization committee met on July 9, 1946. It set up working subcommittees to prepare recommendations on the NPC's scope and procedure, its organizational and personnel needs, and the legal issues raised by establishing the NPC. On September 24, 1946, the council as a whole approved the organization committee's recommendations. These recommendations formed the NPC's Articles of Organization, which became the basis for the operation of the council.[18]

Reflecting the continued concern about antitrust, the organization committee devised a mechanism to ensure that discussions in the council took place only after the secretary of the interior or the director of the Oil and Gas Division referred a matter to the NPC. The committee proposed the creation of a standing Agenda Committee to serve as a gatekeeper, evaluating government requests to determine whether they were appropriate, practicable, and unlikely to create antitrust problems. Within the Agenda Committee a small group of NPC members could meet and vigorously debate the merits of a specific request.[19] They could recommend to the NPC as a whole acceptance or rejection of the request, or they could send it back to the DOI with advice for changes that might make approval of the council as a whole more likely. The work of the Agenda Committee prepared the way for efficient consideration by the NPC of government requests, and the council as a whole seldom opposed its recommendations.

UNDER WAY: FIRST REPORTS SHAPE THE
NPC RELATIONSHIP WITH OGD

Only hours after its creation on September 26, 1946, the Agenda Committee turned to the consideration of the first DOI requests for studies. Davies and Krug felt that the NPC needed to move quickly and authoritatively to establish its usefulness, and they submitted to the NPC six different proposals for studies. In responding to these initial requests the NPC began to define its mode of operations and its relationship with DOI, federal and state agencies, and industry groups such as the API. At the same time the dialogue that developed over Davies's first proposal helped shape the OGD's operations and its relationship with the NPC and the petroleum industry as a whole.

By moving quickly in 1946 Davies avoided a period of drift between the dissolution of the PAW and the beginnings of the NPC. He sought to preserve the spirit of cooperation developed during the war. Krug supported Davies in order to solidify the OGD's role as the key federal agency concerned with petroleum.

The new members of the NPC's Agenda Committee, however, would not be rushed. They were deliberative, indeed cautious, in responding to the government's initial proposals. At the meeting on September 26 they referred only three of Davies's six proposals to study committees. The acting chairman of the Agenda Committee, George A. Hill Jr., president of the Houston Oil Company, was reluctant to act on the other, more problematic requests in the absence of a full committee. With some members absent, the newly created Agenda Committee postponed consideration of three of Davies's proposals until December 10, 1946, the date set for a special meeting of the committee in Washington at the NPC's temporary headquarters in the Investment Building, Fifteenth and K Streets.[20] Soon after, the NPC moved to its still-current headquarters in the Commonwealth Building at 1625 K Street.

Davies's requests embraced both narrowly defined and broadly focused studies of issues on which the government needed help. Three of his proposals received the committee's approval on September 26; it approved the fourth after some consideration at a special Agenda Committee meeting on December 10, 1946. These first four studies established precedents for what was to become an enduring type of NPC report: the detailed analysis of conditions in specific sectors of the petroleum industry. They provided basic data needed by the government to examine the ability of the industry to meet a national defense crisis while also allowing the DOI to monitor the general health of a vital industry.

The first such study—a narrowly focused effort—examined the impact of "a shortage of pressure tank cars for the transportation of liquified petroleum gases." Because other industries used these cars too, the government might need to set priorities to meet both industrial and civilian needs.[21] The next approved study focused on "an acute shortage of materials of various kinds needed by the oil and gas industry, particularly materials containing steel, lead and other materials, which is affecting various activities of the industry that are vital to the national welfare."[22] The third request led to the appointment of a committee to study and make recommendations about the "proposed revisions of the regulations implementing the Federal Mineral Leasing Act."[23] The fourth study was an analysis of "present domestic refining capacity for the production of fuels for military aircraft."[24] All four of these studies produced useful data that the government could not have easily obtained without the cooperation of the industry.

In their dialogue over the other two proposals, the NPC and the OGD established important aspects of their relationship. The Agenda Committee postponed consideration of the two requests on September 26 before rejecting them two months later.[25] The first rejected proposal requested the NPC to make a "compilation and analysis of petroleum statistics on a world-wide basis." The council concurred with its Agenda Committee that there was no need to collect data already being assembled for decades by the API and the Bureau of Mines. The second rejected proposal asked the NPC to develop a general statement of an appropriate national oil policy. The Agenda Committee observed that a report adopted by the PIWC near the end of the war constituted a "current document which presents a comprehensive expression of the industry's views on policy." The Agenda Committee opposed taking on such a large and potentially contentious set of issues, and the NPC as a whole agreed and rejected the request.[26]

Max Ball, the new director of the OGD, responded to the rejection of the two requests by asking the NPC to consider two new requests for roughly the same studies. He submitted to the NPC new proposals for the collection of worldwide data on the productive capacity and availability of oil and natural gas, and for the development of a national oil policy. At a meeting of the Agenda Committee on January 20 the rejected studies and the renewed requests were the first topics for discussion. Ball attended the meeting, at which the committee accepted in modified form his request for the collection of statistics, recommending the focus on "the improvement and simplification [of] the methods of assembling and disseminating statistics." The committee added that "the National Petroleum Council should not be the medium for securing estimates of reserves and availability."[27] In rejecting for the second time the request to define a national oil policy, the committee struggled to establish the nature of the issues appropriate for it to address. The Agenda Committee recommended to the council that "instead of the appointment of a general and continuing committee to which special problems may, from time to time, be referred, appropriate special committees to consider such problems as they arise would be appointed in the discretion of the Council on written request submitted to it."[28]

On antitrust grounds the committee strongly opposed an OGD request to create a general, permanent committee on the military's petroleum needs working in secret and exempt "from some of the procedural rules relating to [the NPC's] committees in general."[29] Members of the Agenda Committee adamantly opposed the creation of a permanent secret committee. This proposal, the committee believed, challenged directly the understandings worked out with the Department of Justice in regard to the NPC. It opened the possibility that OGD might ask such a committee to make studies that had not been considered first by the NPC as a whole. The Agenda Committee concluded that "all committees of the Council must report to it and not to the Oil and Gas Division or others."[30] Ultimately the NPC became heavily focused on preparedness studies in its first twenty years, but these studies went forward in open proceedings on terms satisfactory to antitrust officials and to the NPC's membership.

The NPC had a strong predisposition to conduct its business in public and in the open, and it also wanted its mission clearly defined. To avoid possible conflicts, the council at times declined to undertake studies that it deemed the responsibility of others. In the letter of January 14, for example, Ball requested a study of "one of the significant remaining problems in the field of conservation . . . the continued flaring or blowing to the air of natural gas." He requested that the NPC "survey the over-all problem" and "submit such recommendations as are deemed proper for industry, State, or Federal assistance in the problem." The Agenda Committee recommended that the NPC reject the request on the grounds that it fell "within the exclusive jurisdiction of the states." For the NPC to produce such a study "would be going beyond its proper scope" by involving itself in the states' rights issues raised by regulation of offshore oil and gas. The OGD, in the council's opinion, would do better to cooperate with the Interstate Oil Compact Commission.[31]

The Agenda Committee's recommendations demonstrated the council's sensitivity to the competitive structure of the industry. Ball, for example, requested that NPC "create a committee to undertake a survey of the Nation's petroleum transportation from the standpoint of its adequacy to meet national defense and other emergency needs." To avoid the appearance of conflicts of interest, the Agenda Committee recommended that "the various phases of transportation, such as rail, pipeline, truck, tanker and barge . . . be dealt with by separate committees." Confining NPC analyses to highly specific factual issues also minimized the possibility of disputes. "In view of the competitive aspects of these problems," the Agenda Committee said, study "committees should not suggest plans or programs for meeting the nation's security needs but should confine their work to findings of fact."[32]

The initial wariness of 1946–47 gradually gave way to a general pattern of cautious cooperation between the NPC and the OGD. As mutual confidence and understanding grew, cooperation proved easier. By the end of the 1940s a close working relationship had developed between officials at each organization; each helped the other. The OGD turned to the council for assistance in recruiting suitable staff and in defending its budget before Congress. Similarly, the OGD defended the NPC during periodic attempts by Congress and the president to alter the design and operations of industry advisory bodies.

Walter S. Hallanan was the key figure within the NPC in nurturing a solid, businesslike relationship with the OGD. As chairman from 1946 to 1962 he helped the council become an important intermediary between industry and government. Hallanan was known for his tact and patience, and he had the ability to stay focused on the big picture. As an experienced politician he understood that controversy would deflect the NPC from its major objectives. He emphasized what people agreed on rather than what divided them.[33]

Equally important to the council were the chairmen of its Agenda and Appointment Committees. After George Hill finished his service as chairman of the Agenda Committee, Hallanan worked closely with Alfred "Jake" Jacobsen of Amerada Petroleum Corporation, who chaired the committee from 1950 to 1965. Another significant early member of the NPC was W. Alton Jones of Cities Service, the first chairman of the Appointment Committee. That committee, in consultation with the Department of the Interior, chose the members of study committees.

The early development of the council also owed much to the first full-time director of the OGD, Max W. Ball. He was, as Hallanan said, "no stranger to the oil business. He knows it up and down and backward again."[34] An attorney also trained in geology, Ball left a flourishing consulting practice to take over the OGD from acting director Ralph K. Davies, who retired from government service at the end of 1946. When Ball returned to his consulting practice in 1948, he accepted appointment to the council and served on its Agenda Committee.

Ball proved to be a catalyst and an innovator. Davies had seen the NPC as a peacetime version of the wartime PIWC. He did the political and organizational work needed to launch the council. Ball helped NPC define more specifically its mission and operations. He emphasized the needs of business-government cooperation in the postwar era, a dangerous time for the United

States. Ball thought that a good working relationship with government would allow the industry to avoid the kinds of perceived failures that could lead to increased regulation. "Cooperation," as he said, "can be the best antidote to the danger of control."[35]

Ball had an expansive view of the NPC as a "supplier of knowledge." As he said in his first formal remarks to the council, "when I have been talking about information, I have been thinking not alone in terms of factual information; I have been thinking also of the intangible type of information that men have in their heads, that constitute[s] judgment, that constitute[s] ability, that can't be put down on paper and added up in a column of figures."[36]

Ball recommended an important change in outlook by encouraging NPC members to be proactive in suggesting studies. "There is no impropriety in such submissions, and no danger with respect to the Department of Justice, so long as the suggestions are made to the Oil and Gas Division and we approve them for the consideration of the Council," he stated. He wanted the council to feel free to make suggestions "as to something that should be done, or something that should be undone."[37] Instead of a straight line of requests from the OGD to the NPC, Ball favored a circular process in which the council could suggest studies to the OGD, which could then choose to include them in its normal requests to the NPC, which could then choose to accept, reject, or recommend modifications to them.

As a full-time government official Ball had many opportunities to press the NPC toward fulfilling his broad visions. He did not always succeed. But in the dialogue and, at times, conflict that developed, the working relationship between the industry and the OGD grew closer and more clearly defined.

Ball, for example, pressed the NPC to reconsider its January, 1948, rejection of a study on national oil policy. Circumstances had changed dramatically since the end of the war. Issues of scarcity in the immediate postwar years had turned to those of oversupply. At Ball's urging and after "intensive consideration" the NPC authorized the study in July, 1948. Ball also urged attention to issues of controversy with the government, such as the ownership of tidelands. The NPC's leaders shied away from this issue to avoid antagonizing the Truman administration over an issue that had been in the courts and before congressional committees. Ball argued simply that the NPC should not silence the industry by dodging discussions of important, yet controversial issues.[38]

During Ball's tenure the NPC's sustained expansion forced it to reexamine its organization and financing. Shortages and inflation in 1947 caused a public outcry and congressional investigations that produced the Taft Anti-Inflation Act (Public Law 395) "to aid in stabilizing the economy of the United States, to aid in curbing inflationary tendencies, to promote the orderly and equitable distribution of goods and facilities, and to aid in preventing maldistribution of goods and facilities which basically affect the cost of living or industrial production."[39] By an executive order President Truman authorized government agencies to consult with industry to prepare voluntary agreements that would achieve the goals of the new legislation. The DOI received authority over petroleum, and the secretary turned to the NPC to make recommendations on establishing voluntary agreements. He envisioned the agreements providing for the allocation of transportation facilities, as well as "for priority allocation and inventory control of scarce commodities which basically affect the cost of living or industrial production."[40]

The NPC complied and undertook a series of studies that cost more and involved larger numbers of participants than any previous effort had. The increased costs forced the NPC to change its method of funding. To avoid relying entirely on contributions from the largest companies for funding, the council's Articles of Organization as written in 1946 had specified that contributions to the NPC would be prorated by the size of each company. But as expenses increased, the council changed this policy to one that in effect became "those who can best afford to pay will be asked to pay."[41]

In regard to the voluntary agreements, the council recommended regional, voluntary allocation plans. In consultation with state and federal officials the NPC appointed regional committees that cooperated with other industry groups to prevent shortages of heating oil during the particularly cold winter of 1947–48. In addition the council responded to requests to study, as Ball said, the "quantities and kinds of steel needed by the American petroleum industry in the United States and abroad in order to further the purposes" of the Taft Act.[42]

In both instances Ball wanted the study committees to continue to provide information and advice during the several months authorized in the legislation. Such a role caused renewed concerns within the council about antitrust. Indeed, before beginning the studies the NPC insisted on receiving assurances from the Justice Department that it could legally fill the part it had been asked to play.[43]

In September, 1948, the NPC took on a similar role in response to a strike against six large oil companies. To prevent severe shortages and a rapid increase in prices, the DOI turned to the NPC to appoint a committee for information and assistance, much as the government had relied on the industry in World War I and World War II emergencies. In its report the committee described its purpose as having been "to exchange information and products during the emergency, recommending limitations on deliveries to customers in order to meet the current demands of essential business and to recommend to the industry, the public, and the Government, whatever action seemed in the interests of augmenting the availability of . . . petroleum products."[44]

The NPC viewed these expanded activities as nothing more than responding to the government's request for assistance in an emergency. But there were other new activities in the two years that Ball served as director of the OGD. After Ball made a pitch to the council about the need for additional personnel in the OGD, the NPC authorized Hallanan to make "proper representations to the appropriate Congressional Committees to provide an adequate appropriation for the Oil and Gas Division."[45]

The OGD needed the NPC's support at times on other issues before Congress. In 1949 the DOI turned to the council for a report on a proposed "Petroleum Policy Council," to be made up of representatives from various government agencies with interests in the oil industry. Had Congress adopted this legislation, the OGD would have been out of business. And, at the very least, the NPC would have had to change.[46]

Ball's departure from the OGD at the end of 1948 had indirectly contributed to closer working relations between the council and government. From the beginning of his tenure Ball had indicated that he could not afford an extended stay in government service. A consultant who stays away from his business too long, he said, might not have a business to go back to. In April, 1948, Ball asked the NPC to help the OGD find his successor. He argued that it was in the interest of the industry to find someone who understood it from practical experience. Ball also wanted assistance in staffing other positions in his division. Indeed, because government salaries were lower than those in the industry, he suggested that the NPC investigate the possibility of the industry "lending" men needed in the OGD, as the industry had done in staffing the PAW and PIWC in World War II. In response to Ball's suggestions the council established a committee on government personnel "to canvas the field to see if competent persons can be secured for the jobs that Mr. Ball has in mind in the Oil and Gas Division."[47]

The committee failed to find industry candidates willing to be considered for the director's position. As a result Carroll Fentriss, one of Ball's assistants, took over when he left at the end of 1948. But the committee continued to exist to identify industry people who might serve in other government posts.

Ball's tenure had covered a critical time in which the NPC took on some new and expanded responsibilities. In those years the council proved willing to articulate controversial positions and to take on studies that confronted more directly the competitive divisions within the industry. But there were limits. Hallanan and other council leaders remained sensitive to the antitrust implications of proposed studies. They also preferred to steer the NPC clear of issues that might cause sharp controversies within the council. The petroleum industry was made up of competing interests with numerous strongly held views on key issues such as oil imports. When such contentious subjects were addressed, the NPC emphasized facts, rather than policy recommendations, in its reports.

Hallanan and other leaders of the NPC also sought to avoid controversial issues that might strengthen the powers of government. Hence, in 1950 the NPC refused to make a study of the interrelationships among the "energy" industries—that is, coal, oil, gas, and nuclear power. It rejected the secretary of the interior's request to study "the supplies of and requirements for natural and manufactured gas and heating and fuel oils by geographic areas and by classes of uses." The NPC saw the proposed investigation as beyond the "scope of the activities of the council under its Articles of Organization." The council was not interested in studying the "complex problems" brought about by the "substitutability of energy products."[48]

By the time Ball left, the council and OGD had worked out the ground rules of their relationship. This was a fortunate state of affairs because there was much to do, especially in regard to preparedness and then the war in Korea.

CHALLENGES TO THE NPC

The Korean War (1950–53) proved again the utility of an industry advisory board in time of military emergency. But the war also raised anew the Justice Department's concern about the workings of such groups. During the war the department examined the activities of business advisory committees, singling out the petroleum industry for special scrutiny. On October 19, 1950, it used the enactment of the 1950 National Production Act to issue new recommendations about the organization of business advisory committees. Truman's attorney general, Howard McGrath, had some stern warnings about the need of committees to remain purely advisory. To minimize the possibility of prosecution, McGrath suggested that government set the agenda for all advisory committees and that their chairmen be government officials.

With the declaration of a national emergency in December, 1950, Interior Secretary Oscar L. Chapman sought Department of Justice clearance for petroleum industry advisory functions under the Department of the Interior (including the NPC) and the newly created Petroleum Administration for Defense (PAD). Atty. Gen. Peyton Ford balked. Secretary Chapman opposed the recent "suggestions" of the attorney general, and he solicited and obtained the direct intervention of President Truman to preserve the existing organizational structure of the NPC.[49]

Secretary Chapman, however, required changes in the operation of the NPC. These specified (1) that the council make provision for the transmittal of minutes of its meeting through the interior secretary to the attorney general; (2) that the council act solely and exclusively in an advisory capacity; and (3) that the council make no recommendations with respect to specific allocation of supplies or materials, or the use of facilities to or among individual units of the petroleum industry. The secretary noted that if recommendations such as the third listed had to be made under the Defense Production Act of 1950, he would use special industry advisory committees headed by "appropriate full-time government officials for such purposes."[50]

In the following year the head of the Antitrust Division and the attorney general sought to limit membership in the council to "persons actively engaged in the operation of business enterprises." They hoped to ban participation of trade association officials unless they also were engaged in the operation of a petroleum business. When the council began its work in 1946, twenty-two members were presidents or representatives of trade associations. Chapman unsuccessfully defended their participation in council affairs, and the trade association people were forced to leave the NPC. Their removal displeased the council, but it made the NPC distinctive and enhanced its standing as an impartial source of information and advice.[51]

In 1955 the nature and role of advisory boards surfaced again during House Judiciary Committee hearings on the attorney general's study of antitrust laws. The ensuing debate was driven by the extreme discomfort of some members of Congress toward larger corporations, especially at a time of heightened merger activity. These debates raised pointed questions about business advisory boards. The committee noted that 1,394 boards subject to Justice Department standards existed but that only 615 complied with the department's 1950 "recommendations." The Eisenhower administration's Antitrust Division had not forced a uniform pattern of compliance, allowing instead voluntary compliance based on the "integrity and good judgment of businessmen." Advisory committee structure, however, proved to be an area in which Congress could address its concerns about concentrated economic power.[52]

Congressional interest in the issue crested with the introduction of legislation in early 1957 that would have enacted much of the attorney general's 1950 recommendation into law. Most of the Eisenhower administration, including the Department of the Interior, opposed the legislation; even the Department of Justice preferred a voluntary system. The NPC closely followed the legislation in the House, and council members became discouraged when it encountered no opposition in the Government Operations Committee. Hallanan enlisted the assistance of a sympathetic congressman to make the NPC's case to other members. The NPC chairman emphasized the council's openness and cooperativeness. Hallanan pointed out that he drew up NPC meeting agendas with the approval of the OGD director's office. The council kept full minutes of all meetings, which the NPC then supplied to the secretary of the interior.

The legislation passed the House narrowly on July 10, 1957, but with an amendment introduced by an NPC supporter requiring that advisory committee meetings "shall be at the call of and under the chairmanship of, *or* [emphasis added] conducted in the presence of, a full-time salaried officer or employee of the Government." The NPC believed that this modification would allow it to conduct business essentially as it had in the past, since government officials had always been in attendance at NPC meetings.[53]

Just when the issue appeared resolved, Eisenhower's interior secretary Fred Seaton sought to reduce support for the pending legislation by proposing that the NPC accept the attorney general's earlier recommendations. His request in December, 1957, that Hallanan make the necessary changes to the council's by-laws threw the council into an uproar.[54] Hallanan responded to Seaton that to "carry into effect the changes in our basic procedure as outlined in the [DOI] . . . memorandum would mean that the National Petroleum Council as it has existed would necessarily be abolished." To emphasize his point Hallanan canceled the upcoming meeting of the NPC. He later speculated that if this meeting had been held, a majority of the membership would have voted to dissolve the council. Hallanan described the reaction of NPC members as a "sense of betrayal," a feeling that was especially strong among veterans of government service in the PAW and PIWC during World War II. They voiced concerns that something more than the "conscientious service of a businessman" was now considered necessary to protect the public's business.[55]

The NPC sought no contributions for 1958. Hallanan and a group of leading members of the NPC (Hines H. Baker, Russell B. Brown, Jake L. Hamon, W. Alton Jones, J. Howard Marshall, J. R. Parten, J. E. Warren) negotiated with Seaton and his assistants, as well as with representatives of the Justice Department's Antitrust Division.[56] They met in January and February. Thereafter Hallanan conducted negotiations with the Interior and Justice Departments with the assistance of only Baker, Jones, and Marshall. These discussions included proposals to establish an official position of "government liaison" or to pattern the NPC after the Department of Commerce's Business Advisory Council (BAC), in which the secretary of commerce served as "ex officio General Chairman" while industry representatives ran the BAC. Seaton found all these suggestions unacceptable.[57]

Negotiations continued until the end of the year, when a compromise finally produced a new organizational format for the NPC that has continued to the present. The council amended its Articles of Organization to provide for a cochair of the organization, who would be the secretary of the interior or a full-time salaried official of the DOI designated by the secretary. The government cochair would approve appointments to special committees and working subgroups, and these units would also have government cochairs. These cochairs had to approve the call and agenda for meetings and certify their minutes.

The council met for the first time in fifteen months on January 27, 1959, to vote on the proposed changes. After a sharp-edged discussion the changes were approved with only one dissenting vote. Capt. Matthew Carson, OGD director, became the first government cochair of the NPC. While some members remained disgruntled at the ordeal, others took a more philosophical view. Hines Baker, a principal in the negotiations, commented to Agenda Committee chairman Jake Jacobsen that, "while the working out of changes in the Articles of Organization has been frustrating and annoying and the occasion for them useless, I do not feel that anything of serious moment has been lost and [the NPC] should be able to render a thoroughly worthwhile service to the country."[58] Such disputes were inevitable given the importance of petroleum and the high visibility of the NPC among business advisory committees; they were challenges that had to be overcome if the council hoped to continue in its role as adviser to government.

ORGANIZATIONAL CHALLENGES
IN THE 1960S AND AFTER

While the council preferred to focus on providing information and advice to the government, its leaders also had to confront serious organizational issues.

Some were internal. The council's founding generation—the men who had created the organization and guided it through its first decade and a half—were leaving the scene. Their departure provided the opportunity to reassess and reengineer the day-to-day workings of the council and its staff.

As in the 1950s, the leadership in the 1960s and after had to face anew questions about the NPC's proper role and its relationship to government. At times the disputes became contentious and politicized. Some members of Congress continued to focus on the interactions between business advisory groups and federal agencies. As a successful organization, speaking for a critical industry, the council at times found itself the focus of congressional attention. Then, too, the new administration of John F. Kennedy weighed in on the issue of business advisory groups. In the 1960 campaign Kennedy portrayed his opponent, Richard M. Nixon, as the heir of an Eisenhower administration beholden to the interests of "Big Business." As president, Kennedy wanted to create at least the appearance of independence from such influences.

In the first months of his term JFK terminated the special relationship of the influential Business Advisory Council with the Department of Commerce. In the months that followed, the administration studied other areas where business might have developed undue influence with government agencies. As a result, on February 9, 1962, the White House issued a memorandum entitled "Preventing Conflicts of Interest on the Part of Advisers and Consultants to the Government." The memorandum purported to be applicable to all industry advisory groups.

Initially council officers believed that its members, and individuals participating in NPC studies, were not affected. They were not "officers or employees" of the government, which the memorandum seemed to single out for attention. Under this strict application of the conflict of interest rules an NPC member would not have been able to appear before a government agency for two years regarding any matter in which he had been involved during his tenure on the council.[59]

The first indication that the NPC could be subject to the conflict of interest restrictions occurred when the Department of the Interior reappointed council members in 1962. Some members accepted reappointment. Encouraged by NPC chairman Hallanan, others declined, believing that acceptance of reappointment under the terms offered would acknowledge that the conflict of interest rules applied to the council. Hallanan reinforced this point by suspending operations of the council. Caught in the resulting bind was the nearly concluded NPC report on Soviet oil and gas, which promised to be a significant element in the government's analysis of the escalating "Soviet economic offensive."[60]

In July, 1962, discussions about the status of the NPC began under the "conflicts of interest memorandum." Not until August did Deputy Atty. Gen. Nicholas Katzenbach inform the Interior Department that the Justice Department considered council members and those serving on its study groups as outside the scope of the memorandum. Katzenbach noted that the DOI used the council to obtain a view of the entire oil industry, that the NPC had been representative of the industry, and that it received no government funding. He concluded that it functioned "as a composite spokesman for the industry and that the council members, as they are intended and expected to do, play essentially an industry role rather than an independent role."[61]

The council also had to respond to another initiative of the Kennedy administration regarding the functioning of advisory committees. The president issued an executive order on February 26, 1962, that made mandatory for all federal advisory committees the changes essentially agreed to by the NPC under the Eisenhower administration in 1959. Though the council already operated with government cochairs, it now also would have to maintain verbatim transcripts of all committee, subcommittee, and task group meetings unless the DOI issued a waiver for unusual circumstances. A special committee to review the NPC's by-laws ultimately incorporated these changes into the organization's charter on March 21, 1963.[62]

The NPC faced other significant changes as well. In the early 1960s the operations and motives of the council were again under fire from the executive branch. This disappointed Hallanan, now retired from the active operation of his company and in poor health, and he announced his resignation on July 18, 1962. Longtime NPC vice chairman R. G. Follis, of Standard Oil of California, became acting chairman while the conflict of interest issue was still unresolved.[63]

After Hallanan died in December, 1962, Follis took over as chairman. His chairmanship represented a continuity of personnel at the top of the NPC. Follis and Agenda Committee chairman Jacobsen had held their positions for more than a decade. The membership voted that they continue in their leadership roles. In many respects the early council had been an intimate organization. When, for example, the first secretary-treasurer (equivalent to executive director), Russell B. Brown, retired at the end of 1962, he was succeeded in the job by his son, Vincent M. Brown, who served until 1974.

In a short period much of this changed. Following Hallanan's retirement, Follis appointed Jake Hamon to chair a special committee on reorganization. The committee was to ensure that the council's by-laws complied with existing executive branch orders, but it also provided Follis an opportunity to

make other changes. In its report on October 4, 1962, the committee recommended, "without any reflection on the devoted and untiring efforts of the
former Chairman, that there be a general understanding that the time limit
of the officer's terms should be two terms, except in an exceptional emergency."[64]

Follis also quickly improved the treatment of the council's staff. Only Brown
had a benefits package at the time, and Follis thought that others on the NPC
staff needed to have "the same sort of general level of human relations treatment that is in effect in similar organizations with which the Council must
compete." The special committee on organization had reviewed the staff organization and proposed a formal contributory retirement plan comparable
to that of groups such as the API, although not at the same level as those of
the oil companies. Other changes made daily operations more businesslike,
including placing the council on a fiscal rather than calendar year basis beginning June 30, 1963.[65]

Finally, Follis announced changes in the way the council determined appointments. Because of the diversity of the petroleum industry, Follis thought
that council offices should rotate on the basis of regions, the size of companies, and whether or not firms were independents or majors.[66] Follis encouraged the regular rotation of the top offices in the NPC at two-year intervals,
with the expectation that representatives of the majors and independents would
alternate in the chair's job.

In July, 1965, Jake Hamon, an independent oil producer, became the new
chairman of the council. At the same time Jacobsen stepped down as chairman of the Agenda Committee. The last of the people who had guided the
NPC through the dramatic changes in government attitude toward the industry in the 1930s and World War II was leaving the scene. As Hamon took
over the chairmanship he thanked Follis, saying that the council owed him a
"debt of gratitude for his hard work in reorganizing the internal affairs of the
Council as well as for his unselfish efforts to keep the Council properly oriented when the future appeared uncertain."[67]

Few could have predicted the uncertainties that dramatically altered the
petroleum industry in the United States during the 1970s. As an era of excess
domestic capacity came to an end, interruptions of foreign supplies provoked
a series of energy crises that greatly increased the public scrutiny of petroleum
companies. Government imposed new schemes of regulation on petroleum,
often in hasty responses to short-term dislocations rather than long-term considerations. A variety of well-organized interest groups asserted stronger voices
often at odds with the position of the petroleum industry in debates on

energy policy. Divisive political debates led to complex new energy policies, including the Emergency Petroleum Allocation Act of 1973, the Energy Policy and Conservation Act of 1975, and the Natural Gas Policy Act of 1978.

Greater public and congressional interest in energy-related issues produced new government agencies with far-reaching powers to regulate aspects of the petroleum industry. These included the Federal Energy Office (1973–74), the Federal Energy Administration (1974–77), and the Department of Energy (1977–present). The council's advisory role was transferred in 1978 to the new DOE, which consolidated some, but not all, government energy functions in one federal office. Until that time the NPC continued to operate under the aegis of the secretary of the interior.

Despite these changes, for much of the 1970s the council continued to function as it had in the past. It responded to requests for advice from the DOI, addressing a broad range of energy-related issues encountered by many government agencies and departments. The DOI continued to request council assistance in a wide range of matters, including issues generated by the new petroleum regulatory apparatus.[68]

Heightened public interest in energy supplies and environmental pollution, however, encouraged continued congressional and White House scrutiny of the general relationship between business and government. Long-standing congressional concerns about business advisory committees culminated in the passage of the Federal Advisory Committee Act (FACA) in 1972, which again forced the NPC to make changes in its membership and procedures. This law emerged after two years of hearings and publicity, which at times focused on the council.

In 1971 Montana's senator Lee Metcalf shined the investigative spotlight of his Subcommittee on Intergovernmental Relations (Committee on Government Operations) on the National Petroleum Council. Testifying before the committee, DOI's assistant secretary for mineral resources, Hollis Dole, freely told Metcalf that the DOI accepted the council's information and analysis. It was, he said, the best way to gather industry information. Dole testified that the council's analyses carried considerable weight because they represented the "balanced" view of the petroleum industry. "You will find," he concluded, "that you have all kinds of people here from all phases of the petroleum industry, large and small."[69]

Metcalf revisited an old issue when he noted that some of the members of the NPC were also active in industry trade associations. Others testifying at the hearings affirmed Metcalf's view that advisory committees such as the NPC existed to provide privileged access for petroleum-industry executives to officials in the Department of the Interior and other government agencies. NPC executive director Vincent Brown attempted to defend the council in what had turned into a rather hostile forum. He emphasized the council's lack of political orientation. Like others before him, he made the point that the government would be hard-pressed to gather the kind of information provided by the council without substantial cost.[70]

Brown then discussed the function of council government cochairs and NPC compliance with Executive Order No. 11007, issued in 1962. The council had maintained for the DOI verbatim transcripts of its meetings since its inception. Since 1962, in compliance with the executive order, the NPC had maintained verbatim transcripts of all council committee, subcommittee, and task group meetings. The council had opened its meetings to the public in 1971.

Metcalf commended the council on its compliance with the letter and spirit of the executive order's requirements. But federal advisory committees were a significant political issue that he was not ready to relinquish. Fueled by well-publicized congressional hearings in 1970, Metcalf and other critics of advisory committees intently pursued what they referred to as the "fifth branch of the government." Two years later Congress subjected advisory groups to tighter executive and legislative oversight in the Federal Advisory Committee Act of 1972.[71]

The FACA became the first federal legislation to address the functioning of advisory committees. It provided standards and oversight mechanisms in the executive departments, the Office of Management and Budget (OMB), and Congress. The legislation required that the membership be "fairly balanced in terms of points of view represented and the functions to be performed."[72] A strict interpretation of FACA's open committee requirements would have had a significant impact on the work of the NPC. FACA section 4a(4), as administered by the Office of Management and Budget, allowed a waiver of those requirements for meetings of "informal subgroups." The council thought this waiver essential for the timely and efficient operations of its study groups.

At the end of 1974 the DOI used the OMB's renewal of the National Petroleum Council's authorization to alter its composition. Earlier in 1974 the assistant secretary of the interior for energy and minerals, Jack W. Carlson, examined the issue of balance in the council's membership. Before this time "balanced membership in the council traditionally meant a broad representation of the companies, by size, geography, and function within the petroleum industry." Advisory committees established under the Federal Energy Administration Act included representatives of "public interest groups" (consumer, environmental, and other voluntary citizen organizations). In contrast, few energy-related advisory committees under the aegis of the DOI (such as the NPC) had such representatives.

Carlson concluded that the council had a fairly balanced number of members in terms of geography, but he thought it needed more representation including independent marketers of petroleum and added membership from among the major "stakeholders" of the industry. To comply, early in 1975 the NPC added new members, including representatives of the AFL-CIO, American Automobile Association, the League of Women Voters, Teamsters, Edison Electric Institute, Sierra Club, National Wildlife Federation, American Farm Bureau Federation, Massachusetts Institute of Technology, Chase Manhattan Bank, National Rural Electric Cooperative Association, and the Audubon Society, among others.[73] This inclusion of new members represented the latest episode in an ongoing effort by the NPC to balance breadth of input with the need for cohesion with which to build consensus.

The addition of new members in the mid-1970s was only a dress rehearsal for more far-reaching change that accompanied the creation of the Department of Energy in 1977. The consolidation of the federal government's energy-related functions had been seriously considered by Presidents Nixon and Ford. The Carter administration finally pushed through change with the creation of a cabinet-level department that contained many of the powers over energy that government had accumulated over two centuries. After much debate and compromise the DOE came to include an array of programs inherited from the DOI, the Federal Energy Administration, the Energy Research and Development Administration, and the Atomic Energy Commission. Significant powers over energy-related issues remained outside the new department, however, including the DOI's traditional management of public lands, the regulation of nuclear power (which came under the newly created Nuclear Regulatory Commission), and the regulation of natural gas (which remained in the hands of the successor to the Federal Power Commission, the Federal Energy Regulatory Commission).[74] Of course, power over many issues that greatly influenced the energy industries remained in the Department of Transportation, the Environmental Protection Agency, and the Department of State.

This reorganization left the National Petroleum Council in limbo for more than a year. From the time of Jimmy Carter's election in the fall of 1976 through the final design, approval, and opening of the DOE in October, 1977, the NPC's future remained in question. Then for the next six months fundamental questions about its organization and powers within the DOE had to be answered. The council's chairman during this era of uncertainty was Collis Chandler, and he was called on to negotiate the transfer of the council from the DOI to the DOE. In extended discussions with the first secretary of energy, James Schlesinger, Jr., Chandler and others in the NPC managed this difficult transition. When the long process finally concluded in May, 1978, the NPC's functional reporting relationship had moved to the DOE while avoiding fundamental changes in its operations and organization.

The debate over the reorganization of federal energy functions hamstrung the NPC with uncertainties. Pending a decision on these issues, the council suspended operations for a year. One major study on the outlook for energy through the year 2000 was suspended, never to be completed. The focus of the council's leadership was, of necessity, on organizational issues, and its future place within the changing government energy bureaucracy was the topic of a series of meetings with officials from the DOI and the emerging DOE.

Throughout these discussions the NPC's leaders assumed that their organization had played and could continue to play a useful role—if it were allowed to function in much the same way as it had in the past. But this outcome was not easy to secure, since the organizational upheaval in energy functions was redefining the way the federal government addressed energy-related issues. The traditionally comfortable fit between the needs of the DOI and the procedures of the NPC could no longer be assumed. And in the politically charged environment surrounding energy policy in the 1970s, fundamental questions long resolved within the DOI were now reopened for debate. In this climate the leadership of the NPC worried that their organization might cease to exist in anything similar to its historical form if an acceptable accommodation could not be reached with the DOE.

In the fall of 1977 Collis Chandler took the initiative in approaching Secretary Schlesinger regarding his thoughts on the future of the NPC. Schlesinger, whose background included a stint with the Atomic Energy Commission but not with oil- or gas-related organizations, viewed the NPC's fate in the context of an ongoing review of all energy-related advisory committees that had been inherited by the DOE. Unfortunately for the NPC, the frame of reference within the DOE was not primarily that of the DOI but rather that of the Federal Energy Administration (FEA), the agency that had grown in the 1970s to regulate oil prices. The FEA had used advisory committees as a conduit for explaining its evolving policies to segments of the affected industries and then receiving feedback on these policies. The rules it had applied to such committees had little in common with those that had governed the NPC's broader, more detailed reports to the DOI.

The initial face-to-face meeting between NPC officials and Secretary Schlesinger and his staff came on December 15, 1977. Chandler sought to use this meeting to educate the new officials in the DOE about the historical mission of the NPC and to offer the secretary the continued services of the council. He anticipated that the DOE's staff might revisit all of the old issues that had been raised in the formative years of the NPC. What would keep it from becoming a self-serving "tool of industry"? Were its operations conducted openly and in compliance with regulations governing advisory committees? Were there antitrust issues concerning its continued operation? What was the balance of members from different segments of the petroleum industry and from stakeholders? Why should the NPC maintain its own staff and funding separate from the government? Such questions were inevitable in a time of transition; the DOI had asked variants of these same questions as it created the NPC after World War II. Now the NPC would answer to a new department, this time in an environment of great skepticism about the power and the motives of the oil and gas industries.[75]

Secretary Schlesinger brought to the table a number of questions of his own. He sought to understand what, if anything, made the NPC different from the numerous other advisory committees he had inherited. He also wanted to know what sort of information in what format to expect from the NPC. Though cordial, the "feeling out" process between the DOE and the NPC was tinged with skepticism on both sides. The December meeting went a long way in relieving this skepticism and convincing both sides that the transfer of the NPC to the DOE was desirable.

The meeting produced a consensus that the council should be transferred, but it left numerous practical issues to be resolved. During the first months of 1978 the resolution of these issues went forward in a series of letters between Chandler and Schlesinger and a second meeting between the two in March. At issue was the extent to which the NPC could remain effective and independent if it were forced to conform to the general guidelines for advisory committees being developed by the DOE from procedures taken from the FEA. Chandler and other members of the council remained convinced of the value of the NPC in its traditional form—that is, as a relatively large, independent group specializing in producing detailed reports that presented the consensus of the industry on technical issues of interest to government officials. They resisted Schlesinger's proposals for reducing the number of members, regularly rotating the membership, including larger numbers of "outside" members, and presenting reports in the form of executive summaries. Negotiations over such changes forced the postponement of the NPC's first meeting under the DOE from April to May, 1978, but acceptable compromises finally assured the council that it could continue to serve its traditional functions in a somewhat altered organization under the new DOE guidelines.

On May 25, 1978, the initial meeting of the NPC as an advisory committee to the DOE took place in the Forrestal Building, the new home of the Department of Energy. In his address to the council and in his subsequent actions Secretary Schlesinger left no doubt that he planned to make aggressive use of the NPC. Indeed, in this initial meeting he requested four new studies, and he continued to make heavy use of the council throughout his tenure at the DOE. The NPC had survived a difficult period of transition in the organization of the government's energy-related functions with relatively minor adjustments in its operations.

Schlesinger requested a reduction in the NPC's membership and the inclusion of more members from outside the petroleum industry. The council had grown to 140 members in 1978, and the Energy Department approved a new charter for the NPC in 1979 that reduced this number to no more than 100 members. In appointing new members to the council in 1979, Schlesinger kept the total number down to 94. As a result of the cut, oil and gas professionals ended up with a smaller percentage of the council seats. Because of their expertise and experience they continued to lead the council, but the tone and tenor of meetings and discussions changed with the reduction in the number of "insiders" who knew each other and the issues well.[76]

Other changes originated from within. As the size and complexity of reports increased, staff grew in the early 1970s to thirty-seven from fewer than ten in the late 1960s. The 1980s witnessed an increase in the role of third-party contractors to provide assistance and expertise to NPC committees preparing reports. These experts were needed in part because of the increasingly sophisticated methodologies and computer modeling available to the council. Yet in the 1980s such experts were harder for the NPC to borrow from the industry, since oil and gas firms were greatly reducing their staffs, especially in the areas of industry analysis, technical expertise, and corporate planning. Firms found it less costly to retain, as needed, consultants who had carved out niches of expertise in industry issues and operations. These developments affected the operations of the NPC, which found it harder to staff its studies with the technical experts from industry who had long been the backbone of its work.

The council's staff and operations also reflected industry changes, including downsizing. Like industry, the council had fewer permanent employees with specialized expertise and relied more on the use of recent industry retirees as temporary employees to supplement the staff. Expenditures for consultants and third-party support services became a larger portion of the costs of NPC studies. In the 1990s these trends led to higher budgets, especially when the NPC responded to DOE requests to take on more than one large-scale project at a time. The higher costs of such studies reflected the expenses of accounting and consulting firms retained by the NPC to conduct studies, protect the sensitivity of each participating firm's data, and undertake sophisticated economic surveying and modeling.[77]

There were other changes in the 1990s as the council and the government refined their relationship. In 1992 the energy secretary requested that the council examine how better to provide the department with short-term information. In requesting the study the secretary noted that "there must be flexible mechanisms within the NPC that will enable me to tap the skills I need when I need them . . . to allow DOE to make better use of the very substantial expertise represented by the NPC."[78]

In response to the request, NPC chairman Ray L. Hunt appointed an Ad Hoc Committee on Structure and Procedures to review the council's methods of operation.[79] After several months of work the ad hoc committee reported in February, 1992, reaffirming that the NPC should continue to produce long-term studies as it had in the past. For studies that would require an answer in less than sixty days, the committee reiterated the council's view that the DOE would need as a rule to look outside the NPC structure. For short-term advice the report advised the secretary to convene ad hoc meetings, to which members of the council as well as government officials and representatives from other groups might be invited.[80]

In making his request, Secretary of Energy James D. Watkins wanted to improve the general working relationship between the council and the DOE. NPC chairman Hunt had also been looking for ways to enhance the dialogue between the two. To do so, the report recommended the creation of a "Co-chairs Coordinating Committee" (CCC). The CCC would include the secretary and deputy secretary of energy; the chair, vice chair, and immediate past chair of the NPC; chairs and members of the Agenda Committee; chairs of active NPC study committees; government cochairs of active NPC study committees; chairs of NPC administrative committees; and five at-large electees to ensure inclusiveness and industry balance. Members of the CCC would be required to attend meetings; they could not send alternates. The secretary and the NPC chair would have to take responsibility for the meetings.[81]

In effect, the CCC was to act as a joint monitoring and steering body for the NPC and the DOE relationship. It would track NPC activities, identify issues of concern to the Energy Department and the industry, review ongoing studies, and consider possible subjects for study. All in all, the CCC was designed to create a more effective relationship between the industry and government through the NPC and the DOE.

After more than fifty years many organizations become set in their ways. Clearly that has not happened to the NPC. While operating within an organizational structure created in 1946, the NPC has proved flexible in the face of changing circumstances in its industry, the government, and the larger global market in which NPC members now compete. With one wary eye on the antitrust laws and the other on real and potential divisions within its industry, the National Petroleum Council has pursued its sole purpose of providing advice to the executive branch by producing valuable reports on fundamental conditions within the petroleum industry. Just as the organizational structure of the NPC has evolved over more than five decades, so has the focus of its reports, and it is to these reports that the remainder of this book now turns.

CHAPTER 2

The National Petroleum Council and Emergency Preparedness

THROUGHOUT THE NPC'S HISTORY most of its studies have directly or indirectly involved preparedness. Its numerous reports on conditions in the petroleum industry kept government informed about the industry's capacity to respond quickly and efficiently to the outbreak of war. In the early 1950s the industry's performance in the Korean conflict proved that it could provide both guns and butter—or, more accurately, aviation fuel and gasoline—for a limited conventional war. After Korea the concept of preparedness expanded to include the possibility of nuclear war, and the NPC contributed reports important in preparing the nation's petroleum industry for this daunting prospect. Later the growing reliance of the United States and its major allies on imported oil added still another dimension to national security: the need to protect the economy from disruptions in the supply of foreign oil. The National Petroleum Council studied the implications of such changes for national security, recommending ways that the petroleum industry should prepare for conventional, nuclear, economic, and ultimately cyber "warfare."

POSTWAR PREPAREDNESS AND THE KOREAN WAR

The industry's experience in World War II initially defined the NPC's thinking about preparedness. The war illustrated how close business-government cooperation could facilitate increased exploration, production, and distribution. Among the first issues the OGD posed to the NPC for advice was readiness for another war. Indeed, from 1946 until the United States entered the Korean War in 1950, most NPC studies dealt directly or indirectly with preparedness (see appendix B).

During World War II expediting and coordinating the flow of petroleum products through the U.S. system of pipelines, tank cars, and barges proved to be one of the PAW's key tasks. Opening bottlenecks and increasing transport capacity to handle growing supplies of petroleum had not been easy. The difficulties of that experience remained fresh when the OGD requested that the NPC examine postwar transportation capabilities. The OGD wanted the NPC to assess the situation and recommend projects to ensure that the petroleum delivery system would be adequate to meet a war emergency.[1] During World War II the government had undertaken special projects to improve waterways and harbors to handle increased barge traffic. Even though these projects were completed on an emergency basis, there had been delays. The OGD requested that the council assess the postwar situation so as to avoid future problems, and the NPC did so in 1947 with the publication of one of its first reports, on barge transportation. In that same year the council completed reports on rail, truck, and pipeline transportation, as well as winter shipping on the Illinois River. The council also produced a general report on petroleum transportation facilities.[2]

Other studies focusing on the transportation infrastructure soon followed. Similar reasoning on the part of the government prompted the study of a shortage of pressure tank cars for the transportation of liquefied petroleum gases. Other industries needed these tank cars too, and the government wanted an assessment of the nature of the demand for this equipment in the petroleum industry. Once the OGD understood the nature of competing demand for the cars, it could make recommendations to other government agencies about priorities for their use.[3]

Another preparedness issue revolved around the capacity of the industry to produce adequate supplies of petroleum products in the event of another war. The refining of extraordinary supplies of 100-octane aviation fuel had been one of the great achievements of the United States during World War II. The significance of air power to modern combat focused the government's postwar attention on aviation fuel. Early on, the OGD requested the council to study the industry's aviation fuel production capacity. Assessing such refining capabilities involved technical issues that the industry itself could best address. In 1947, as a result, the NPC issued three reports on "military aircraft fuels productive capacity."[4]

In its first years the NPC produced numerous other preparedness-related studies. There were council analyses of available supplies of crude oil in 1947, 1948, and 1950. In addition the NPC issued reports on petroleum storage facilities in 1948, 1949, and 1951, and on the industry's manpower needs in 1949 and 1950. Reports on such issues have continued up to the present. Early on, the council also prepared reports on the materials (especially steel) the industry needed to expand capacity to meet growing civilian and government demand for petroleum. As civilian petroleum sales increased, the NPC produced reports in 1948 and 1949 that surveyed the impact of such growing demand on supplies available for the military.[5]

The OGD requested more and more of these studies as relations between the United States and the Soviet Union worsened and the cold war intensified. By 1948 the Soviet Union had created a bloc of dependent countries in Eastern Europe. In 1949 a communist government took power in China, which when linked with the Soviet Union created a Eurasian land mass that appeared menacing to the United States and its allies. As these events unfolded, the director of the OGD requested that the NPC review the industry's experience in World War II and prepare an advisory report on how the petroleum industry should respond to a war emergency. The resulting *Report of the National Petroleum Council's Committee on National Petroleum Emergency* was published in January, 1949, and emphasized two lessons from World War II.

The first lesson was that the PAW had been successful because the government had not placed the petroleum industry under the "horizontal" authority of some broad mobilization agency, such as the War Production Board. The NPC emphasized the PAW's independence as a "vertical" governmental agency run and staffed by experienced industry personnel and justified such a special agency in a future conflict by observing that "the ramifications of oil are so vast, so specialized, so complex, and so unique as to require a governmental organization of experienced oil personnel, authorized to work with the petroleum industry in all its branches." The second lesson was that government acted wisely by not attempting to take over the industry during the war. To do so, the NPC report concluded, would have led to massive inefficiency and the loss of a "large amount of creative and productive effort which can be brought forward by an industry-government partnership such as existed during World War II." Indeed, the NPC believed that neither in peace nor in war was the government capable of effectively administering the production, refining, and distribution of petroleum products. "Only by mobilizing the initiative of individuals all along the line," the report concluded, "can real solutions be found for the new and presently unpredictable situations which another national emergency will inevitably bring to the nation and its petroleum industry."[6]

Thus, when the Korean War broke out in June, 1950, the NPC had already developed for the record how the government should respond to the crisis. The council supported in theory an arrangement much like the PAW for mobilizing the industry for war. Initially, however, the discussions in Congress and the White House focused on establishing a centralized authority for war production. Proposals included moving responsibility for petroleum mobilization to the National Security Resources Board or a new version of the World War II War Production Board. There was also a proposal for a new agency, a Minerals and Energy Administration, under the authority of the secretary of the interior.[7]

For much of summer, 1950, the industry seemed reluctant to encourage government involvement in the petroleum business. But during those summer months problems arose in producing adequate supplies of high-octane aviation fuel and tetraethyl lead. Once North Korea attacked its southern neighbor in June, 1950, the NPC entered the debate about whether the government should create a wartime organization for petroleum. The council strongly opposed submerging the petroleum industry in a broad-based government agency. The NPC's position on the value of close industry-government collaboration modeled after the PAW won over Secretary of the Interior Oscar Chapman. Accepting the NPC's arguments about the need for an independent agency staffed by "oil men," Chapman established the Petroleum Administration for Defense (PAD) on October 3, 1950.[8]

Chapman appointed NPC member Bruce K. Brown as the deputy director of the PAD. There Brown functioned as the key liaison between oil and state much as Ralph Davies had done during World War II. Brown had been assistant deputy director of the PAW during World War II. At the time of his appointment he served as president of Pan-Am Southern Corporation, a subsidiary of Standard Oil (Indiana). Brown's involvement in the NPC had resulted from his membership on the Military Petroleum Advisory Board (MPAB), which had been formed in March, 1947, to bring together industry representatives and high-ranking military officers. Over the years the NPC gladly left classified work to the MPAB and other military-industry groups such as the National Security Resources Board.[9]

The PAD took over the work of the Military Petroleum Advisory Board and the Department of the Interior's Oil and Gas Division. The NPC altered its Articles of Organization to reflect the fact that the council would provide both advice to the PAD and assistance in carrying out its responsibilities. As had been the case with the PAW, the PAD coordinated the industry's efforts to produce the petroleum necessary for the war effort. As such, the NPC cooperated with the PAD in helping determine the military's requirements; the essential materials the industry might need to carry out its responsibilities; and the proper allocation of petroleum and natural gas to the military and the civilian population. The council also assisted Brown in identifying and recruiting industry personnel to staff key positions within PAD. Of the approximately 200 PAD employees, 110 were recruited from industry. Thirty were high-level executives who were paid by their companies and served without government compensation.[10] They helped the nation pursue a limited war while supplying petroleum products demanded by the domestic economy.

As the war came to a close in 1953 and the PAD prepared to disband, its assistant deputy administrator approached the NPC for advice about postwar business-government relations in petroleum. The council responded with a report published in December, 1953, *Report of the National Petroleum Council's Committee on Government Oil and Gas Organization,* which recommended a return to the pre–Korean War arrangements. Government and industry experience since World War II, the report argued, proved the importance of having a "principal point of contact and cooperation between the Government and the petroleum industry." The NPC wanted to resume its role in these arrangements, and the DOI should remain as the governmental point of contact "because of the knowledge the Department of the Interior has gained in oil and gas matters over the past decade." The OGD should be reactivated, and the responsibilities assigned to PAD during the war should be returned to that division. The report also supported the reactivation of the Military Petroleum Advisory Board to carry out classified studies.[11] At war's end the new administration of Dwight D. Eisenhower followed these recommendations by quickly reestablishing the prewar arrangements between the Department of the Interior and the NPC.

The use of nuclear weapons by the United States had been a source of heated debate during the Korean War. President Truman had ruled them out when the People's Republic of China entered the conflict on the side of North Korea in November, 1950. By that time the United States no longer had a nuclear monopoly. The Soviet Union had successfully tested a nuclear device in September, 1949, and was at work on a hydrogen bomb, which it would test publicly in 1954. It was only a matter of time, American military officials believed, before the Soviet Union would have the capability of delivering such weapons.

Ending the Korean War stopped hostilities, but it did not bring peace. There was no reason to relax concerns about national security. International tensions remained high in the 1950s and in the decades following. The realities of the cold war confrontation and the prospect that nuclear weapons might be used in a future conflict posed an entirely new set of preparedness issues. The NPC redefined its approach to preparedness and thus played a key part in the petroleum industry's planning for the realities of this new and dangerous international environment.

CIVIL DEFENSE AND MILITARY MOBILIZATION IN THE ATOMIC AGE

The possibility of nuclear war added difficult new dimensions to the traditional approach to preparedness. How would industry contribute to the military mobilization that would follow such an attack, and how would industry help the civilian population cope with the consequences of such a devastating event? Before the end of the Korean War the government began addressing these issues. For the rest of the 1950s and well into the 1960s the NPC helped examine civil defense and military mobilization in a nuclear environment.

In World War II and the Korean War the PAW and PAD took several months to organize, with the details of mobilization worked out as the conflicts unfolded. Before the Korean War, advanced planning had been general and consisted of the statement of overall principles. Both government and the NPC concluded, however, that in the event of nuclear war the nation would not have the luxury to mobilize after the advent of hostilities. Thus, in the 1950s and 1960s the preparations for the next war became considerably more detailed than in the past.

The NPC became deeply involved in these efforts as it resumed its prewar advisory responsibilities following the Korean War. Nuclear war would demand a strong civil defense program as well as military mobilization, and the NPC became a part of government efforts in both areas in the 1950s and 1960s. The starting assumption for the NPC's work on preparedness for nuclear war was that the government should heed the lessons of the PAW and the PAD in using industry experts to help manage the petroleum industry. Because nuclear war might begin with vast destruction in the United States, however, preparedness would entail much more advanced planning than had been the case in previous wars.

In the months before it closed, the PAD requested that the NPC study preparedness in the new era of atomic weaponry. Early in March, 1954, the acting deputy administrator of the PAD, Joseph A. LaFortune, sought the NPC's advice on the kind of emergency defense organization needed in the event of a nuclear attack. Up to that time the country's mobilization effort assumed a dynamic economy operating under stable internal conditions. As an official of the Office of Defense Mobilization (ODM) said at the March 23, 1954, council meeting, "Now we are faced . . . with the grim fact that if [nuclear] attack is possible[,] a major portion of the [mobilization] capacity thus far established may not only be vulnerable but may be unavailable when most needed."[12]

Preparedness in the nuclear era required greater coordination and more detailed planning between the industry and civil defense officials. As the PAD's letter to the NPC stated, "a study including all levels, from the Federal Government down to and including the community level, is required in order to provide information and make recommendations to the ODM on plans for the reduction and overcoming of attack damage to petroleum and gas facilities. To be effective, these studies must be properly coordinated with civil defense programs in disaster areas, and be designed to assure necessary supplies of petroleum and gas to meet essential military, civilian, and industrial requirements under emergency conditions."[13]

The committee consulted with government officials, as well as representatives of the steel and chemical industries, in preparing its report on the problems likely to result from a nuclear attack. Published in 1954, this initial NPC report on preparedness for nuclear war outlined the general planning problems to be overcome. It emphasized that the planning effort should rely heavily on industry personnel. Since the country had no experience in coping with nuclear attack, the report did not lay out a detailed plan for response. It also did not dwell on precautions that might protect refineries and other facilities in the event of a nuclear attack. Instead it recommended that the secretary of the interior establish emergency committees staffed by industry personnel for oil and one for gas in each of the five regional districts of the country established by the PAW during World War II. These committees would take responsibility for planning for and responding to the circumstances created by an emergency. As had been the case with the PAW and the PAD, subcommittees would focus on the specific issues of supply, refining, transportation, and distribution in each of the regions, with the general committees coordinating their work.

Since such committees would, by necessity, contain representatives of competing companies, antitrust constraints to their activities would have to be removed. To skeptics who doubted that oilmen should be trusted to submerge the individual interests of their companies to the broader public interest, the industry could only point toward its performance in both world wars and the Korean conflict. As in previous wars, federal government oversight of the privately staffed committees would ensure that they worked in the national interest. The NPC's report stressed that federal control was essential to avoid the "chaos" that might result if the initiative rested entirely in the hands of state or local officials. Although such officials had important roles to play, jurisdictional conflicts could not be allowed to disrupt the smooth operations of the national petroleum industry.[14]

The report called for the prompt establishment of standing regional emergency committees, which could be activated by a presidential proclamation in the event of an attack on the United States. It also made the case for the reactivation of a PAD-like organization to report to the secretary of the interior. In addressing the unusual circumstances that a nuclear attack might create, the report made a few general recommendations for the entire industry. Companies were advised to decentralize new refining and storage facilities to minimize the effects of a direct strike on such installations. In addition, mobile transportation facilities would be important following such an attack, and the NPC recommended that the industry ensure an adequate supply of tank cars, barges, and tank trucks.[15]

These general recommendations in the 1954 report spawned a second government request to the NPC for a more detailed study of such issues. In May, 1955, the council produced *Disaster Planning for the Oil and Gas Industries,* a report designed for wide distribution within the industry so that company officials could take part in preparing for a civil defense emergency. At the government's request, the new report examined what preparedness measures should be taken by individual companies. Drawing on the industry's experience in coping with accidents, such as shutdowns caused by equipment failure or fire, the report provided a detailed management checklist of what needed to be done by specific companies to prepare for a nuclear emergency. It emphasized the need to plan for continuity in management, operations, and product availability by training personnel in security measures, emergency procedures, and plant damage control. Members of the industry, the report recommended, would need plans to rotate or recall personnel, to make an inventory of potential contractors to provide services, to provide medical services, and to provide clothing and shelters to protect workers from radiation.[16] This report was a valuable first step in practical thinking about the unthinkable: What could be done to prepare for a nuclear attack that could be expected to destroy much of the nation's petroleum facilities?

The council approved the printing and distribution of five hundred copies of *Disaster Planning for the Oil and Gas Industries* and a manual on security principles. The NPC had prepared the latter in 1952 by utilizing a group of industry experts on safety, fire prevention, and sabotage. It had not been published at the time. The council targeted the manual for industry personnel at the plant level, whereas the larger report was designed for distribution to managers responsible for such planning at the corporate level.[17]

At about the same time in the 1950s and 1960s the government planned the staffing of emergency civil defense committees. It was one thing to have plans in place at the industry level, but it was quite another to ensure that personnel were ready to staff civil defense operations and mobilization efforts in an emergency. Government bureaucracies with some responsibility for civil defense and military mobilization had proliferated in the decade after World War II. As a result, in 1955 Congress authorized the president to establish the National Defense Executive Reserve (NDER), a group of experienced executives capable of coming into government service on short notice. In 1956 President Eisenhower issued an executive order creating such a body. Selected and trained before an emergency erupted, its members would be ready to assume executive posts in the federal government at the onset of an emergency.

During his second administration President Eisenhower sought to streamline and centralize the government's efforts to prepare for nuclear war. In reorganizing the executive branch in 1958, Eisenhower gave the Office of Civil and Defense Mobilization (OCDM) the power to manage all of the federal government's civil and defense mobilization activities. The newly created office delegated responsibility to the secretary of the interior for ensuring adequate supplies of oil and gas in a major crisis. In turn, the DOI's Office of Oil and Gas (formerly the Oil and Gas Division) drafted a plan for the petroleum and gas industries during a national emergency. Operation of the plan centered on the eight regions created by the Office of Civil Defense Mobilization. In January, 1959, the DOI asked the NPC "to review [the] proposed plan and submit such comments and recommendations as it deemed appropriate for consideration for possible future revision of the plan." In addition the DOI requested "the names of industry personnel qualified to fill key positions in the emergency national and field organizations as outlined in the plan." The NPC provided three names for each essential position in both the headquarters and regional organizations. If chosen by the DOI, these individuals would become members of the NDER.[18]

The Office of Oil and Gas proposal embodied earlier recommendations of the NPC. The council's study of the government's proposal reached out across the nation for the input of the petroleum industry. The council convened meetings in each of the OCDM regions for industry reaction to the report. While soliciting the industry's opinion, these meetings also explained and interpreted what the government would require from members of the industry. In this regard the NPC had become something of a middleman, providing information to the government from the industry (its original role) but also providing information directly to the industry (beyond those appointed to the council) that the government wanted it to have.[19]

The new Kennedy administration expanded the role of the National Petroleum Council while taking further steps to ensure the country's "readiness" for nuclear war. In 1962 President Kennedy issued an executive order instructing the Department of the Interior to develop readiness programs for petroleum and natural gas. In response in August, 1963, the secretary of the interior established the Emergency Petroleum and Gas Administration (EPGA), with offices in the regional headquarters of the Office of Emergency Planning, Office of Civil Defense.[20] Following a request to the council, Lawrence Rawl (Humble Oil and Refining and later CEO of Exxon) chaired a committee that developed a pro forma organizational structure for the EPGA that included twenty divisions and offices.

In an emergency the EPGA would be staffed by industry officials, many of whom had already enrolled in the National Defense Executive Reserve (NDER). All executives invited to work with the newly created EPGA were required to join the NDER and receive briefings and training. Approximately six hundred executives subsequently went through training sessions and received voluminous information about preparedness and mobilization.[21] This cadre of trained executives would be activated by the EPGA in the event of a national emergency affecting the petroleum industry.

The secretary of the interior turned to the council to help in the implementation and assessment of the EPGA. In 1964 the NPC published a two-volume guide to assist companies in developing their own emergency plans. That same year the NPC produced a detailed analysis of the adequacy of the EPGA and other emergency government planning efforts for oil and gas. Following the completion of these assignments the Department of the Interior asked the NPC to provide general information to the industry about the government's programs. Of equal importance, it requested that the council prepare procedural manuals for the various divisions of the EPGA. These manuals included detailed information to guide the actions of different segments of the petroleum industry in the event of nuclear war. The first of these manuals completed was *Domestic Production and Natural Gas Processing*, which was approved by the NPC in early 1966 and became the prototype for the other manuals. As the work went forward, the coordinating subcommittee appointed an editorial task group composed of three members from industry and one representative from the DOI's Office of Oil and Gas. This group shouldered the burden of editing the nineteen remaining volumes and then assembled the twenty into ten volumes for printing. The council approved the manuals in January, 1967, and they were widely distributed throughout the industry.[22]

The preparation of these detailed manuals involved the NPC in some of the most painstaking, demanding work of its existence. The council worked closely with federal officials in the EPGA to plan how industry would work with government in response to a nuclear emergency. These manuals outlined how industry should prepare for such a catastrophe and how industry and government would respond after a major attack on the United States. The chaos of nuclear war would have provided the ultimate test for any type of advanced planning, with little time to adapt existing plans to realities altered by nuclear destruction. With the guidance of the NPC, the petroleum industry cooperated with government in an attempt to anticipate the requirements of the ultimate challenge to national defense.

Individuals from the National Defense Executive Reserve were recruited from industry to fill key positions, both at headquarters in Washington, D.C., and in regional offices. Each reservist was furnished with the appropriate manual for the position and was required to obtain secrecy clearances with the DOI. Regional training exercises took place, along with a national training exercise in Washington, D.C., in 1972. Although manuals were used in these exercises, fortunately the nation avoided nuclear war and has not needed to mobilize the EPGA and industry reservists.

NATIONAL SECURITY AND THE
DISRUPTIONS OF SUPPLIES OF FOREIGN OIL

As important as these efforts were, a nuclear attack was not the only threat the United States faced in the postwar era. Serious disruptions of the foreign oil supply, while less catastrophic to the country than a nuclear war, were a more likely occurrence. Difficulties in Iran in 1951–53 and Suez in 1956 alerted government, industry, and the council to the serious problems caused by major disruptions. In the 1950s temporary cutoffs of Middle Eastern production presented difficulties primarily to U.S. allies in Europe and Japan. But as foreign oil came to supply more of the American market in the 1970s, the potential problems of disruption hit closer to home. Planning for foreign oil shutdowns became another important responsibility of the federal government, which turned to the NPC for assistance in understanding this relatively new threat to the nation's economic security.

In meeting the emergencies caused by disruptions of foreign supplies to its allies and later to itself, the United States generally turned to voluntary agreements among affected parties to alleviate the impact of shortages. The government's commitment to volunteer programs grew out of the World War II experience. The cooperative arrangements used to ensure that oil needed by the armed forces was supplied before other needs served as a model for facing the nation's postwar problems. Indeed, one of the earliest reports the NPC produced recommended a cooperative agreement of oil producers to meet a heating oil shortage during the winter of 1947–48. The NPC's Committee on Voluntary Petroleum Allocation Agreements studied the supply/demand situation. Such agreements had been used in 1947 to meet supply problems following a strike that idled refineries west of the Rocky Mountains. In reports in January and April, 1948, the council produced a series of recommendations on how to increase supply and ensure a fair distribution of heating oil supplies to New England.[23]

Government and industry turned to such proven voluntary agreements when first confronted with disruptions of foreign supplies of oil. The Defense Production Act of 1950, which created mechanisms by which the government mobilized to fight the Korean War, provided the legal basis for such cooperative arrangements. Thus the United States again turned to the Voluntary Allocation Agreements when the Iranian prime minister nationalized the holdings of British Petroleum in June, 1951. The British government vigorously opposed the Iranian policy and organized a boycott against oil produced by a new national Iranian petroleum company. The nationalization and the following boycott further destabilized the country. Under pressure from Western governments, the shah of Iran tried to fire the prime minister, Mohammed Mossadeqh. Instead the shah himself was deposed, although the military returned him to his throne in August, 1953, following bloody confrontations in Tehran.[24]

During the two-year Iranian crisis (1951–53), a voluntary agreement allowed American companies with overseas petroleum operations to cooperate in alleviating shortages created by turmoil in Iran and the war in Korea. The Petroleum Administration for Defense took nominal responsibility for the voluntary agreement. Nineteen American companies participated, developing and implementing their plans through a Foreign Petroleum Supply Committee. The companies shared terminals, storage facilities, tankers, and pipelines. Because of the emergency, the Justice Department agreed not to prosecute the companies after the fact for violating the antitrust statutes.[25]

The NPC did not play a major role in the voluntary agreement that covered the Iranian crisis. As with the earlier voluntary agreement on heating oil, however, it paid attention to the antitrust implications of such understandings. The council consistently supported efforts of the secretaries of the interior and defense to ensure that the Justice Department approve the cooperative understandings among industry members.

Following the Iranian crisis and the end of the Korean War, the government retained the option of using a voluntary agreement to allocate petroleum in international commerce. The Foreign Petroleum Supply Committee (FPSC) and several subcommittees continued as liaisons between the industry and the government, especially the Department of Defense. In 1955 and 1956 the FPSC collected detailed data about international oil operations for the use of foreign policy and defense officials. Pressed by the Justice Department, however, the FPSC and its subcommittees changed their mode of operations in spring, 1956. Henceforth federal officials chaired the FPSC and its subcommittees; government employees took over staff positions from industry; and data was presented in such a way as to minimize individual company information being placed in the hands of competing firms.[26]

The 1956 crisis over the Suez Canal restored the role of industry representatives in the FPSC and the voluntary agreement for international oil operations. Their plan of action developed cooperative arrangements and schedules of shipments among the major international oil companies. The plan also called for a Middle East Emergency Committee (MEEC) to coordinate the government's response to the crisis. The secretary of the interior administered the plan of action and appointed members of the MEEC, which included representatives of major American petroleum companies. Government officials also turned to the NPC to assist in the United States' long-term preparations to meet the threat posed by the Suez Canal closing. While the Eisenhower administration coped in 1956 with the immediate threat of dealing with the loss of oil through the canal, it also began plans for a longer-term response to such disruptions. In each instance the NPC had a role to play.

The Suez crisis unfolded during the summer and fall of 1956. It began on July 26, 1956, when Egyptian president Gamal Abdel Nasser nationalized the Suez Canal Company. Great Britain and France threatened military action and began economic reprisals. Through the summer and fall the United States sought a peaceful solution to the crisis. Cold war politics complicated the situation when the Soviet Union took the side of the Egyptians. Britain, France, and Israel moved troops into the canal area in October. On October 31, Britain bombed Egyptian military bases. The Egyptians responded by sinking ships in the canal, putting it out of operation. Acting together through the United Nations, the United States and the Soviet Union brought about a cease-fire; the removal of British, French, and Israeli troops; and the introduction of a UN peace-keeping force into the canal area.

But the damage had been done: Egypt had closed the canal. International oil operations were further disrupted after supporters of Nasser in Iraq sabotaged that country's pipelines. Before these events about 2 million barrels per day of petroleum had moved through the canal and pipeline, and the loss of much of this oil from international markets created a serious shortage in Europe. Individual American and Venezuelan companies at first met European demand for oil by shifting crude oil supplies and tankers. Some oil also made it around the difficult Cape of Good Hope. In addition, from the beginning of the crisis in summer, 1956, European countries increased crude oil inventories. When the canal closed, their governments instituted rationing. Such ad hoc solutions provided adequate supplies for essential public and business needs in Europe. By spring, 1957, the market had adjusted to the new situation; by summer the United States government disbanded its emergency coordinating agencies.[27]

The NPC closely monitored the development of the Suez crisis. Some of its members took part in the various government efforts to meet the challenges created by the canal closure. The council provided assistance to the government, for example, in helping find individuals to work in the Washington Voluntary Allocation Agreements offices and to assist on a technical level the Middle East Emergency Committee.[28]

Traditional NPC data gathering also contributed to the government's response to the Suez crisis. According to the DOI's director of the Office of Oil and Gas, the accumulated data found in NPC (and MPAB) reports put the government "in a position to analyze and meet practically any petroleum emergency which may arise" and supply "those who need basic petroleum information and sound data, thereby assuring a sound basis for all petroleum planning."[29] Events moved too fast in the Suez emergency to allow time for the NPC to conduct a detailed study of the best short-term response to the crisis.[30] But in examining the long-term implications of the Suez crisis, the NPC played its most important role in shaping the nation's planning for future disruptions.

The Suez crisis prompted the Eisenhower administration to examine the long-range needs of international petroleum distribution. Large tankers capable of economically shipping Middle Eastern oil around Africa appeared to be a solution to the unreliability of the Suez Canal. Both Secretary of State John Foster Dulles and President Eisenhower thought such "supertankers" could counter the threats Nasser had posed. Indeed, the president instructed the interior secretary to have the NPC call a conference on the future of petroleum distribution. In October, 1956, the NPC hosted such a conference, which included representatives from the Departments of State, Treasury, Defense, Commerce, and the Interior. Following two meetings the secretary of the interior requested that the NPC make a study of tanker transportation. The resulting *World Petroleum Tanker Construction Reports* (1956 and 1957) made projections through 1965. The government used the reports to develop policies for tanker construction to ensure that the United States and its allies could cope with future disruptions of oil shipments through the Suez Canal and Middle East pipelines.[31]

For more than a decade after the Suez crisis the United States and its allies did not face a comparable challenge to international oil operations. During those years, however, there were incidents that might have led to disruption of international flows of oil. The Middle East became unsettled in 1958, following a revolutionary change in government in Iraq. At that time both Lebanon and Jordan requested the landing of American and British troops to protect them. Matters quieted down quickly, but the government prepared to turn to voluntary agreements, as it had during the Suez crisis.

During the Cuban Missile Crisis of 1962 and following the June, 1967, "Six-Day" Middle East War, the U.S. government prepared to reactivate the Foreign Petroleum Supply Committee, which would have reintroduced voluntary agreements. In neither case did an emergency develop that disrupted supplies as did that following Suez. During the month after the 1967 war the canal closed and pipelines from Iraq and Saudi Arabia shut down, disrupting supplies to Europe. But the eleven years since the Suez crisis had witnessed the development of giant tankers five times larger than those available in 1956. Indeed, by 1967 the Japanese had built six tankers, each with a capacity seven times greater than those common at the time of Suez. The availability of these vessels lessened the crisis for Europe. Then, too, the Arab countries quickly returned their production to prewar levels. As in 1956, producers in the United States and Venezuela also increased their output to make up shortfalls brought on by the war and the embargo the Arab producers instituted against the United States, Germany, and Great Britain.[32]

The outbreak of still another Middle East war in October, 1973, again shook world oil markets, creating problems for countries allied with the United States. During the crises of the 1950s and 1960s the United States could call on its ample domestic supplies of petroleum to cushion the impact of supply disruptions on its domestic economy and on the economies of its allies. But by the 1970s the situation had changed dramatically with the growing dependence on imported oil. As imports rose to account for one-third to one-half of the nation's petroleum supply in the 1970s, the potential for drastic economic consequences from the loss of imports became an urgent matter of national security. With the United States and its allies becoming increasingly dependent on oil imported from politically unstable regions, questions of oil supply loomed large in shaping foreign policy as well as energy policy. Preparedness had taken on a pressing new dimension.

During the 1970s serious disruptions of oil shipments from the Middle East remained an urgent issue for both the government and the industry. War between Israel and its Arab neighbors in October, 1973, brought a selective embargo by Arab oil producers against supporters of Israel, including the United States. Before this crisis had begun, the NPC was at work on a report on emergency preparedness, and this report grew into an important source of information about the nation's capacity to withstand current and future disruptions in the supply of imported oil.[33] In the crisis that followed the embargo, the shah of Iran increased production to help offset the reduced shipments from neighboring countries. At the end of the decade, however, the shah's government fell and he fled into exile. During the crisis in 1978–79 that forced him from power, Iran could not maintain its oil shipments. Moreover, soon after taking over from the shah, the new government of Ayatollah Ruhollah Khomeini faced a war with neighboring Iraq, which attacked Iran on September 22, 1980. The beginning of a conflict between two of the major Middle East oil producers provided another major shock to world petroleum markets.

In response to its demonstrated vulnerability to such oil shocks, the United States launched a series of initiatives to reduce the country's vulnerability to disruptions of critical supplies of foreign oil. Because of the NPC's long experience with preparedness-related issues and its close ties with the petroleum industry, the government called on the council to study conditions in the industry and the nation's policy options regarding imported oil. The 1973–74 embargo prompted the creation of an emergency international program to share oil under the auspices of the International Energy Agency (IEA), which was a logical extension of the voluntary agreements to share oil adopted following the crises of the 1950s and 1960s. The IEA quickly became an important forum for the consideration of joint actions by the major oil-consuming nations in response to the joint actions of oil exporters through OPEC. Another major energy policy initiative was the creation of the Strategic Petroleum Reserve (SPR) of oil stored in the United States for use as an insurance policy against future disruptions of oil supplies. As will be discussed in chapter 4, National Petroleum Council studies helped shape the design, development, and use of the SPR. Both the IEA and the SPR were creative responses to the new realities that preparedness now involved measures taken to protect economic-energy security, not just military security. The two had become too intertwined to be treated as separate issues.

These two issues remained at the forefront when the petroleum industry planned responses to a variety of national emergencies. In September, 1989, with events in the Middle East much on his mind, Secretary of Energy Watkins requested the help of the NPC in designing an effective emergency response system. The council answered his request with *Industry Assistance to Government: Methods for Providing Petroleum Industry Expertise during Emergencies.* This publication outlined an approach in which the industry would be prepared to respond to three distinct levels of energy emergencies, depending on their nature and severity.

Level 1 would include all types of supply emergencies, including regional and local emergencies created by floods, hurricanes, earthquakes, and severe weather affecting refineries and distribution facilities. Under these scenarios key individuals designated by their companies became the contacts for informal one-on-one discussions with DOE officials. The NPC noted that while the DOE already maintained such a list, it should be updated regularly.

Level 2 scenarios included larger supply disruptions and national security emergencies, a description that included the Iraqi invasion of Kuwait in 1990. Under such circumstances a cross section of the petroleum industry, represented by no more than a dozen executives serving as an advisory committee, would give individual assessments of the specific situation and the actions they believe the secretary of energy should take. The report warned, however, that existing antitrust statutes might limit the ability of industry executives to respond fully to and participate in government-sponsored action to combat energy shortages.

Level 3 scenarios were the most extreme and included severe national security emergencies such as full military mobilization and war. Such events could trigger a Level 3 response if the United States were experiencing real or impending severe shortages in oil supplies; if the government were intervening or about to intervene in the marketplace; if the need for activation had been approved by the president; and if all antitrust and conflict of interest issues had been legislatively remedied. The NPC report also stated that a crisis that reduced Persian Gulf oil exports by 50 percent might also activate Level 3.

In these cases a petroleum National Defense Executive Reserve (NDER), designated and trained in advance, would be called to active duty. In many respects quite similar to the EPGA created with the assistance of the NPC in the 1960s, the NDER would assist the DOE in the management of its emergency programs, including the SPR, and direct, where necessary, activities of the oil industry to ensure that supplies meet the nation's essential military and civilian requirements. In discussing the role of the NDER, the council's report acknowledged that decisions on the SPR were the government's to make and that members of the industry could merely advise the government. The report recommended that the NDER should consist of fewer than fifty positions and should rely upon the petroleum industry to operate under competitive free market forces.

While the Defense Production Act of 1950 gave the president the power to create NDER organizations, its authorities had expired in October, 1990. In addition, antitrust and conflict-of-interest issues pertaining to DOE officials had a chilling effect on the industry's desire to participate in such an organization. The Departments of Defense and Commerce and a handful of other government agencies currently had NDER programs in place. The DOE had NDER units for electric power, coal, and natural gas, but no such organization existed for crude oil and petroleum products. The idea for a petroleum NDER was not new in 1991. The council's own 1981 emergency preparedness report had recommended the creation of such a body. President Ronald Reagan had in 1983 pushed for the establishment of an "emergency executive manpower reserve," a pool of oil industry officials upon whom the government could call for organizational help, advice, and an information-gathering clearinghouse to help direct and speed the operation of the market in an energy crunch. His efforts were without success. The GAO held that conflict-of-interest and antitrust laws would have prevented many if not most oil industry executives from participating in such an organization. And the 1991 industry assistance report commented that the main reason a petroleum NDER had still not been implemented was that such an organization would potentially run afoul of existing antitrust and conflict-of-interest laws. For example, in the event of the activation of the NDER, reservists called up from industry would be required to disassociate themselves from their companies, divest themselves of all energy-related financial holdings, and even restrict the functions they could perform upon their return to the private sector. The report urged that the George H. W. Bush administration press for the passage of the proposed January, 1990, amendment to the 1950 Defense Production Act.

Such considerations seemed to block the sort of cooperation that had been the hallmark of business-government cooperation in both world wars. The NPC report urged the passage of an amendment to the 1950 Defense Production Act to facilitate future cooperation by loosening the existing restrictions of those in industry who wanted to serve their country in the event of a national emergency. But even without the amendment, industry could look to history to see that a major war would undoubtedly overwhelm any restrictions on business-government cooperation deemed vital to successful mobilization. Such concerns might hinder peacetime planning for wartime cooperation, but they had never stood in the way of the defense of the nation.

To minimize legal problems, the report recommended that the DOE use an ad hoc approach in which twelve or fewer industry executives would be called on to give their advice and to express their views, in an informal setting, on current or future conditions. Such an approach would avoid existing antitrust and conflict-of-interest concerns while also getting more candid views from industry officials than might otherwise be the case in a larger group and a more formal setting.[34]

Such difficulties were to be expected in forging plans for cooperation between business and government to meet future national security crises. Preparedness for future crises raised a complex set of issues in a democratic society with a long-standing commitment to antitrust. In times of shooting wars antitrust had been suspended for the duration so that immediate threats to national security could be met with the combined efforts of industry. In times of peace—including even times of serious national peril short of war—antitrust considerations remained in effect and close cooperation was more difficult. The move from concerns about conventional war to cold war to nuclear war to economic and diplomatic "warfare" over oil supplies redefined preparedness, while making it much more difficult to pursue.

Still another important dimension to preparedness emerged in the 1990s, when cyberterrorism captured the attention of industry and government planners. The growing dependence on computers to manage the smooth flow of energy—and other vital commodities—posed a new threat to national security, since these computers were vulnerable to breakdowns from technical problems or from terrorist activities. In response to widespread concerns about the security of the computers that had become central to the operations of the nation's infrastructure, government officials called on the NPC to study ways to enhance the security of the petroleum industry by safeguarding it against potential disruptions in computing and telecommunications services.

This new focus on electronic bits, not bombs, as threats to national security first grabbed headlines as the year 2000, or "Y2K," approached, when many experts warned of massive problems from the breakdown of a computer system not programmed to operate in the new century. Potential Y2K problems caused information technology experts in business and government to seek ways to safeguard the nation's computer systems from the chaos that seemed imminent. At the same time, these experts began to look past the immediate issues raised by the coming of the new millennium to examine more general security issues raised by the nation's growing reliance on sophisticated computing and telecommunication systems.

In May, 1998, President Bill Clinton issued a White Paper on the vulnerabilities of the nation's "critical infrastructures"—including telecommunications, energy, banking and finance, transportation, water systems, and emergency services—to "equipment failures, human error, weather and other natural causes, and physical and cyber attacks."[35] The White Paper called for the creation of new approaches to planning that reached across the traditional boundaries of the public and private sectors.

In response to the president's request, Secretary of Energy Bill Richardson turned to the National Petroleum Council for a study of these issues as they affected the petroleum industry. In a letter to NPC chairman Joe B. Foster in April, 1999, Secretary Richardson made a formal request for the NPC to "review the potential vulnerabilities of the oil and gas industries to attack—both physical and cyber—and to advise me on policies and practices that industry and Government, separately and in partnership, should adopt to protect or recover from such attacks."[36] After an exchange of letters with Foster, Richardson formally approved the establishment of the NPC Committee on Critical Infrastructure Protection in August, 1999.

To chair the new committee, the council named Richard B. Cheney, then chairman and CEO of Halliburton Company, a major service company with working ties to most segments of the petroleum industry. When Cheney stepped down in August, 2000, to campaign for the vice presidency, he was replaced as committee chairman by his successor at Halliburton, David Lesar. In addition to representatives of major oil and gas companies, the committee included members from major service companies and from the financial community. In an economy and an industry increasingly interconnected by computers, the intent of the committee was to take a broad view in identifying potential problems and beginning to forge cooperative endeavors to address them.

Published in June, 2001, the committee's final report, *Securing Oil and Natural Gas Infrastructures in the New Economy*, began by defining the new security challenges facing the petroleum industry in an age of computers. At the heart of the matter was a simple reality: "Electronic tools have been developed at a rapid pace and have been quickly incorporated by the oil and natural gas industries in their electronic infrastructures. The pace at which these changes have taken place has been so fast that adequate measures for critical infrastructure protection have lagged behind."[37] Without the development of adequate safeguards, the petroleum industry was vulnerable to severe disruptions caused by technical problems as well as by the actions of hackers and terrorists. Such disruptions represented threats to the national security as real as those caused by traditional wars.

For solutions, the committee looked at the "Y2K model," which had used the sense of urgency created by the immediate threat of widespread problems to forge broad cooperation and information sharing. Since no imminent disaster loomed in the near future, the committee faced a difficult educational task in building the sense of common purpose required to address problems that clearly transcended the operations of individual companies. One key conclusion was that business and government needed greater cooperation in sharing information and experience about the best ways to manage the new risks produced by the growing reliance on modern computers. Officials in industry and government needed to plan unified responses to future breakdowns in computer services.

Of particular importance to the industry as a whole was greater coordination of the efforts of individual companies to enhance the security of vital information technology processes. The NPC's study concluded that the best mechanism for industrywide coordination to improve the security of computer operations would be what it called "an industry-directed service provider."[38] To this end, the report recommended that the petroleum industry should "establish a secure information-sharing mechanism to collect, assess, and share with its members information on physical and electronic threats, certain vulnerabilities, incidents, and solutions/best practices."[39] This information sharing and analysis center (ISAC) would become the focus of industry cooperation in safeguarding vital cybersystems.

The NPC report recommended several governmental actions needed to ensure that an industry-directed approach could succeed. Foremost was the loosening of legal and regulatory constraints to information sharing; close cooperation could not move forward under existing antitrust laws. Industry-directed coordination could also be improved if government would make available to the ISAC current information about pressing threats to the petroleum industry's computer systems. The federal government should also take the lead in researching and developing new safeguards and in improving cooperation with foreign governments on the adoption of global standards and protections for computer systems. In the tradition of civil defense planning, government agencies should continue to prepare for recovery efforts in the event of widespread problems with the nation's cybersystems.

Securing Oil and Natural Gas Infrastructures in the New Economy highlighted the growing need for coordination within the petroleum industry and between industry and government in planning to ensure the smooth flow of the nation's energy to markets. With oil and gas supplying approximately 62 percent of the United States' energy in 2001, any disruption of supplies had immediate implications for national security. As had been the case throughout its existence, at the turn of the new century the National Petroleum Council retained an important role in preparing the vital oil and gas industries for a variety of challenges.

For more than half a century, the NPC has helped identify and study new threats to the security of the petroleum industry and recommend ways to safeguard national security by protecting the flow of oil and natural gas. Throughout its history, the council's reports have played an important role in ensuring that the petroleum industry remains ready to step forward and meet the demands of national emergencies. While compiling reports on various aspects of preparedness, the NPC also has assisted government officials in planning and maintaining an organizational structure for business-government cooperation that could be activated in times of emergencies. Beginning with the efforts of its predecessor, the Petroleum Industry War Council in World War II, the NPC's work on preparedness in all of its many forms has been and continues to be the council's most significant contribution to the nation.

CHAPTER 3

A New Outlook on U.S. Energy Policy

EVENTS IN THE LATE 1960s moved the National Petroleum Council beyond its traditional emphasis on emergency preparedness. As basic assumptions about energy changed, the council faced a variety of new questions concerning the long-term outlook for oil and gas and other forms of energy. In previous decades of energy abundance, ample supplies of oil and gas at stable prices seemed ensured and the balance between foreign and domestic supplies of oil seemed manageable. Such assumptions began breaking down in the late 1960s under relentless pressure from rapidly expanding demand for oil and gas, both in the United States and abroad. The inability of domestic supply to keep pace with demand raised serious new questions about America's energy future, and the Department of the Interior turned to the National Petroleum Council in its search for answers.[1]

The key problems in this era of energy transition were evident in the late 1960s, several years before they became pressing concerns in the wake of the Arab oil embargo of winter, 1973–74. Given proper incentives, could domestic oil and gas production expand to meet the growing demand for energy? If not, what were the logical alternatives? What was the proper role of imported oil in America's energy mix? What was the proper role of government and of market forces in energy?

In late 1970 the secretary of the interior asked the NPC for answers to such questions. For the next three years the council mobilized the efforts of some 250 energy specialists to produce the multivolume *U.S. Energy Outlook*, its most ambitious study to date.[2] The report used past energy trends to project possible energy futures for the United States. Published on the eve of the energy crises of the 1970s, this landmark study was at once the last major document of the era of energy abundance and the first of the new era of scarcity. It could not avoid the influence of traditional assumptions about energy demand and supply, nor could it predict the far-reaching changes wrought by OPEC's assertion of control over crude pricing. But it helped set the terms of debate about energy policy in the 1970s by providing for policy makers a comprehensive, market-oriented analysis of several possible energy futures for the nation.

PREVIOUS PETROLEUM POLICY STUDIES

In 1949 and 1966 the NPC had prepared reports on petroleum policies that foreshadowed much about the writing of *U.S. Energy Outlook.* In each of these studies the task of building a consensus within the NPC proved difficult. Tensions inevitably accompanied the debates within the diverse membership of the council on such divisive issues as, for example, the role of imported oil in supplying America's growing demand for energy. When the topic turned to the position of petroleum in the energy mix of the nation, the NPC's reports drew criticism from representatives of other energy industries, most notably coal. Because of the great significance of energy and the high visibility of the NPC, its reports on oil policy also attracted intense political scrutiny from critics who did not share the oil industry's views. Amid the tensions that swirled around its reports on petroleum policy, the NPC generally avoided specific policy recommendations, choosing instead to issue broad statements of the market-oriented principles that policy makers should follow in defining specific oil and energy policies.

Reaching agreement within the NPC on even a broad statement on oil imports proved difficult. Since well before World War II the import issue had ripped apart all efforts at consensus building within the industry. In the 1920s the American Petroleum Institute led the fight to define an industrywide accord on the closely related issues of imports and restrictions of domestic production. This proved impossible in an era of glut, when domestic producers passionately argued that every barrel of imported oil allowed into the nation meant one less barrel sold by U.S. companies. Failing to find common ground for the international companies that depended on import markets for their growing supplies of foreign oil and the domestic producers that considered the U.S. market as their preserve, the API stepped away from this volatile issue and watched as the federal government imposed a tariff on oil imports in the 1930s. Thus, even before oil imports became a significant part of the U.S. energy mix, the battle had been joined. Independent producers saw themselves as the backbone of a healthy domestic oil industry. They understood that unrestricted imports from giant foreign fields with much lower production costs than the older, smaller domestic fields spelled their economic doom, and they made the restriction of imports their top priority. Emphasizing the argument that national security required a healthy domestic industry, these independents defined the agenda for the political debate over imports for almost half a century.

Near the end of World War II the Petroleum Industry War Council grappled with this issue in its general statement, *A Petroleum Policy for the United States*. Included was the following statement on imports: "It should be the policy of this nation to so restrict amounts of imported oil so that such quantities will not disturb or distress the producing end of the domestic petroleum industry."[3] From the point of view of the independents, World War II had shown again the key lesson of World War I: oil won modern wars. The first principle of U.S. oil policy thus should be to encourage the expansion of the domestic industry with promotional policies such as preferential tax treatment for oil exploration and easy access to public lands. Such policies would be for naught, however, if cheap imports were allowed to overwhelm domestic oil in the marketplace.

Facing difficult and controversial choices on postwar oil policy, the Department of the Interior turned to the newly created National Petroleum Council for advice. Among the earliest requests to the NPC from Ralph Davies, acting director of the Oil and Gas Division of the DOI, was a letter in September, 1946, asking for a report on broad issues of oil policy. The letter noted that "various questions of great national importance relating to the adequacy of crude oil and its products, of access to foreign reserves, and of actions by the Government relating thereto which should be taken to insure the adequacy of oil supplies for the United States are continually arising." Citing instructions from President Truman that the secretary of the interior should seek to coordinate and unify federal petroleum policies, the letter observed that "these are matters on which the advice and counsel of the petroleum industry are vital if Governmental action is to be intelligent and effective and based on a full understanding of all of the facts."[4] Be that as it might, the NPC's Agenda Committee declined the request, responding that the PIWC's proclamation on oil policy near the end of World War II "is still a current document" and that "restating such policy at this time would serve no constructive purpose."[5] Indeed, the effort to define a general oil policy acceptable to the diverse membership of the NPC might have proven quite destructive within the council, since there was no easy consensus on such issues as oil imports.

As the debates over oil policy intensified within government and in the broader body politic, the NPC found itself on the inside looking out. It had a strong working relationship with the Oil and Gas Division, but it had little voice outside of the DOI. As the Truman administration considered its options in oil policy, a variety of voices from outside the oil and gas industries put forward proposals for greatly increased government involvement in energy. In 1948 Eugene Rostow, a Yale professor of economics, angered segments of the industry with a much-discussed book entitled *A National Policy for the Oil Industry*, which proposed radically restructuring the oil industry, ending prorationing, and increasing imports.[6] At the same time strong voices within the federal government called for a government-led program to develop synthetic fuels from coal and shale oil, and the Federal Trade Commission was gearing up to pursue an antitrust case against the international oil companies.[7] Such proposals for government programs convinced the NPC to reconsider its previous decision to refrain from putting forward a broad statement on oil policies. The desire to respond to external critics overrode the desire to avoid potentially divisive internal debates.

In June, 1948, Max Ball, director of the Oil and Gas Division, wrote to NPC chair Walter Hallanan with a request that the council reconsider its decision not to prepare a report on national oil policy. Ball was "most anxious to avoid the possibility of the refusal of the Council to advise the Government on a matter of such high national importance," and he submitted a draft letter so that the NPC's Agenda Committee could consider the request informally and make any revisions "deemed necessary or desirable."[8] The Agenda Committee made minor revisions to the request letter, which noted that "during the past year the subject of national oil policy has been a matter of intensive consideration and discussion by several branches of government, the public, and the petroleum industry." Its chairman, George Hill, then declared that this request represented an emergency under existing NPC rules, thus allowing the Agenda Committee to speed its deliberations by using written opinions as opposed to a formal meeting. In July, 1948, the committee recommended that the NPC appoint a committee to "restudy and supplement" the PIWC's report on oil policy.

After the council as a whole approved this recommendation, the process of writing the report moved quickly. A twenty-four-member Committee on

National Oil Policy met four times between July, 1948, and January, 1949. Chaired by the president of Amerada Petroleum Corporation, this committee contained more than one-fourth of all the members of the NPC, and it had a balanced representation of majors and independents. Chairing the drafting committee was Joseph Pogue, a noted oil economist and a vice president of Chase National Bank of New York, which had prominent majors as clients. Pogue previously had published an article entitled "Oil and National Policy," and the committee received copies of this along with copies of the original PIWC statement on oil policy and "National Oil and Gas Policy," recently published by the Independent Petroleum Producers of America (IPPA).[9] These documents became the starting point for the seven-man drafting committee consisting of Pogue, Charles Harding (a director of Socony-Vacuum), Eugene Holman (president of Standard of New Jersey), Stuart Crocker (president of Columbia Gas, a large gas distribution company), Frank Porter (president of the Mid-Continent Oil & Gas Association), George Hill (president of the Houston Oil Company, a large independent Houston oil company and chair of the NPC's Agenda Committee), and Russell Brown (general counsel of the IPPA). This committee had the difficult task of putting into words the principles for oil policy that would be acceptable as the consensus view of the NPC and the industry as a whole.

Hammering out such a consensus was no easy matter, for the oil industry remained deeply divided on the issue of imports. Years later, as the NPC prepared to revise the 1949 report for reissue in 1966, several of those involved in the debates in the late 1940s reminded their younger colleagues of "the many hours it took to write" the 1949 report and "the rather conflicting opinions" that had to be resolved in the process.[10] At Max Ball's urging, the NPC had agreed to put forward a broad position paper on oil policy so that the industry's voice would be added to the "increasing activity among committees of Congress and other groups of civilians urging the formulation of a national policy regarding oil and gas."[11] Yet on imports, competing views within the industry were fundamentally at odds. Citing the needs of national security, independent producers argued strongly that domestic markets had to be protected from rising imports. The major international companies that controlled these imports obviously had a different self-interest and a different view of the national interest. They argued that increased imports would allow the nation to retain its domestic reserves for use in future national emergencies.

Published in 1949, the final report, *A National Oil Policy for the United States,* contained generally worded compromise on the divisive issue of imports. It concluded that the participation of U.S. companies in the development of foreign fields was needed to promote free enterprise around the world, but that imports into the United States from these fields could not be allowed to undermine the health of the domestic industry. Indeed, "the availability of petroleum from domestic fields produced under sound conservation practices . . . provides the means for determining if imports are necessary and the extent to which imports are desirable to supplement our oil supplies."[12]

On other issues the NPC report gave voice to a general position that might best be characterized as a call for an "American-style free market" in oil and gas. This view embraced government promotion of a healthy petroleum industry at home and abroad, including prorationing of oil production by state governments in the interest of conservation, state control of offshore lands, continued easy access to public lands, and the continuation of existing tax incentives for oil and gas exploration and development. It opposed government regulation of gas prices or end uses of energy, touting the virtues of a free market in which "price functions effectively as a regulator of supply and demand." It opposed government-owned synthetic fuel plants, arguing that "synthetic fuels will attain an orderly and economic development by private industry, if normal incentives are free to operate." Government prorationing and its impact on the price of oil were not addressed; by the late 1940s government controls over levels of production in the interest of conservation and stable prices had been widely accepted by the industry as a part of the normal workings of the free market. The report justified government controls of imports, since the "national security and welfare require a healthy domestic oil industry."[13]

A National Oil Policy for the United States reflected the shared assumptions of the oil fraternity on the eve of the cold war—as well as its divisions on several key issues. Abundant and relatively inexpensive petroleum would flow from a free enterprise system nurtured by government promotion. Market forces, not government direction, would shape the rise of new energy sources, which would enter the market when called forth by price. Aggregate consumption and specific end uses for oil and gas would also be dictated by price, which would ensure adequate supplies. The major limit of the market suggested by the report was its inability to ensure the health of the domestic industry in the face of growing imports. On this issue the voice of domestic producers was heard loud and clear: Given the vital role of oil in times of war, domestic production should be encouraged and protected, if necessary, from imports. Anticipation of the needs of future wars did not require the setting aside of oil reserves in the public lands or offshore. Instead oil policies should encourage the expansion of the domestic industry, since "the greater the civilian consumption at the outset of a war, the larger will be the supplies available through rationing."[14]

This was the voice of a confident industry, poised to expand in the United States and throughout the world and strongly committed to a vision of American-style capitalism. The NPC's initial report on oil policy laid out the framework for an oil/energy policy shaped by market forces in the domestic arena and national security considerations in foreign affairs. Through careful choice of words the NPC's committee crafted a general statement that could be supported by most segments of the oil industry. The creation of this fragile consensus was no small accomplishment given the deep divisions of interest within the industry on several fundamental issues, and the process of writing this report illustrated the capacity of the council to serve as a powerful unifying force within its industry.

THE BATTLE AGAINST SYNTHETIC FUELS

By the time of the report's publication in 1949, however, the Truman administration was headed in a different direction, and its secretary of the interior, Julius Krug, responded with public indignation at the report. He voiced his displeasure directly to the industry in an address to the American Petroleum Institute in Pittsburgh in April, 1949. In particular, Krug found the report lacking in its treatment of the government's roles involving safeguarding the consumers' interest in low prices and protecting the independent producers and small refiners. He disagreed fundamentally with the report's easy reliance on free markets in energy: "The government must view with suspicion the prices and profits of recent years in the petroleum industry and cannot trust the industry to determine prices because free markets do not exist continuously."[15]

One of Krug's assistant secretaries went even further in his criticism of the NPC's report, noting that it disagreed directly with the secretary's positions on the tidelands and synthetic fuels and that its general principles "are now almost too trite to need repetition." He concluded, "Although we have an Oil and Gas Division charged with the responsibility for developing policy and program in the field, we, in effect, transferred that responsibility to the National Petroleum Council."[16] The Truman administration was beginning to push for much greater government involvement in the oil and gas industries, including government-owned synfuels plants, federal government control of offshore leasing, regulation of gas prices, and antitrust against the major international oil companies. In these critical areas the administration was at odds with the NPC's recommendations in *A National Oil Policy for the United States.* For the next four years the industry would fight President Truman on all of these fronts.

The NPC aggressively questioned the economic wisdom of the president's push to develop a synthetic fuel industry in the United States. "Synthetic fuels," a term used to include a variety of liquid and gaseous fuels produced from shale oil and coal, had been put forward in the 1920s as a huge new source of domestic energy. After being submerged under the oil glut of the 1920s and 1930s, synthetic fuels enjoyed a resurgence of interest in the late 1940s, when the Department of the Interior championed them as a way to develop dependable domestic reserves to meet the increasing demand for oil. With access to patents shared by Standard of New Jersey and I. G. Farben before World War II and to captured German documents that contained detailed information about the Nazis' massive synthetic fuel industry during the war, the DOI spearheaded the postwar effort to build a large new synthetic fuel industry.

Citing the needs of national security, both Julius Krug, secretary of the interior, and James Forrestal, secretary of defense, backed substantial public investment in synfuels in the late 1940s. They sought the immediate construction of demonstration plants and the creation in the long term of a new industry capable of producing as much as a million barrels of synthetic fuels a day. Initial estimates of the costs of such fuels were quite optimistic, with the Bureau of Mines in the DOI asserting in 1949 that the production costs of gasoline from coal would be within several cents per gallon of the cost of gasoline. Such estimates were used to justify the government-financed construction of demonstration plants heralded as "the forerunners of a new basic industry that ultimately may free the United States from dependence on foreign oil."[17] Federal funding would be used to launch the new industry and support it until it became competitive with oil.[18]

The NPC forcefully opposed such funding.[19] The battleground was the projected cost of synthetic fuels. Council members from large oil companies with experience in this area found the Bureau of Mines's cost estimate decidedly low. In April, 1950, newly appointed secretary of the interior Oscar Chapman asked the NPC to review the cost projections of the Bureau of Mines and prepare independent cost estimates. The council agreed and created a study committee headed by W. S. S. Rodgers of the Texas Company and staffed largely by representatives of major oil companies. To complete its study the NPC called on 49 subcommittee members and as many as 150 technical personnel from the oil industry. The goal was "an authoritative evaluation . . . of definite value, both to government and industry . . . indicating the probable future of synthetic liquid fuels."[20] For three years, from 1950 until its final report in 1953, the NPC looked closely at potential synthetic fuel prices and estimated them to be substantially higher than the earlier cost figures put forward by the Bureau of Mines. The council concluded that "all methods of manufacturing synthetic liquid fuels proposed by the Bureau of Mines are definitely uneconomical under present conditions."[21]

The synthetic fuels debate pitted coal against oil, parts of the DOI against the NPC, and advocates of New Deal–type government activism versus proponents of market forces. In the heated debates over the use of government subsidies to encourage the creation of a major new energy industry, the NPC played a crucial role in reminding all involved of such a program's economic costs. The American-style free market approach advocated by the NPC had no room for large government subsidies to develop a new source of energy as yet unable to compete economically with oil and gas. Many within the NPC believed that foreign oil provided a viable option to make up any foreseeable shortfall in domestic oil production. The NPC had examined closely the economics of synthetic fuels in this era and found them wanting. Most observers acknowledged the significant role of the council's reports in delaying the expansion of President Truman's synthetic fuels program until the election of a new president who was less sympathetic to this initiative. In this case the NPC helped block a new government program that it viewed as premature and unwarranted by the market.

Ironically, as President Eisenhower moved to shut down government synthetic fuels programs in his first term, a new source of energy unmentioned in NPC reports of the 1940s and early 1950s, nuclear power, would become the recipient of government supports far in excess of those proposed for synthetic fuels. During the decades of the 1950s and 1960s nuclear energy became the consensus choice for a dramatically expanded role in the nation's energy future, and speculation about the prospects for synthetic fuels largely disappeared. But the projected transition to nuclear power was not in the nation's immediate future. As the demand for energy grew sharply in response to the postwar boom, other sources of energy could not compete economically with oil and gas, and the nation's reliance on these fuels increased.

Within the oil industry and the NPC, tensions over oil imports continued to grow during the 1950s and 1960s. Despite the imposition of voluntary restrictions on imports in the early 1950s and mandatory import controls after 1959, domestic production could not keep pace with domestic demand. Booming production of oil in the Middle East, Africa, and other regions supplied the surging demand in Europe and Japan while also supplying much needed oil to the U.S. market. The NPC periodically issued short reports on petroleum imports, and its message remained consistent with that of *A National Oil Policy for the United States:* Imports should be restrained to ensure the health of the domestic industry in the name of national security. But as demand for oil in the United States moved higher and higher and domestic production began to level off in the late 1960s, the NPC and the industry as a whole had to confront an old nemesis, the debate over the proper place of imports in the domestic market.

The opportunity to do so came in 1965, when the Department of the Interior requested that the NPC review its 1949 statement of the proper principles underlying oil national policy and "report its views based upon its appraisal of conditions as they are today and as they may be anticipated to evolve in the future."[22] After a lengthy discussion of the appropriateness of revisiting the 1949 report, the Agenda Committee recommended approval of the request. One member acknowledged, "I would rather see a committee appointed by the council take a crack at it than some others I can think of."[23] A twenty-seven-person committee led by Dean McGee of Kerr-McGee and dominated by independent producers set about the task of "modernizing" the previous statement of oil policy. A nine-person drafting committee led by Richard Gonzalez of Houston took the primary responsibility for writing the report. An experienced economist for Humble Oil and a director of that company from 1951 to 1965, Gonzalez drafted much of the original report, which embodied his strong devotion to market-oriented principles and deep concern for the national security implications of oil policies.

In several long meetings during fall, 1965, the committee went through the 1949 report "clause by clause" and suggested revisions. The initial meeting identified several basic changes since 1949, including the growing importance of oil and gas in the nation's energy mix, price regulation of natural gas by the Federal Power Commission, and a shift from an era of rapidly increasing demand after World War II to a time of slower demand growth in the 1960s. Also noted was the substantial decline of domestic exploration since 1956 and the growth of imports to about 20 percent of domestic oil consumption. After extended discussion of the issues covered in the 1949 report, the committee decided to add fuller treatments of natural gas and government research in energy. It rejected inclusion of several additional issues suggested by individual members, notably the need for stockpiling of oil supplies for use in future emergencies and discussion of the oil industry's record of good citizenship. Agreed upon was use of the word *petroleum* to include oil and gas; there was also agreement about the need to focus on petroleum policies—oil, gas, and synthetic fuels—instead of attempting to define broader energy policy.[24] Two days of meetings in October, 1965, gave Gonzalez input to write a working draft of the new report. After receiving comments on this draft, he prepared second and third drafts for use at the drafting committee's next meeting on November 30. A final report was submitted to the NPC in early 1966.

Though much had changed in the world of oil and gas since 1949, the report as published on March 1, 1966, under the title *Petroleum Policies for the United States* differed little from the earlier report. It began with a strong restatement of the industry's firm commitment to free enterprise and limited government. While acknowledging that government regulations were at times "required for reasons of national security and conservation," the report cautioned that government "should interfere as little as possible with normal competitive forces that encourage efficient operations."[25] It advocated strong government support for U.S. nationals abroad and the continuation of existing state-led conservation and pollution control programs, as well as the continuation of provisions in the tax code aimed at encouraging exploration for oil and gas. Although the report stopped short of advocating deregulation of natural gas prices, it called for more efficient regulation to encourage expansion of gas supplies. Competition based on price would produce the proper mix of energy sources without government intervention.

The report did, however, call on government to maintain flexible quotas on imports to "provide opportunity for and encourage expansion of all phases of domestic petroleum operations in keeping with increasing demands insofar as practicable."[26] Coming as it did in the midst of a general argument for free markets, this somewhat convoluted statement on import policy reflected all too clearly the new reality of the petroleum industry: Domestic production could no longer keep pace with the oil demand reserved for it under the import quota system.

Petroleum Policies for the United States elicited little response from government or from the larger society. As a restatement of the industry's belief in traditional American-style free markets, it contained nothing new or particularly controversial. Its assumption of energy abundance reflected the mindset that had guided oil policies throughout most of the postwar era. Its lack of pressing concern about the nation's growing reliance on imported oil reflected a generally held assumption that oil from the major exporting nations would continue to flow freely and at traditional prices for the foreseeable future. A more demanding analysis of the changing balance of domestic and foreign production might have helped educate the public and government officials about the implications of the nation's growing dependence on imported oil.

U.S. ENERGY OUTLOOK: DISPATCH
FROM BETWEEN TWO WORLDS

In the late 1960s fundamental changes in the world oil economy steadily undermined the basic assumptions underlying the post–World War II energy order, raising serious questions about the nation's energy future. Driving these changes were two related trends: the continuing surge in U.S. and world oil consumption and the decline in the discovery rate for domestic oil. Strict new environmental regulations that placed constraints on the use of coal and other relatively dirty domestic fuels heightened the demand for oil and gas. The figures on supply and demand did not lie. By 1970 the traditional as-sumption of abundant supplies of cheap oil could no longer be taken for granted.

A series of events that year brought this fact to the attention of policy makers in business and government. First came a stern warning from a promi-nent group of domestic producers that surplus capacity within the United States was fast disappearing. Then in July, 1970, the Libyan government of Mu'ammar Qaddafi played hardball in its negotiations with international oil companies by temporarily cutting off the shipment of four hundred thou-sand barrels per day of crude oil. Libya's low sulfur crude was much in de-mand in the United States, and this episode served as a stern warning about the perils of the nation's growing dependence on oil imports from politically unpredictable countries. Later that same year the closing of the Trans-Arabian Pipeline reinforced this warning by removing another five hundred thousand barrels per day of Middle Eastern production from shipment via the Mediter-ranean Sea, creating a scramble for large tankers to ship this oil around the African cape to markets in Europe and the United States.[27] With increases in domestic supplies lagging behind increases in U.S. demand, these events raised serious doubts about the nation's capacity to withstand future cutoffs of the now-vital supplies of imports from OPEC nations.

The voluntary and mandatory controls of the 1950s and 1960s had sought to limit imports to about 12 percent of the total U.S. demand for oil.[28] Vari-ous administrative adjustments allowed this figure to ease up toward 20 per-cent in the years before the energy crisis. But a simple, disturbing, new reality was becoming evident: Domestic oil could no longer automatically fill the demand protected for it by import quotas. In short, with demand for oil outrunning available domestic supplies, greater reliance on imports or some other source of energy could not be constrained by unrealistic quotas.

One response was the creation by Richard Nixon of a task force on import control under the direction of Secretary of Labor George P. Schulz. With information from numerous sources, including the NPC and individual oil companies, this task force looked hard at existing import controls and found them wanting. Published in early 1970, its report suggests the difficulties that would face the NPC's more ambitious study *U.S. Energy Outlook.* The task force held numerous traditional assumptions about oil and energy—notably that foreign oil would remain less expensive than domestic, that the risk of cutoffs of imports for political reasons was low, and that oil from the North Slope of Alaska would reach the lower forty-eight states in three years.[29] Even with these "friendly" assumptions, the task force concluded that import quotas should be replaced by a more efficient system based on some form of tariff.

The import quota system was the most visible symbol of the traditional, post–World War II order in oil. One key assumption underlying energy policy in this era had been the need to protect the health of the domestic industry in order to promote national security. In the decades before the energy crises of the 1970s, this protection meant barriers to the growth of imports, a series of tax laws aimed at directing investment toward domestic exploration, and a system of prorationing of production aimed at conserving domestic oil while maintaining the price of oil. As the nation entered what proved to be a tumultuous decade in the 1970s, easy access to greater supplies of domestic and foreign oil at traditional prices could no longer be assumed.

In the years before the shock of the Arab oil embargo of winter, 1973–74, numerous specialists in industry and government sought to understand the far-reaching changes transforming the petroleum industry, to interpret them to a broader audience, and to suggest government policy responses to changing conditions. In 1970 the secretary of the interior asked the National Petroleum Council to join in this effort by undertaking the most comprehensive study of energy policy in this period. Like the task force on import controls and numerous others in these transition years, the NPC faced the daunting task of peering into the future through lenses colored by traditional assumptions about energy.

The original request letter from the secretary of the interior for the study that became *U.S. Energy Outlook* asked the NPC to examine oil and gas supply and demand in the Western Hemisphere "projected into the future as near to the end of the century as [is] feasible." A lively debate about this letter within the Agenda Committee helped sharpen the focus of the study. Several members protested that such broad studies had not proved effective in the past, noting that "the National Petroleum Council did prepare a tentative . . . petroleum policy in 1949 and again in 1966 . . . but it was produced and then it [lay] there, so to speak."[30] Skepticism grew after comments about the difficulties of projecting conditions far into the future—reminders that the NPC had never before ventured outside of the United States to study trends throughout the hemisphere and warnings of the controversy that would accompany discussions of issues such as the oil depletion allowance. Jake Hamon, chairman of the Agenda Committee, argued forcefully that the "imponderables" involved in projecting trends to the end of the century meant that "whatever report we make . . . is going to be wrong either on the high side or the low side." He went on to say that "it is utterly ridiculous to me to say in this uncertain world that we, the National Petroleum Council, attempt to say what is going to happen in the year 2000. . . . I do not think we ought to undertake this study. I think it is impossible; and that is all I have to say." Then bowing to what he considered the will of the remainder of the Agenda Committee, Hamon concluded, "Now, I suppose I will entertain a motion to undertake this study."[31]

After the Agenda Committee redrafted parts of the request letter from the Department of the Interior, the NPC agreed to undertake the study. The revised letter stressed the need for a broad study of energy in an era of transition: "A number of events affecting basic policies of government and the social and physical environment of the Nation have occurred or appear imminent which will set the stage for a new era in the petroleum industry in the United States." Citing the "important and pervasive nature of the changes which may be engendered by these events," the request letter concluded that "there is need for an appraisal of their impact on the future availability of petroleum supplies to the United States." It gave the NPC general guidelines for the scope and focus of the study, asking for the inclusion of the oil and gas outlook in the Western Hemisphere "projected into the future as near to the end of the century as [is] feasible." It asked for a comprehensive study of the conditions in the oil and gas industries, including government energy policies, and concluded, "The Council's final report should indicate ranges of probable outcomes where appropriate and should emphasize areas where Federal oil and gas policies and programs can effectively and appropriately contribute to the attainment of an optimum long-term national energy policy."[32] The NPC agreed to undertake the study, which would focus on three fundamental questions raised in the request letter: How much energy would the United States need? From where would it come? And what changes in government policies and/or economic conditions in the energy industries would be required to improve the nation's energy posture?[33]

From the outset it was clear that *U.S. Energy Outlook* would be unprecedented in scope. The NPC mobilized the resources and personnel of the energy industries into task groups organized to examine selected aspects of the nation's energy future. Almost 250 energy experts worked on the various task forces, with 163 from council member organizations, 41 from non-council-member organizations, 35 from government, and 9 staff members from the NPC. Representatives from electric utilities and the nuclear, coal, and synfuels industries provided the study committee with "the best talent on these matters available in the United States today," according to the committee's chairman, John McLean, then president of Conoco.[34] This diverse mix represented a sharp departure for the NPC, which never before had drawn so heavily on expertise from outside the oil and gas industries.

The final cost of the study is impossible to determine given the contributions in time and resources of council members. Estimates of the direct cost to the NPC ranged up to $1.5 million. The total cost to the industry as a whole came to perhaps $10 million. More than three years of labor produced volumes of information about energy, as well as a computer bank of energy-related statistics and computer models made available to numerous universities. In undertaking a comprehensive view of all energy forms, not just oil and gas, the NPC broke new ground for itself. In the process it produced a valuable and controversial study that became a starting point for the intense debates about energy futures and energy policies spawned by the supply crises of the 1970s.

The results of this massive study came forward in three distinct stages. The first product came out fairly quickly with the publication of *U.S. Energy Outlook: An Initial Appraisal, 1971–1985,* in July, 1971. The final report, published in December, 1972, projected energy supply and demand under four different sets of circumstances. This "scenario" approach allowed the NPC to examine various alternatives facing the nation, and these projections could be extended to discuss possible trends in the years after 1985. The task groups subsequently published a series of detailed reports on their work. These came out according to the time clocks of the different task forces, with the last reports published in 1974. This project's final product was a set of computer models showing aspects of energy supply and demand. These were developed to analyze future trends and were made available to universities upon completion of the study.

The publication of the interim report focused public attention on the changing realities of energy. The report made projections of the supply and demand for energy "under certain assumed conditions which involve minimal changes from present policies, practices and economic climate."[35] In assuming the regulatory and economic environments as stable, this report essentially projected energy trends from the post–World War II era into the years from 1971 to 1985. This was a useful exercise for those involved in the broader study, since it gave them a basic starting point from which to work. The contemporary reader—who could not know that sharp discontinuities in the overall patterns of oil supply and demand loomed just over the horizon— could take some comfort in the tone of the report, which suggested that America's short-term energy problems, though real, were manageable.

Assumptions spawned by a long era of energy abundance shaped the interim report. As listed on the first page of the report, they included the following: extension into the future of recent trends in oil and gas exploration and discovery rates; "relatively constant" investment trends in oil and gas exploration and production; the continued use of oil imports to satisfy shortfalls in domestic production and the lack of "political, economic and logistical considerations" that restrict the availability of imports; the use of all "presently feasible sources of gas supply" from both domestic and foreign sources; the maximum use of nuclear power "consistent with a feasible development program"; and a rise in coal production to the extent allowed by economic, technological, and environmental requirements. Taken as a whole, this set of assumptions reflected what the study's members acknowledged was an optimistic projection of future trends based on patterns that had held true in the past.

A closer look at these assumptions is useful in understanding the conclusions of the interim report, the difficulties facing those working on the project, and, indeed, the problems facing the United States if and when easy access to imports ended. At the heart of the matter was the balance between domestic production and imports. On this vital issue the interim report could only assume some variation of what was considered the status quo. But everyone involved in writing the report understood that the status quo was changing; this was, after all, the reason for undertaking the report.

Could domestic production continue to grow as in the past under any reasonable set of assumptions about the future? Would imports continue to be available to make up the gap between domestic supply and demand at anything approaching the prices of the recent past? What were the realistic expectations for other domestic energy sources, especially the much-heralded nuclear option? What would be the long-term impact of the growing body of strict environmental laws on energy supply and use? All of these difficult questions had to be answered in order to put forward a reasonable guess concerning the nation's energy future. But the reality in the summer of 1970 was that none of them could be addressed with any certainty. The nation approached a crossroads in its energy history, but there were no signposts pointing the way to a sustainable energy future.

In its interim report the NPC placed its own signpost of sorts, a disclaimer on the first page that the report was "not a forecast of what will probably happen in the future and [that] it should not be so interpreted. It is solely a set of projections, reflecting an optimistic view of what might happen without major changes in present government policies and economic parameters."[36] In both the interim report in 1970 and the final report in 1972, the NPC's experts sought to understand what America's energy situation might be in the year 1985 and beyond. In fairness, they could not have predicted that unforeseen events in the immediate future would drastically change the nation's energy options. In this sense the projections in *U.S. Energy Outlook* reflected a problem common to almost all other energy-related projections in the late 1960s and early 1970s. Extending trend lines from World War II to the early 1970s into the future, specialists might predict what appeared at the time to be significant departures from past trends. But almost no one foresaw the sharp departures in energy supply, demand, and price brought by the energy crises of the 1970s.

The NPC's interim report projected continued growth in the domestic demand for energy at roughly the historic rate of more than 4 percent per year, and this led to a projection of oil demand to about 26 million barrels per day (MMB/D) in 1985, up from almost 15 MMB/D in 1970. Even under the optimistic assumptions of the interim report, however, the projection of growth in domestic production in this period was far from encouraging. The report suggested that domestic production would grow slightly from 1970 to 1975, increasing from 8.5 to around 9.1 MMB/D. But from 1975 through 1985 production in the lower forty-eight states would decline sharply for the first time in modern petroleum history, leading to an estimated 7.9 MMB/D in production in 1985. While acknowledging that as much as 2 MMB/D from Alaska would boost total domestic production in 1985 slightly above the corresponding figure for 1970, the interim report sounded a bleak note in its overall conclusions on the future of domestic production. Noting recent trends such as the decline in the real price of domestic crude and the decline in drilling activity, the report warned that "unless the assumed improvements actually occur, the available domestic petroleum supplies could prove to be less than projected herein."[37]

Although some in the petroleum industry previously had warned about declining domestic production, this was the strongest, most convincing statement on record in 1970 that the wolf was at the door. A historical pattern of steady growth in production in the United States could no longer be sustained without fundamental changes in the situation facing domestic producers. Americans might choose to ignore this warning as the self-interested pleading of the oil industry, but in a forceful, authoritative voice the oil industry through the NPC had issued fair warning to citizens and policy makers alike. Greater supplies of domestic oil could no longer be taken for granted under anything approaching existing economic and technological conditions.

The interim report organized its information on energy trends around a general overview of energy supply and demand, followed by a section detailing trends affecting each major energy source. This was a pathbreaking approach for the NPC, which had focused on oil and gas, not energy as a whole, in its previous work. The overview of energy conditions was put forward in the form of an energy "balance sheet," which set out the expected supply and demand for the various forms of energy. In making this departure the NPC ventured beyond its traditional expertise and its traditional measures of oil in barrels and natural gas in cubic feet. Instead, in this report the NPC made use of a measurement that later moved center stage in the energy debates of the 1970s, the British thermal unit (BTU). By translating the supply and demand for all different energy forms into BTUs, the report allowed the reader to make quick comparisons of conditions in various energy sectors. The common measure used in the interim report was a trillion BTUs, and the report came complete with a handy guide for converting more-traditional measures of oil, gas, coal, and electricity into BTUs. By the mid-1970s such BTU-based measures had become common, with a new convention of recording broad trends in energy in terms of quadrillion BTUs, or "quads."

The statistics on BTUs from different sources of energy reflected the work of numerous task groups organized to report on conditions in various energy sectors long organized into separate industries. Combined with its traditional reliance on oil and gas experts, the NPC used the expertise from industries considered freestanding concerns, rather than interlocking pieces of the same broad energy puzzle, and put together a convincing portrait of how these pieces fit together. In addition to its treatment of trends in domestic and imported oil, the interim report included sections on gas, coal, hydroelectric energy, nuclear power, synthetic fuels, and new energy forms such as geothermal energy. Combining the projections from all of these separate sections into a general overview of energy placed the position of oil and gas in a broad perspective. It reminded readers of the vital importance of oil in the nation's energy mix while emphasizing how dramatically the impending trend toward much greater imports would affect this mix.

In June, 1971, just before the publication of the interim report, President Richard Nixon altered the context within which the study was moving forward with a speech to the nation on U.S. energy policy. As the first presidential address to the nation offering a comprehensive message on energy issues, Nixon's speech emphasized the notion that energy issues could no longer be ignored or discussed as industry-specific problems; rather they would have to be addressed in terms of a comprehensive energy policy. Nixon focused on programs through which the government could help to expand nuclear power, develop coal gasification processes, accelerate leasing on the outer continental shelf, and push forward practical environmental programs. He called for the creation of a new Department of Natural Resources in which federal government powers over energy and resources would be centralized. Although Congress largely ignored Nixon's call for action on these assorted issues, the speech highlighted the growing need to take a hard look at the nation's energy situation, including key government energy policies such as the import quota system and the regulation of natural gas prices. In the altered context created by Nixon's speech the *U.S. Energy Outlook* study took on added significance.

In its final report the committee sought to project what might occur under a variety of conditions, not just in the "status quo" case developed in the interim report. These general scenarios described a variety of supply-and-demand conditions that might shape future energy developments. The task groups mobilized information and analyzed it using computer models showing the likely responses of the different energy sources—oil, gas, coal, hydroelectric energy, nuclear power, synthetic fuels, and new energy forms—to these alternative energy futures. As the hard work of accumulating and analyzing data about each of these sectors went forward, a committee under the direction of Warren Davis (director of economics at Gulf Oil) sought to coordinate the work of the various task forces. John McLean's oversight committee, which included ranking members from the various task forces, sought to keep the entire endeavor moving smoothly toward publication of the final report, whose target publication date of summer, 1971, finally slipped back to December of that same year. As the data from the task forces became available, a government policies subcommittee under N. G. Dumbros of Marathon Oil pushed ahead with a vital part of the overall committee's work—the formulation of a list of recommendations on government policies.

The scenarios of energy demand and supply were the glue that held the work of the various task groups together. These scenarios embodied the committee's best guesses about the parameters of the supply and demand for energy in the years from 1970 through 1985. They became the focus of much of the attention given to the published report. Inevitably, they were shaped by committee members' perceptions concerning the most likely pattern of events in the future, which meant that they reflected many of the traditional assumptions about energy. When the energy crisis shattered these assumptions less than a year after the study's completion, many of the report's conclusions appeared to be outmoded almost before the ink was dry.

Nonetheless, a detailed look at the assumptions and conclusions of the study is instructive in understanding the context within which the energy crisis occurred in the early 1970s. A look back at the study thirty years after its publication allows readers to look past the temporary impacts of the boom and bust in oil prices in the 1970s and 1980s in an effort to place conditions at the turn of the twenty-first century on the long-term trend lines for energy supply and demand that were the focus of *U.S. Energy Outlook*.

The committee began with three estimates of future demand, using figures that seemed to cover the most likely possibilities in light of past trends and future conditions. The three scenarios of future energy demand included a high demand future with a projected annual growth in demand of 4.4 percent; an intermediate estimate similar to that used in the interim report's 4.2 percent annual growth; and a low demand future that would result if annual demand dropped below its historic rate and fell to 3.2 percent. At first glance the difference in 4.2 percent and 3.2 percent growth rates seemed relatively minor, but when projected over fifteen years this 1 percent difference produced dramatic changes in the total demand for energy. Thus by 1985 the high demand rate would require 130 quads of energy per year; the intermediate, 124.9 quads; and the low, 112.5 quads. Obviously, the greater the demand for energy, the more pressure on domestic suppliers.

In retrospect, it is clear that the study's demand scenarios embodied two traditional assumptions that did not hold after 1973. They assumed that the price of oil and competing energy sources would stay in the relatively narrow ranges that had prevailed since World War II, and they assumed that economic growth would continue to require energy growth in roughly the same proportion as that which had characterized the postwar boom. Given conditions that had prevailed before 1973, neither of these assumptions was questioned by the committee nor did the majority of energy experts of this time question them. When the price of oil exploded off the historical trend lines in 1973 and again in 1979, market forces kicked in to dampen demand in ways unforeseen by the committee. Likewise, these much higher prices called forth sweeping measures to conserve energy, measures that challenged the traditional assumption that economic growth could not go forward without corresponding growth in energy use. Thus while the demand projections at the heart of the study were based on logical assessments of past trends, they proved dramatically high—as did almost every estimate made in the early 1970s of future demand for any form of energy in America.

A second set of scenarios guided the estimates of energy supplies in the years up to 1985. Each of the individual fuel supply task groups conducted "supply-economic studies" that examined possible ranges of energy supplies under different sets of government policies. Four scenarios framed the studies of each of the task groups. Case I represented the best possible case for the production of energy, since it assumed an all-out effort to develop domestic energy sources of all sorts, a high success rate for oil and gas discoveries, the rapid growth of nuclear power and coal, and the maximum development of synthetic fuels. Case IV, the worst case for energy suppliers, assumed that little would be done to facilitate domestic energy production and that recent declines in discovery rates for oil and gas would continue, nuclear sitings would remain difficult, and financial and environmental constraints would continue to hamper coal development. Case II put forward a less optimistic future than did Case I but assumed marked improvements in the conditions affecting the supply of oil and gas, nuclear, coal, and synthetic fuels. Case III was less optimistic for oil and gas and nuclear fuel than Case I but the same as far as coal and synthetics were concerned.[38]

Using these four scenarios, and at times collapsing Cases II and III into a single "intermediate case," the task groups set about the detailed work of projecting the supply of energy from the various domestic sources under different conditions. "Parametric studies" examined the potential effects of, for example, federal land leasing policies, environmental considerations, and changes in the tax system. With the data provided by the individual task groups, the coordinating committee could construct general "energy balance sheets" combining the projections of the supply and demand of all the energy sources for each of the scenarios. This impressive exercise used experts' analyses of the inner workings of the individual energy industries as building blocks for an overview of the nation's possible energy futures.

As the committee began drafting the results of the task group studies, it debated the proper way to present the tricky problem of energy prices in the different energy futures. A compromise solution was to include figures that looked for all the world like prices but putting the word *price* in quotation marks and inserting numerous disclaimers that read as follows: "As used in this study, 'price' does not mean a specific selling price as between producer and purchaser and does not represent a future market value." The statement then went on to say that "price" was used "to refer generally to economic levels which would, on the basis of the cases analyzed, support given levels of activity for a particular fuel."[39] Though such an explanation might satisfy an economist that these figures were not price projections, the average reader was left to ponder just how "price" differed from price. Many no doubt simply disregarded the quotation marks and the disclaimer. The "price" figures put forward in the report came back to haunt its authors several years later, when critics of the industry argued that the NPC had concluded after intensive study that prices lower than those that actually prevailed in the mid-1970s would be sufficient to sustain domestic oil development.

Numerous NPC members questioned the way parts of the report were presented. Richard Gonzalez, the primary drafter of the NPC's report on oil policy in 1966, decried the use of "price" in the report. He argued that "any calculation of 'prices' by the methods used in the report invites misinterpretation of the estimates in the same manner that the initial [interim] report resulted in erroneous impressions that the U.S. could not escape rapidly increasing dependence on foreign oil."[40] He recommended the substitution of the phrase "estimated revenue requirements to yield specified rates of return" for the word "price." Several other readers reacted to the initial draft by raising questions about price elasticity. John McLean summed up such responses by asking, "Do we disavow it [price elasticity] too much?" Such responses recognized that any discussion of oil pricing was bound to attract public and political attention, and that the NPC should therefore be careful in its presentation of projections of price. Thornton Bradshaw, president of Atlantic Richfield, recommended a different tack on the related issues of price and price elasticity: "Why do we shed price elasticity? If you get away from price, you get away from the main issues. Why don't we charge it head on?"[41]

Other readers within the NPC worried that the pessimistic conclusions of the draft might lead readers to write off the domestic oil and gas industries as major concerns of public policy makers. Minor Jameson, executive vice president of the Independent Petroleum Producers Association, strongly argued this point in a series of letters to the NPC. Giving voice to the fears of domestic producers, Jameson asked for clarification of a variety of issues, ranging from the issue of the relatively low contribution of domestic petroleum projected under even the most optimistic scenarios to the wisdom of treating oil and gas as distinctly separate industries in the modeling for the study.

Jameson's complaints elicited a detailed response from the committee, which summarized for him the reasons for the draft's stance on a variety of issues. Here was the historical tension between the domestic producers and the international companies being played out one more time in the drafting of a major NPC report that, when published, would have profound implications for public policy. But this time the independent's concerns could not override the report's basic data on the bleak future of U.S. production. This caused one critic within the NPC to observe, "The industry must decide on how much, and how good, information it should give." He then posed the question "Are we helping ourselves? If not, what are we doing it for?"[42]

Others on the committee debated the issue of how best to present the information gathered and analyzed for the report. Several readers asked if the overly optimistic Case I should be edited from the published report, since it seemed to set the NPC up for criticism while deflecting attention from Cases II and III, which study participants generally recognized as the most likely scenarios. After much discussion John McLean voiced the opinion that "the consensus is to leave Case I in with qualifications." On numerous other issues involving both the content of the draft and the review process itself, consensus—though often shaky—resulted when the NPC used its time-honored methods for reaching compromise: It argued about the issues in question until either dissenters gave up the debate, most members seemed satisfied by changes in the words used to convey an idea, or dinnertime arrived.[43]

After the internal discussion had played itself out, the final report was published in December, 1972. The NPC went to unprecedented lengths to ensure that the report found an audience worthy of the work required to write it. The council initially published 7,500 copies of a 380-page, one-volume summary of the entire study. It also printed 2,600 copes of the full report and distributed widely 125,000 copies of a 40-page "guide," a reprint of McLean's presentation to the NPC as a whole describing the procedures used to compile the report and summarizing its primary findings. Also distributed were thousands of pamphlets explaining the resulting primary recommendations for public policy. The council distributed summaries of the report in Spanish, French, and Japanese. Considerable fanfare accompanied the publication of *U.S. Energy Outlook,* which at that point was the most ambitious study undertaken by the NPC.

The contents made important, if controversial, contributions to a growing national debate on energy and energy policy. The most discussed aspects of the report were its projections on domestic and imported oil. The four scenarios yielded quite different projections. In even the most optimistic case domestic oil would drop from 31 percent of total energy consumption in 1970 to 28 percent in 1985; at the same time, oil and gas imports would drop from 12 percent of the total to 11 percent, with greatly expanded supplies of coal and nuclear power making up much of the difference. These figures were in sharp contrast to those generated by the worst case scenario, in which imports would grow to 38 percent of the nation's total energy supply with a sharp dip in domestic oil to 17 percent and gas to 13 percent. In practical terms this meant that imported oil, which stood at 3.4 MMB/D in 1970, might rise to a Case I projection of 7.2 MMB/D or a Case IV projection of 19.2 MMB/D; the giant disparity between the two figures obviously had far-reaching ramifications for the nation.

The body of the report discussed in detail how the different energy industries might respond to the conditions embodied in each of the scenarios. The optimistic scenario (Case I) showed healthy growth in a dynamic nuclear industry, a coal industry freed from environmental deadlocks, a gas industry unleashed by more permissive regulations, and an oil industry with production figures pushed upward by successful exploration and production programs. The pessimistic scenario (Case IV) showed just the reverse, with little if any relative expansion of coal and nuclear fuel and a dramatic decline in domestic oil and gas production requiring the nation to turn increasingly to imported oil to feed its growing demand for energy. The intermediate scenarios (Cases II and III) fell between the two extremes, with levels of oil and gas production being the critical variable shaping the nation's energy balance as a whole.

U.S. Energy Outlook thus depicted three general ways America could respond to the growing gap between energy demand and domestic energy supply. The first, and obviously the preferred approach for NPC members, was increased emphasis on the development of domestic supplies. With proper economic incentives, early resolution of environmental issues, and easier access to public lands for resource development, all of the major domestic energy industries could be expected to supply significant additions to the nation's energy supply. A second general approach relied more on foreign imports, which the report argued "would not serve the Nation's security needs nor its economic health because of uncertainties regarding availability, dependability and price."[44] Of course, the growth of imports had been one of the factors that motivated the study, and this option was clearly the least acceptable to the NPC. The final approach was labeled "restraints on demand growth" and included using government policy and market forces to reduce the rate of growth in energy demand. The report noted that such restrictions could prove "expensive and undesirable" and, according to calculations used in the study, would have limited impact on energy demand in the era from 1970 to 1985.

An important part of the final report was an extended concluding chapter entitled "Recommendations for a United States Energy Policy." This fifteen-point program laid out a specific set of policies that would move the nation toward the healthiest possible energy future. The list began with a general proclamation of the need to adopt a national sense of purpose to solve the energy problem. There followed more specific programs described under the general headings of national security, energy in the marketplace, environmental conservation, energy conservation, access to U.S. energy resources, energy research and development, taxation, and concluding comments. The policy recommendations under each of these headings held few surprises. They were, in general, updated versions of the recommendations of the 1966 report on oil policies, with several aspects expanded to include discussion of energy sources in addition to oil and natural gas.

The policy recommendations sounded a theme familiar from earlier NPC reports with a call for programs to protect and expand the domestic oil industry. Despite President Nixon's earlier call for changes in the mandatory oil import program, the NPC called for this program to remain a "fundamental part of the national energy policy of the United States." The report advocated the creation of a better economic environment for domestic oil and gas development, including a carefully worded recommendation that "field prices of natural gas should be allowed to reach their competitive level." As in the NPC's oil policy report in 1966, this was not an outright plea for deregulation, but rather a call for regulators to allow gas prices to rise. The report's call for "a balance" between "environmental goals and energy requirements" preceded a long list of ways that environmental regulations could be eased to permit more rapid development of energy supplies. The report also called for continued efforts from industry and government to promote energy conservation, policies to encourage the growth of domestic refining, easier access to public lands, an accelerated program for leasing offshore lands, assistance in energy research and development, tax policies that fostered energy development, and support of American energy companies abroad. Mixed in with these recommendations were calls for policies to encourage the growth of the domestic uranium industry and for the coordination of "the many competing and conflicting agencies dealing with energy."[45] In sum, this was the

American-style free enterprise approach previously applied to oil and gas by the NPC and now extended to include all of the domestic energy industries.

RESPONSES TO *U.S. ENERGY OUTLOOK*

The initial response to *U.S. Energy Outlook* was favorable, especially within the oil and gas fraternity. The *Oil & Gas Journal* presented a detailed analysis of the contents of the report in a lengthy article entitled "Historic NPC Study Lays Out U.S. Energy Options." The story included charts from the report illustrating the various scenarios and the complete list of recommended government policies, as well as an extended discussion of criticisms of the report by Richard Gonzalez and several others who had worked on the study. An editorial accompanying this story called the report "an effort for the first time to quantify the energy options for the future open to this country" and applauded its recommendation for "developing all domestic sources of energy." After noting criticism of the report's pessimistic tone and its methodology, the editorial concluded that no one in the industry could argue with its overall conclusions on the proper direction for energy policy and its suggestion that "it's time to get cracking" on solutions. *World Oil* echoed the same general tone in its reports on *U.S. Energy Outlook,* and numerous national newspapers made liberal use of press releases supplied by the NPC to conclude that "energy is a problem, but not a crisis."[46]

The report's policy recommendations found sympathy in the White House as President Nixon's energy advisers prepared for his second address on energy in spring, 1973. Charles DiBona, the president's special consultant on energy, looked favorably on a more market-oriented approach to energy development, and he helped prepare the energy address delivered by President Nixon on April 18, 1973. This address presented a laundry list of policy initiatives favored by the administration, and much of the list would have fit comfortably within *U.S. Energy Outlook.* The policies to reduce dependence on oil imports proposed by the president included partial deregulation of natural gas, accelerated leasing of offshore lands, enforcement of environmental regulations that took into consideration the need for energy development, and changes in the mandatory import program.[47] A month after the president's speech, on May 10, 1973, DiBona attended a meeting of the NPC and discussed the specific policies put forward in Nixon's address. From his comments it was clear that the NPC's work had helped shape the thinking of the president and his assistants.

Congress remained largely unmoved by the president's call for action on energy issues until fall, 1973, when events in the Middle East forced the hand of policy makers in Washington and around the world. In October, 1973, came the outbreak of the latest wars between Israel and its Arab neighbors. This time the major Arab oil-producing nations decided to use the "oil weapon" against nations supporting Israel. The United States was a prime target of the resulting oil embargo, which caused chaos throughout the international petroleum industry as companies and countries alike had to adjust to suddenly altered patterns of oil supply. At the same time it became evident to the major producing nations in OPEC that world supplies were stretched thin and that scarcity of energy from sources other than OPEC gave that organization effective power to establish world oil prices.

The oil embargo by Arab members of OPEC had severe consequences. The U.S. government estimated that the embargo cut the nation's petroleum supply by 14 percent, causing an estimated 500 thousand person increase in unemployment and a $10 billion to $20 billion drop in GNP. Against the potent political symbol of long lines at gas stations, President Nixon responded with a call to arms for an energy war of sorts in which Americans would work toward a goal of zero oil imports by 1980 while warning the OPEC nations that they should be careful how far they pushed the United States and other industrial nations. Such posturing could not, however, alter the newly discovered reality that OPEC now had effective power to set world oil prices. In a startlingly rapid transformation with far-reaching implications for the oil industry, OPEC successfully enforced a series of price hikes that fundamentally altered all previous calculations of the supply and demand for energy.

One response to the new situation was a wave of new energy studies, many of which began with the basic data of *U.S. Energy Outlook* and then sought to analyze this information in the light of radical changes in world oil since the publication of the NPC's report in December, 1972. The Federal Energy Administration (FEA) under John Sawhill led the way with *Project Independence,* a massive effort to sort out the impact of recent changes on the nation's energy future to the year 1985. *Project Independence* borrowed more than its target year from *U.S. Energy Outlook;* it also took the same sort of scenario approach that soon became the stock-in-trade of many energy studies. Using much the same baseline as that established in the NPC's interim report, the FEA report began with a brief look at energy trends to 1985 as they might look in the absence of new government action. Like the council's previous report, *Project Independence* then examined ways to enhance domestic energy production, while adding an extended discussion of emergency programs to guard against the impact of future shortages or embargoes. In its projections of demand, *Project Independence* compared its own estimates to those of *U.S. Energy Outlook* and several other energy studies of the era. Even the announcement of the report took on a tone similar to that which earlier accompanied the release of *U.S. Energy Outlook,* with Sawhill proclaiming that this "massive interagency effort . . . represents the most comprehensive energy analysis ever undertaken."[48]

The most significant difference between *Project Independence* and *U.S. Energy Outlook* was, not surprisingly, in their treatments of price. Unrestrained by the threat of antitrust, the government agency could make direct calculations of the impact that changing prices would have on supply and demand for different forms of energy. Unfettered by traditional assumptions about the relatively narrow price band in which almost all energy experts before 1973 expected oil prices to stay, *Project Independence* created scenarios with oil prices ranging from seven dollars per barrel to eleven dollars per barrel—numbers unthinkable before the energy crisis for most who had long worked in an oil industry characterized by stable prices in the two-dollar to four-dollar per barrel range.

Project Independence injected a healthy dose of realism into political debates about self-sufficiency. As in the *U.S. Energy Outlook* report before it, the figures did not lie. Zero imports by 1980 or 1985 was not an option. Any projected cut in energy use due to higher prices combined with all conceivable advances in the production of domestic alternatives to oil imports could not make the United States completely self-sufficient in the near future. Instead, the report concluded that the United States should pursue policies aimed at decreasing its vulnerability to cutoffs in foreign supplies while encouraging the growth of domestic energy supplies. The NPC supported this economically realistic approach, which was far removed from the politically and diplomatically attractive call for complete energy independence. Many of the policy recommendations in the FEA's report were similar to those earlier put forward by the NPC. Both embraced a form of American-style free enterprise focused on using government policies to expand supplies.

The nation was never to learn if the comprehensive supply-side policies called for in *Project Independence* could move the nation toward increased self-sufficiency. With the Watergate scandal came the departure of President Nixon and his programs, and the beginning of a swinging door to the White House in the remainder of the 1970s that frustrated the effort to define a consistent energy policy by producing one shift after another in the content and focus of the government's energy initiatives.

The absence of coherent energy policies placed a premium on the capacity of markets to adjust to the new world of domestic energy shortages. Price-driven conservation became one important component of the nation's response to the energy crisis. Growing fears of shortages led Rogers Morton, the secretary of the interior, to ask the NPC to fill one obvious gap in *U.S. Energy Outlook,* its lack of a full treatment of energy conservation. In July, 1973, citing the usefulness of this earlier report, he asked the council "to further assist us in assessing the patterns of future U.S. energy use" by studying the "possibilities for energy conservation in the United States and the impact of such measures on the future energy posture of the Nation."[49]

The council's Agenda Committee was initially wary of a request that raised hard questions about the prospects for government regulation of the end uses of energy. But one member acknowledged that *U.S. Energy Outlook* had been "deficient" in its analysis of conservation before speculating that "the Secretary wants to give us the chance to come out strong for conservation."[50] The Agenda Committee decided to take advantage of this opportunity. With the approval of the council as a whole, it began work on an ambitious study on the elimination of waste and the more efficient use of energy. While certainly not likely to meet the approval of those who advocated zero growth, the conservation study presented the NPC with a chance to take a new look at an issue of growing importance to the nation.

Under the direction of Maurice Granville (chairman of Texaco), the NPC's Committee on Energy Conservation organized its study around the detailed analysis of past and future energy use in four general sectors of the economy: industrial, electric utilities, residential/commercial, and transportation. A study group for each sector contained representatives of major energy consumers. A separate "consumer task group," including representatives from labor, environmental groups, academia, state government, and consumer advocacy organizations, contributed insights on the impact of conservation on society in general.[51]

The starting point was a study that extended trends in past energy use into the future, providing benchmarks for measuring the potential impact of conservation. Once it had established such benchmarks, the committee moved quickly to prepare an interim report that would help the secretary of the interior understand the prospects for conservation in a society racked by the energy crisis of winter, 1973–74. The interim report came out in March, 1974, followed by four detailed volumes on the potential for conservation in the four general sectors. The final report for this first phase of the study, which looked at the years from 1974 to 1978, appeared in September, 1974. A second phase of the study examining the potential for conservation from 1979 to 1985 produced a final volume in August, 1975.[52]

Taken together, these volumes marked a sharp departure in the treatment of conservation by the NPC. The reports considered three different sources of conservation: measures to reduce energy consumption, measures to use energy more efficiently, and measures to substitute plentiful fuels for scarce fuels in the generation of electricity. In all sectors of the economy the NPC found substantial opportunities for conservation. The council remained true to its long-standing commitment to market forces by examining primarily opportunities for conservation driven by higher prices rather than by government policies. While acknowledging that projections were made difficult by lack of experience with increases in energy prices rivaling those brought by the energy crisis, the report nonetheless found impressive evidence that conservation would occur as a rational response to the new realities of much higher energy prices.

The thoroughness of these reports on conservation was unprecedented in the petroleum industry, as was their conclusion that solutions to the nation's energy problems "will require conservation and an awareness and acceptance of a 'conservation ethic' by the American public." This conclusion was followed immediately by a reminder of the importance of "a comprehensive national energy policy" that encouraged increased production as well as conservation. In these reports on conservation by the NPC, the petroleum industry acknowledged that the age of energy abundance had ended and that the more efficient use of energy could help create a sustainable energy future.[53] In presenting a road map of sorts for identifying potential pathways toward energy conservation, the NPC made a valuable contribution to the debate on responses to the energy crisis.

As the studies on energy conservation neared completion in 1975, a final interesting footnote to *U.S. Energy Outlook* was written when the Department of the Interior requested that the NPC undertake "an update of the NPC's 1972 energy outlook study." The rationale from a spokesperson for the DOI was that "most of the information that we've worked off of in government" took basic information from *U.S. Energy Outlook* and *Project Independence,* "did a few wiggles on top of it and essentially lived off of it," and will soon be "out of date."[54] After much discussion the NPC agreed to launch the requested update and organized the effort in two parts: an initial critique of existing energy studies followed by a comprehensive study on the nation's energy outlook. This project continued until 1977, when the NPC finally suspended work on it, in part because of uncertainty over the council's future in the impending reorganization of the federal government's various energy functions and the council's move in 1977 to the newly created Department of Energy. But before the suspension of work on the study, a committee including some of those who had worked on *U.S. Energy Outlook* conducted a critique of this earlier report.

Texaco's Maurice Granville expressed the most pessimistic view when he argued that the "nation would have been better off without this study." As some had foreseen, the major problem raised by the study involved the use of the word "price" to designate the approximate cost for oil and other energy forms that would be required to support a certain level of production. But the numerous disclaimers placed throughout the study had not driven home this distinction even to careful readers. Additional confusion stemmed from the fact that the drafters had lacked the "courage to separate replacement costs versus average costs," in part for fear that a more realistic view of the replacement costs for oil in the future would appear so high that readers would dismiss it as the self-interested pleading of the oil industry. Because of these problems the report's projections "had been greatly misunderstood in some quarters," including the U.S. Congress.[55] Prominent congressmen such as Les Aspin in the House and Henry "Scoop" Jackson in the Senate had made use of the "price" projections in the 1972 report to argue in the mid-1970s that the industry itself—through the NPC—had already established that prices far below those actually prevailing in 1975 and 1976 would be sufficient to sustain the level of domestic production. The NPC clearly was plagued by its earlier choice to label cost extrapolation as "prices," a choice dictated in part by the need to stay on the safe side of the antitrust laws.

In other respects the report remains an intriguing document. Though dismissed in the 1970s and 1980s as relics of an era made obsolete by the energy crises, the projections in *U.S. Energy Outlook* hold considerable interest as a historical effort to make projections on the volatile issues of oil supply, demand, and price. The "high" scenario for the demand for energy and the most optimistic case for energy production proved far removed from the real trends, as many who wrote the report suspected would be the case even before the energy crisis. These "best case" scenarios had, after all, been included as one part of a set of "bookends"; along with the most pessimistic projections, they served as a logical context for the analysis of the "intermediate case" scenarios that most participants in the study assumed would be close to the actual path taken by energy supply and demand. Ironically, the "low cases" turned out to be "not so bad" when OPEC's price hikes slowed demand.[56]

Indeed, long-term trends have been much kinder to those who worked on *U.S. Energy Outlook* than were the trends in the 1970s and early 1980s. By the end of the twentieth century, petroleum price trends had settled back down closer to the long-term paths with which the NPC's members were familiar in 1972. The dramatically higher oil prices established by OPEC in the 1970s undermined all projections made in the early 1970s, but the subsequent decline of OPEC's power over price after the mid-1980s pushed both price and demand back toward the trends established from 1945 to 1973. While serving as a reminder of the impact of booms and busts on projections of oil supply and demand, *U.S. Energy Outlook* remains useful as a pioneering effort to make careful projections during eras of relatively stable prices. Unfortunately for its authors, almost thirty years of relative price stability gave way to chaotic surges in price just after the completion of the report.

U.S. Energy Outlook nonetheless made an important contribution when it pointed out the limited prospects for domestic oil production. This controversial issue was at the heart of the most serious tensions within the NPC committee, as it had been at the heart of the most significant debates within the earlier oil policy committees and, indeed, within the industry as a whole. All of the scenarios showed variations of the same pessimistic trend for domestic oil production, and even much higher oil prices in the era from 1973 to 1985 did not produce domestic production significantly greater than that projected in the report. The end of historic growth rates in domestic production was one half of the new reality of the U.S. oil industry. The other half—the uncertainty posed by OPEC pricing in an import-dependent nation and world—became quite clear the year after the publication of *U.S. Energy Outlook.*

That those working on the study could not predict the impending energy crisis and all of its far-reaching impacts on supply and demand meant only that they were not seers. It also pointed to the hazards of long-term projections, recalling warnings from inside the NPC during initial debates on the project of the "imponderables" inherent in such undertakings. In the years after 1972 the NPC would dodge such imponderables by focusing less on long-term projections and more on narrower studies of specific policy options, such as the Strategic Petroleum Reserve and alternative energy production. Its work would continue to be informed by the basic market-oriented approach highlighted in the oil policy reports and *U.S. Energy Outlook.* But in the policy process the NPC's voice of industry would face ever-growing competition from other voices presenting policy makers with decidedly different perspectives on energy-related issues.

CHAPTER 4

Redefining National Security: The NPC and the SPR

THE ENERGY CRISES OF THE 1970s produced a wave of new energy policies, as government sought ways to adapt to a new era marked by OPEC-led crude oil pricing. The quest for sustainable energy policies was at times chaotic and often confusing. There was little continuity across the four presidential administrations in the decade after the first energy crisis in 1973. Nor was there coherence among policies aimed at different energy industries. As government officials struggled to sort out the policy choices posed by the nation's dependence on imported oil, they regularly turned to the National Petroleum Council for advice. The council compiled major reports on key issues facing the Department of the Interior and the Department of Energy, the latter of which was created in 1977 as one response to the need for a more comprehensive view of energy issues. This was a busy and challenging time for the NPC, which informed the debates on energy policy with a series of data-rich reports.

Of special significance in the long term was a series of studies on the creation and operations of the Strategic Petroleum Reserve (SPR), an initiative designed to enhance the nation's energy security by storing large quantities of crude oil as an insurance policy against future cutoffs of imports. Of the many stops and starts in energy policy in the 1970s, the SPR proved to be the most durable, in part because of the NPC's work in shaping its evolution.

The concept of stockpiling oil for use in an emergency had been debated in various forms throughout the twentieth century. But the devastating economic impact and the implications for military security of the Arab embargo put such historical debates in a new perspective. What, if anything, could be done to dampen the impact of future embargoes? The long-term answer was obvious, if difficult to achieve: Cut the nation's reliance on oil imported from unstable, unpredictable producing areas. In the short term, access to a reserve supply of crude oil might give the nation temporary respite from the impact of oil embargoes, thereby reducing the incentive of producer nations to use them.

A petroleum reserve could be justified on the grounds of a broad definition of national security, since it could make the nation less vulnerable to a sort of energy blackmail capable of bringing the economy to its knees and bringing the nation to the brink of war. As one way to take back a measure of control of the nation's energy future, the SPR quickly gained wide political support, including that of many in the oil industry and in the NPC. Given the vital importance of oil to the nation's economic and military well-being, "preparedness" now included planning aimed at blunting the impact of economic warfare that used the weapon of oil embargoes to weaken the American economy.

An SPR could, of course, take many different forms depending on its size, content, location, ownership, and management. In a series of reports compiled over several decades, the NPC shaped government policy by helping government officials understand the implications of various choices regarding the design and operations of the reserves. The council provided input from industry on the original decision to create the SPR, the subsequent choices on its size and organization, the practical issues of how to use it in an emergency, and finally the successful use of the SPR in the early days of the Persian Gulf War in 1991. In so doing, the NPC exercised the most direct, sustained influence on a specific energy policy in its history.[1]

IDENTIFYING THE NEED

The idea of creating a government-owned SPR was not new in the 1970s. Security of oil supplies needed by the U.S. Navy had been the force behind the early-twentieth-century establishment of the Naval Petroleum Reserves in California, Wyoming, and Alaska by Presidents Taft, Wilson, and Harding. The Teapot Dome scandals of the 1920s raised questions about the management of these reserves, but not about the need for them in a world where oil had become a key to national security. In the 1940s the growing recognition of the economic aspect of national security prompted Interior Secretary Harold Ickes to propose the creation of U.S. government–owned reserves in Saudi Arabia to be managed by a Petroleum Reserves Corporation. Ickes's efforts to expand the government's oil reserves continued after the war, when he unsuccessfully sought to have selected coastal wetlands and the outer continental shelf declared part of the Naval Petroleum Reserves. The idea of a set-aside area of offshore oil reserves was also put forth by President Truman's Materials Policy Commission (the so-called Paley Commission) in its 1952 study, *Resources for Freedom*. In the mid-1950s President Eisenhower put forth the idea of storing oil for national security in abandoned mines and oil wells. In the late 1960s the shah of Iran suggested selling Iranian oil to the United States for storage underground for emergency use. Except for the Naval Petroleum Reserves set aside in the early twentieth century, however, none of these proposals was adopted.

Government officials first turned to the National Petroleum Council for advice on the technical feasibility of a petroleum reserve during the Truman administration. In May, 1951, H. A. Stewart, acting director of the Oil and Gas Division of the Interior Department, wrote to Walter S. Hallanan, chairman of the National Petroleum Council, "It would be of material assistance to the government to have an authoritative study on the feasibility of the use of underground storage for petroleum products, including liquefied petroleum gas." The need for such a study was prompted by two postwar phenomena: shortages of steel and other critical materials, and the strategic importance of oil in the cold war. Steel tanks were a primary medium for industrial storage of oil and petroleum products, but they were expensive to build, especially amid a steel shortage. Underground storage, Stewart wrote, "would reduce the steel requirements of the [oil] industry, would make available to the industry additional storage capacity during this period of materials shortage, and would be less vulnerable to enemy attack."[2]

Hallanan referred Stewart's request to the council's Technical Subcommittee of its Committee on Underground Storage for Petroleum, which completed its report in April, 1952. The report, *Underground Storage for Petroleum*, found that storage in underground salt domes was feasible with attendant economies of manpower and equipment infrastructure, with high levels of safety. The study compared various forms of above-ground storage, including atmospheric pressure storage and pressurized surface storage. The subcommittee favored leached salt domes over conventionally mined caverns on the basis of lower cost, steel infrastructure required, and labor and maintenance costs per barrel of oil or petroleum product stored.

The council reported that salt and brine were impervious to oil and gas, making salt domes excellent containers for petroleum and its products. It also found that while salt had a strength comparable to concrete under the weight of the underlying rock, deep underground it also acted like plastic to seal any fractures. At those depths oil and petroleum products would be safe not only from evaporation, but also from natural disasters and sabotage. Previous studies had revealed that crude oil could be stored for months or even years without suffering degradation in quality; petroleum products, on the other hand, tended to degrade and thus had to be cycled more regularly, usually seasonally. But properly leached and maintained underground salt-dome caverns could be used to store crude oil indefinitely, the subcommittee concluded.

The subcommittee conceded that its broad conclusions needed to be backed up with more specific and detailed studies. Numerous tests, including taking rock-core samples and checking for adequate pressure in the salt domes, were needed before storage could begin. It seemed likely, the subcommittee concluded, that private companies would continue their investigations of underground storage. The report noted that underground storage capacity for some 7 million barrels of petroleum products (mostly liquefied natural gas) were under construction or in operation. The subcommittee pledged to continue to study the issue as industry increased its use of salt-dome storage.[3] By contributing to the acceptance of the idea that large petroleum reserves could be effectively stored underground in salt domes, this early NPC report helped prepare the way for the subsequent emergence of the concept of a large SPR stored in such salt domes.

As the threat of energy shortages grew in the early 1970s, the idea of government-owned-and-operated SPRs gained renewed interest. In August, 1971, economists Walter Mead and Phillip Sorensen published an article entitled "A National Defense Petroleum Reserve Alternative to Oil Import Quotas," which recommended that the existing system of import controls be replaced with an emergency petroleum reserve. They noted that import controls had been instituted on the grounds of national security but that these had "fail[ed] in several respects as a solution to the national security problem." The quotas had kept prices artificially high, accelerating the depletion of domestic reserves. "The most attractive alternative of providing a reliable future petroleum supply for security purposes," they contended, "appears to be a shut-in domestic petroleum reserve." To this end they recommended expanding the Elk Hills and Teapot Dome Naval Petroleum Reserves and buying out nearby private developers to avoid drainage. They also recommended that the federal government acquire offshore oil tracts for in situ reserves, much as Ickes had wanted. Mead and Sorensen favored shut-in reserves over salt domes on the basis of cost.[4]

The strategic reserve idea gained momentum as realization grew that exist-ing Naval Petroleum Reserves could not provide substantial assistance in stem-ming the growing tide of imported oil. In January, 1973, the comptroller general's office of the GAO assessed the oil-producing capacity of the Naval Petroleum Reserves and the Naval Oil Shale Reserves and found no reason for optimism about their future contributions to energy security. Only the Elk Hills and Teapot Dome sites had any near-term potential for significantly increased production in an emergency, and together they could provide less than 100,000 barrels per day in additional production. With the American energy economy demanding over 17 MMB/D, including imports of 6.4 MMB/D, the Naval Petroleum Reserves provided scant relief in the event of supply disruptions.

On Capitol Hill, Sen. Henry M. "Scoop" Jackson (D-Wash.) sounded the warning about energy security and the need for strategic reserves. In April, 1973, Jackson introduced the Petroleum Reserves and Import Policy Act (S. 1586), which called for the creation of a system of government-owned oil reserves stored in salt-dome caverns and managed by the Department of the Interior. The bill also called for limits on imports of oil and gas, mandatory minimum inventory requirements for oil importers, and mandatory "surge production capacity" requirements for domestic producers in an emergency.

Much of this bill encountered strong opposition within the oil industry. Domestic producers opposed requirements for surge capacity, which they felt would force reductions in their production. Oil importers objected to the mandatory inventory requirements, which they argued amounted to a dead asset. Nixon administration officials, while in favor of the idea of strategic reserves, stated that more time was needed to study stockpiling options. Such opposition blocked the bill. The debate over energy policies would not move to the top of the legislative agenda until some dramatic crisis forced the na-tion to come to grips with the changing situation in energy. That crisis, the Arab oil embargo and the OPEC price increases of 1973–74, was not long in coming.[5]

Even before the debates over Jackson's bill, the National Petroleum Coun-cil had launched a study of the potential impact of energy shortages. In De-cember, 1972, Assistant Interior Secretary Hollis M. Dole, recognizing the "risk involved to the Nation's economic well-being and security" posed by the "rapidly increasing dependence on imported petroleum," requested a new study by the NPC. Dole noted that while *U.S. Energy Outlook* had been valuable in suggesting long-term methods to reduce energy dependence, the government needed a study that recommended short-term responses to energy supply disruptions, including "possible emergency supplements to or alternatives for imported oil, natural gas liquids and products." He asked the council to consider two possible disruptions: a cutoff of 1.5 MMB/D for sixty days and a cutoff of 2 MMB/D for ninety days. Dole requested that the council explore the possibilities for stepped-up domestic production, interfuel substitution, conservation through demand reduction, and the temporary relaxation of environmental standards. So pressing was the need for the study that Dole asked the council to submit a preliminary report by July, 1973. After the council had agreed to undertake this study, Interior Secretary Rogers C. B. Morton revised the original request by asking the NPC to consider short-term responses to a 1.5-MMB/D supply disruption lasting three months and a shortfall of 3 MMB/D lasting six months.

To prepare the study the council turned to an Emergency Preparedness Committee comprising executives from the international integrated majors, domestic independent producers, and natural gas transmission companies; Interior Department officials; petroleum industry consultants; and financial specialists. Subcommittees on emergency petroleum production, fuel convertibility and use curtailment, and petroleum logistics brought together the specialists needed to collect and analyze data. The study sought to summarize the impact of petroleum shortages on the energy industries and on the economy as a whole and to examine the potential effectiveness of different policy options to respond to such shortages.

In July, 1973, the committee submitted an interim version of their ongoing study, *Emergency Preparedness for Interruption of Petroleum Imports into the United States*. Amid discussions of many different short-term policies that might weaken the impact of supply interruptions, one conclusion stood out: An SPR could give the nation an effective tool for responding to cutoffs of imported oil. This interim report and subsequent NPC reports helped solidify the place of the SPR on a political agenda crowded with an array of proposed energy policies.[6]

The interim report examined hypothetical oil supply disruptions in January, 1974, and in January, 1978, the earliest time by which the council's recommendations could begin to take effect. In response to the near-term crisis, the council recommended curtailment of consumption, including gasoline reduction measures such as carpooling, lower speed limits, and rationing; and interfuel substitution, with emphasis on utilities switching from petroleum to coal-based energy sources. Increased production could be achieved by temporarily lifting the statutory requirements for the maximum efficient rate of crude oil production and by opening the Naval Petroleum Reserves

(NPR) at Elk Hills for increased development by oil companies. By 1978 longer-term programs and policies, such as an emergency petroleum reserves system, could be in place. In particular, the NPC committee found that an oil stockpile of 500 million barrels would protect against a 6-MMB/D short-fall lasting ninety days. After examining numerous types of storage facilities, the council concluded—as it had in 1952—that underground salt domes provided the most secure and efficient means of storing a large reserve.

The NPC committee found better possibilities for interfuel substitution, but not for increased production, in the 1978 scenario than in the 1974 scenario. The availability of a petroleum reserve made the projected problems in 1978 far more manageable than those in 1972. The report left the clear impression that the creation of an SPR could make a significant difference in the event of a future interruption of oil imports.

What had been hypothetical became all too real in October, 1973, when the major Arab producing nations embargoed crude oil shipped to the United States. In attempting to punish supporters of Israel in its war against Egypt and Syria, the Arab oil-producing states discovered the power of their oil weapon. The major consuming nations had become so dependent on imports from the Middle East that they were vulnerable to concerted efforts to withhold this oil. The consequences for the United States and its allies were dire. During the winter of 1973–74 the embargo cut 2 to 3 MMB/D of crude oil and refined products from the supply available to the United States, which at the time consumed about 17 MMB/D. Long gasoline lines quickly became the symbol of the resulting energy crisis, but increased inflation, a lower GNP, higher unemployment, and balance-of-payment problems all flowed from the shortage of oil needed to fuel the nation's economy. The deep, painful economic impacts of the 1973 embargo proved that future embargoes posed fundamental threats to national security.

On October 26, 1973, Assistant Interior Secretary Stephen A. Wakefield requested that the NPC prepare a supplement to the recently published interim report. Recognizing that the council was completing its report on responses to oil import supply disruptions, Wakefield explained that "recent events have added new urgency to this scenario."[7] History thus had presented the NPC with a rare opportunity to use an ongoing study to help government respond to an unfolding crisis. The council responded quickly, reaching deeply into the petroleum industry for information needed to help guide the nation through a crisis in oil supply.

Responding to the government's need for immediate information, the council's Emergency Preparedness Committee completed and submitted its supplemental interim report in mid-November. Before examining the short-term responses that might ameliorate conditions spawned by the sudden shortage of oil, the report noted that "the U.S. energy supply was tenuous even before the Arab embargo." It recommended a number of actions to increase energy production and reduce demand. In the near term increased production could come from the Elk Hills NPR, the lifting of requirements for most efficient production methods from domestic producers, and increased interfuel substitution. Reduced demand could come from voluntary reductions in consumption by individuals and corporations, as well as possible mandatory measures such as gasoline rationing. Such measures, the report made clear, were not offered as long-term solutions to the nation's energy problems, but rather as emergency responses in times of severe economic dangers.[8]

The NPC rushed to collect basic information in a useful form and presented these data to the government in November. In December the council published still more data in a supplement to the interim report consisting of background papers and information that the coordinating committee of the committee on emergency planning had used in compiling the November report.[9] Given the urgency of the times, these papers went forward without the approval of the NPC as a whole. Together these two reports painted a bleak portrait of the economic impact of the embargo and a pessimistic outlook on the effectiveness of short-term policies to increase energy supplies and reduce energy demand. Later studies by the NPC found these reports to be overly pessimistic, especially with regard to the prospects for conservation induced by much higher oil prices. Although they did not directly discuss how an SPR might be useful in future energy crises, their pessimism about other options for energy policy represented at least an indirect argument for the creation of an oil reserve.

As the nation slowly adapted to shortages, the NPC completed *Emergency Preparedness for Interruption of Petroleum Imports into the United States*. Published in September, 1974, the final report presented greater detail than the interim reports had on possible responses to supply disruptions. It also went beyond short-term responses to include a lengthy discussion of the prospect for an SPR. The final report noted that the existing Naval Petroleum Reserves could not mitigate national energy shortages and that a Strategic Petroleum Reserve was needed for this purpose. The National Petroleum Council noted the depletion of reserves and the lack of existing productive capacity. It also reminded readers that the NPR sites could be produced only when the navy secretary, in accordance with the president, found that the reserves were needed for national defense; production would then have to be authorized by a joint resolution from Congress. The NPC concluded, "The legal and economic problems involved [with] the Naval Petroleum Reserves precluded a timely response" to an emergency. Moreover, the Naval Petroleum Reserves had been created to give the navy a secure source of fuel oil, not to provide spare energy capacity to the American economy in general. Another sort of oil reserve, one built specifically to provide an energy "buffer" for the American economy in general, would have to be built.[10]

After dismissing the prospects for significant future production from the NPR, the report focused on more practical alternatives in planning for a future oil import disruption, including conversion to alternate fuels, emergency production from existing fields, reduction of consumption, and emergency standby petroleum supplies. Conversion to alternate fuels had limited future potential because the conversion of industrial and utility boilers from petroleum to coal burning was an ongoing process. Emergency production had limited viability. The committee's proposals from its interim report for increasing production had not yet been adopted, suggesting that they had limited political appeal. The NPC committee projected that voluntary efforts such as carpooling and thermostat adjustment could reduce American energy consumption by as much as 1 MMB/D by 1980. If voluntary efforts proved insufficient, then the government should implement mandatory consumption reduction measures such as rationing and allocation. Such emergency measures, however, could be maintained for weeks, not months or years. "Solutions to the long-term supply shortages," the NPC committee declared, "lie in providing a free marketplace . . . which encourage[s]. . . energy self-sufficiency, rather than in temporary emergency measures."[11]

The NPC committee weighed in strongly in favor of an emergency petroleum reserve. It recognized that market forces could bring energy self-sufficiency only in the long run and that the current political climate did not permit the elimination of price controls and the allocation system that had been put in place as one of the initial responses to energy shortages. The committee looked at the prospects for the creation of shut-in reserves, the storage of crude oil, and the storage of refined petroleum products. As presented in the report, the NPC's study had examined the use of steel tanks, salt domes, and hard-rock mines. By providing basic information on the potential costs and benefits of each of these approaches, the NPC helped shape political debate on the organization of the petroleum reserve.

The final report stated that protection against an import interruption of 3 MMB/D lasting 180 days would require a 540-million-barrel reserve of either crude oil or refined products. The committee decided that shutting in reserves of this size would reduce the supply of domestic oil, encouraging imports and increasing the nation's dependence on foreign oil. Far superior, the report concluded, was the storage of crude oil in underground reserves in salt domes. The Texas-Louisiana Gulf Coast provided the most logical sites for the SPR, since this region had abundant salt domes, a vast refining and pipeline transportation complex, and first-class seaports for handling oil.

The bulk of crude oil for the reserve, the NPC indicated, would likely be imported. The use of imports to fill the reserve would, of course, temporarily increase the nation's reliance on foreign oil. But such short-term problems were outweighed by the long-term benefits of the reserve. High prices were a concern. At then-current prices of $12–$14 per barrel, a 500-million-barrel reserve would cost from $5 billion to more than $6 billion and take several years to fill. The purchase of such vast amounts of imported oil depended upon the continued oil production and political goodwill of producer nations. A practical problem was the high sulfur content of some imports, which might pose problems for U.S. refineries while challenging existing environmental laws.

Such potential problems would have to be overcome since domestic oil was simply not available in sufficient quantities to fill the reserve. The most logical possibilities for domestic oil for the SPR were oil from the Elk Hills Naval Reserve and royalty entitlement from private producers on other federal lands. The 1974 report made it clear that a strategic reserve would be difficult and expensive to create in the midst of a growing shortage of domestic oil. But the nation had little option if it hoped to reap the benefits of such a reserve in the future. With excellent data from the oil industry and detailed, convincing analyses of key issues, the NPC's 1974 report on emergency preparedness became an authoritative source for those seeking to create an SPR.

DESIGNING THE RESERVE

Soon after the report's publication the political debate on the SPR became a part of the broader debate on energy policy that dominated American politics in the mid-1970s. When Gerald R. Ford assumed the presidency in August, 1974, he inherited the energy crisis, as well as the Federal Energy Administration's efforts to develop a legislative package based upon its report, *Project Independence.* The FEA recommended a 500-million-barrel crude oil reserve for the three-month (or ninety-day) disruption scenario, and a 1-billion-barrel reserve for the six-month disruption scenario. In his original energy legislation presented to Congress in January, 1975, President Ford proposed the creation of a government-owned-and-funded domestic civilian oil reserve of up to 1 billion barrels. This proposal was part of an omnibus bill containing a package of other far-ranging proposals, including an oil import tariff fee, decontrol of domestic crude oil and natural gas prices accompanied by a windfall profits tax, increased development of coal, interfuel substitution for utilities, and a synthetic-fuels program. The SPR was one of many significant parts of this bill, though at times it became lost in the controversies engendered by the many different parts of Ford's energy package.[12]

As debate went forward, the NPC stepped front and center with a new comprehensive report on the design and operation of an SPR. Acting Interior Secretary Jack W. Carlson's letter to council chairman John E. Swearingen in December, 1974, noted that the council's recommendation for "an emergency petroleum security storage system" had been of "particular interest" to the Interior Department. Inasmuch as "the United States is now in the position where it needs to move decisively and promptly in this most critical area of national security," Carlson requested that the council "undertake as a matter of urgency a study of the major factors involved in the implementation of a security storage system similar to that recommended by you in your summary report," the council's *Emergency Preparedness for Interruption of Petroleum Imports into the United States.* Carlson requested that the NPC examine the issues of the optimum size for the reserve, including the 500-million-barrel and the 1-billion-barrel targets; the choice to store crude and/or petroleum products; storage medium alternatives; the source of financing for the reserve; actions that might expedite the establishment of the reserve; and any geographical, logistical, or environmental issues that might relate to the building of the reserve.[13]

This request raised several important questions for the NPC's Agenda Committee. The first was the relationship of the proposed SPR to military needs for petroleum. The Naval Petroleum Reserves had been established on the basis of the traditional definition of national security; they were set aside specifically for the use of the military. The SPR at first appeared to have two components, military use and civilian use. The Agenda Committee sought clarification on whether all or part of the SPR would be set aside for military use. Once it was clear that the proposed SPR would be for civilian use only, the discussion could focus on the many practical issues raised by its design and construction.

One of the most obvious issues to NPC members was the huge cost of any program that hoped to purchase and store 500 million to 1 billion barrels of expensive oil. Swearingen put the issue of financing the SPR in perspective: "If you are talking about a billion barrel storage system . . . you are talking about $12 billion that has to be raised somewhere, and this is equal to about the whole industry's annual capital expenditures in the United States." He concluded, "I ought to almost start from the standpoint there is no way the industry can finance this itself," a statement seconded by others at the meeting.[14] To be large enough to be effective, the proposed reserve inevitably would be a big-ticket budget item.

After additional debate on possible methods for financing the reserve, the Agenda Committee moved on to the issue of the study committee's makeup. With the appointment of Carroll Bennett (chairman of Texaco) as chairman of the committee and Edward DiCorcia (from the supply department of Exxon) as chairman of a coordinating committee, the study group began to take shape. Swearingen remained deeply involved in its work.[15]

On August 6, 1975, the NPC completed *Petroleum Storage for National Security.* Its basic conclusion repeated the conclusion in the September, 1974, report on emergency preparedness that underground storage of approximately 500 million barrels of crude oil in salt domes along the Gulf Coast was the best approach to creating a petroleum reserve. But the 1975 report provided fuller analyses of the logistical, economic, and environmental considerations of the program, including the need to ensure that at least one-third of the reserve would be filled with crude oil of low to medium sulfur content.

The council projected that between 1980 and 1990 the United States would import an average of 8.1 MMB/D of crude oil and petroleum products, and 5.5 MMB/D of crude oil alone. Conservation could reduce demand by 1.0 to 1.1 MMB/D by 1980. A complete interruption of crude and petroleum product imports thus would leave a shortfall of 7.0 to 7.1 MMB/D. A cutoff of all crude imports would yield a shortfall of 4.4 to 4.5 MMB/D. A 500-million-barrel reserve could, therefore, "protect against a total imports denial of about 70 days, and a crude-oil-only denial of about 110 days." A smaller volume, the committee reasoned, would not provide enough import protection; a larger reserve would be excessively costly, diverting needed manpower and resources away from industry while providing "diminishing security benefits." The report read, "Moreover, over the longer term, genuine security can be obtained only by reducing the Nation's dependence on imports."[16]

Unlike the previous reports, *Petroleum Storage for National Security* addressed the environmental issues raised by salt-dome storage. The report recognized that proposed surface storage area requirements, fresh water requirements, pipeline construction, and brine disposal all posed potential environmental threats to the marine life offshore, as well as in local bays, marshes, and estuaries. To address these concerns the report recommended biological, chemical, botanical, and oceanographic studies of the program's potential effects on the local and regional environment. The committee also recommended that the brine created during leaching be disposed far enough out in the Gulf of Mexico to allow for dispersion. Monitoring of the leaching and filling process should ensure that the SPR's operations complied with environmental permits requirements. With such safeguards the program could move ahead quickly while meeting environmental standards.

The 1975 report also included a fuller discussion of the economic costs of the program. Its estimate that a 500-million-barrel reserve would cost up to $7 billion was slightly higher than previous estimates. The report examined a range of approaches to private financing, including industry inventory requirements and control by an industry consortium. It concluded that private financing was inappropriate. In presenting the report to the secretary of the interior, John Swearingen acknowledged that, given the general commitment of the NPC and the oil industry to the free market, "the decision that the Federal government should own and control the entire security storage capability was a difficult recommendation to make."[17]

The key consideration pointing the NPC away from its traditional commitment to free markets was the fact that "a national security petroleum storage program is designed to provide insurance against a threat to the Nation's economic well-being and its military security." The energy crisis had forced a redefinition of national security to include economic well-being as well as the traditional concern for military security. In its first twenty-five years the NPC had regularly conducted studies related to military preparedness; many of its studies after the early 1970s would examine the impact of possible energy policies on the nation's economy, implicitly recognizing that the vital economic role of energy meant that it had broad, if indirect, implications for national security.

Swearingen's submittal letter for *Petroleum Storage for National Security* went to great lengths to justify this redefinition of national security and the policy recommendation of a government-owned reserve that flowed from it. The beneficiaries of the reserve would be "the Nation as a whole, its economy, and all its people in their roles as producers and consumers." Further, the "very large financial burden of the program" should not be placed upon private industry, which needed to be left unencumbered by additional regulations so that it could set about the "very formidable task of increasing domestic energy supplies." The industry could not build the strategic reserve while also increasing energy supplies for America and for international markets. "There simply is not enough money," according to the report, "for the petroleum industry to undertake both efforts simultaneously." Swearingen concluded that as a national security initiative, the strategic reserve should be financed and controlled by the federal government and paid for with general revenues.[18]

A final recommendation of the 1975 report represented a shift from earlier studies of the NPC. After consideration of available options for acquiring crude to fill the SPR, the report concluded that the best choice was oil from the government's Elk Hills Naval Petroleum Reserve site. If authorized by the president and approved by Congress, Elk Hills production could be stepped up to 130,000 barrels per day "within several months." Ultimately the report projected that Elk Hills could produce 267,000 barrels per day, supplying enough crude to fill a 500-million-barrel reserve in six to seven years.

This conclusion sharply contrasted with the council's emergency preparedness report of 1974, which argued that "legal and economic problems" precluded the NPR's "timely" use in energy emergencies. This shift in thinking was justified with an assertion that the use of NPR oil was the only available option that did not divert much-needed domestic production or contribute to a rise in reliance on imported oil. It also reflected concerns about the government entering into the marketplace and driving up the price of oil. Using Elk Hills NPR oil would help to limit the federal role in the oil marketplace, since the government would be using its own oil. Although foreign oil ultimately proved vital in filling the SPR, the concept of using Elk Hills oil, once introduced, had staying power. When the Carter administration suspended SPR oil purchases during the oil shock of 1979–81, Congress responded by enacting legislation that forced the DOE to use oil from the Elk Hills NPR.

Petroleum Storage for National Security presented useful information about reserve programs in other oil-consuming nations, noting crucial distinctions between their economies and that of the United States. Japan and the nations of Western Europe had "more compact logistical systems with smaller volumes of unavailable stocks" than did the United States, where greater transportation requirements forced companies to hold a higher level of working stocks. Moreover, those stocks were widely dispersed over the nation's large geographical area. Compulsory industry inventory requirements, which comprised a significant portion of the petroleum reserve systems of the other IEA member nations, were therefore undesirable in the United States. These conditions, the report implied, gave further evidence that the American petroleum reserve should be a centralized program under the government's control.[19]

The council recommended a number of steps to expedite the SPR's creation. First, one federal department should be created to direct the petroleum security storage program. In addition the Defense Production Act of 1950 should be used to expedite delivery of materials to the program, and the responsible department or agency should be empowered to exercise the right of eminent domain to obtain needed land and rights of ways. The report concluded that enabling legislation allowing for the use of Elk Hills NPR oil should be enacted and that the legislation creating the reserve should provide an operational definition of an energy emergency, which required conservation measures prior to withdrawals.

The strategic reserve, the committee concluded, should include sufficient capacity to "insure against a reasonable range of anticipated risk." Facilities should be designed and located for "quick and efficient movement of security stocks into the U.S. supply system to replace lost imports." The report called for an "expeditious" construction schedule, since "import levels and vulnerability are already significant and growing." Emphasizing the idea that the reserve should be controlled by the government, the council concluded that the "petroleum security stocks" should be "clearly distinguished from working stocks of crude and product maintained by industry" and that the reserve should "provide the benefits of petroleum security storage without reducing energy resource development."[20]

The report recommended a so-called "rainy day policy" that used the SPR only as a last resort after a presidential declaration of an energy emergency. It advocated that "the government should require that all other provisions of a national emergency preparedness plan be implemented before security storage supplies are called upon." The NPC committee concluded that it was time to get moving on the creation of the SPR: "It is imperative to underscore the urgency of the Federal government's proceeding immediately with a crude oil security program."[21]

The road to SPR creation led through a minefield of competing interests in Congress. By 1975 competing visions of the nation's energy future had generated varied ideas about the proper direction for energy policy, with well-organized interests pushing Congress in numerous directions at once. During the tumultuous year of 1975 political debate continued on many different energy policies, and a much-compromised collection of policies finally emerged from Congress as the Energy Policy and Conservation Act of 1975 (EPCA).[22] Included in this omnibus energy act was authorization for an SPR with a capacity of up to 1 billion barrels and not less than 150 million barrels of petroleum products, to be in place in three years.

Congress's version of the SPR was similar to that described by the NPC's *Petroleum Storage for National Security,* but several differences reflected the intense political controversies that had accompanied the EPCA's passage in 1975. Upon the insistence of the New England congressional delegation, the act authorized the FEA administrator to create a regional petroleum reserve for the storage of crude oil, residual fuel oil, or any refined petroleum product in areas and regions extremely dependent on imports for their residual fuel oil needs. Although the council had opposed this in its reports, the New England congressional delegation and representatives from the Hawaiian Islands successfully pressed for authorization for the SPR to store residual fuel oil in their regions.

The SPR as approved by Congress contained the Industrial Petroleum Reserve (IPR) provision, under which the FEA administrator had the discretion to "require each importer . . . and each refiner to acquire, store, and maintain" petroleum products "in readily available inventories." *Petroleum Storage for National Security* had opposed such industry inventory requirements, and importers and refiners continued to resist mandatory industry inventory requirements. Proponents of the IPR countered that it would force the heaviest users of petroleum products—importers, refiners, and consumers—to pay some costs of the SPR, ensuring that the entire burden would not fall upon the general taxpayer.[23]

The EPCA required the FEA administrator to submit a plan for the SPR by December 15, 1976. Included would be descriptions of the creation and operation of the reserve, analyses of its economic and environmental impacts, and discussions of how the Industrial Petroleum Reserve and regional reserve provisions would be implemented. The EPCA authorized $1.1 billion from general revenues for the planning and development of the SPR plan. The legislation pointedly excluded the acquisition of petroleum products, although the bill did provide that funds for oil acquisition would come from future appropriations from the government's general revenues.

The National Petroleum Council's recommendations proved influential to the FEA in its completion of the SPR plan. The EPCA of 1975 placed the newly created SPR office within the FEA, charging the office with the responsibility for providing detailed plans and realistic goals for the development of the SPR program. The FEA bore the responsibility of reporting to Congress within one year of the EPCA's passage. The newly created SPR office would carry out the task of designing and creating the plan.

In writing the SPR plan FEA officials made use of studies on salt-dome storage that had been under way within the FEA since early 1975, as well as the council's 1974 and 1975 reports on the SPR. On December 15, 1976, the

FEA presented its larger report on the entire SPR program, the *Strategic Petroleum Reserve Plan,* to Congress. On most significant issues the SPR office accepted the logic put forth in the council's previous reports and the FEA's *Project Independence.* The FEA accepted the council's 500-million-barrel target size for the reserve, estimating that when combined with conservation measures, such a reserve could replace lost imports for up to six months in the most likely interruption scenarios, with only a 3 percent loss in oil consumption. Following logic earlier developed in the NPC's reports, the FEA chose underground storage in Gulf Coast salt domes. Plans called for the initial use of salt domes previously created by industry, with the gradual development of new salt-dome caverns created by solution mining or leaching specifically for the SPR. As earlier recommended by the NPC, the FEA decided against storing petroleum products, arguing that crude oil offered greater flexibility.

In consultation with industry representatives and the National Petroleum Council, the FEA concluded that the most flexible and cost-effective mix of crude would be about 60 percent intermediate density–high sulfur (or "sour") crude and about 40 percent low density–low sulfur (or "sweet") crude. Since more than 90 percent of the SPR's costs would be in oil acquisition, the FEA hoped to control costs by using as much of the cheaper sour crude as possible to fill the SPR. Even with such cost cutting, the FEA estimated that a 500-million-barrel SPR would cost between $7.5 billion and $8 billion.[24]

On two controversial issues, the regional reserves and the industry reserves, the SPR plan agreed with previous NPC reports in deciding against having the FEA exercise discretionary authority provided by Congress in the 1975 EPCA. The SPR plan pointed out numerous potential problems with imposing mandatory inventory requirements on importers and refiners. In the large and diverse American petroleum industry such a requirement might have significant, yet highly unpredictable, competitive effects. Moreover, industry-held reserves could easily become an administrative and regulatory nightmare. The industry overwhelmingly opposed such reserves in hearings held in July, 1976, arguing that they would face challenges in court for taking property without just compensation. Such litigation would inevitably delay the SPR program. While promising to continue to study industrial reserves, the FEA's SPR plan concluded that their budgetary benefits were "outweighed by the resulting [higher] national cost, by the programmatic, legal, and environmental problems that would result from creating such a reserve, and the potential adverse impact on the competitive environment in the petroleum industry."[25]

The FEA again accepted the council's recommendations when it refused to exercise its discretionary power to create regional reserves. As the FEA noted in the SPR plan, storage of refined petroleum products such as residual fuel oil was considerably more expensive than the storage of crude oil. The FEA's report argued that lower-cost, centralized crude oil storage in Gulf Coast salt domes would provide adequate protection for New England, since sufficient refining capacity and transportation existed to refine SPR crude into residual fuel oil on the Gulf Coast and then transport it to the New England region. The FEA promised to continue to study the need for regional petroleum reserves, but its promise gave scant consolation to New Englanders who had expected the FEA to establish in their region a reserve containing residual fuel oil.[26]

The SPR plan put forward an ambitious schedule for filling the reserve. It called for the SPR to have 10 percent, or 50 million barrels, in place by June, 1977; 150 million barrels by December, 1978; 65 percent, approximately 325 million barrels, in place by December, 1980; and 100 percent, 500 million barrels, in place by December, 1982. Anything less than 500 million barrels, the FEA contended, would not provide sufficient protection. Its plan provided, however, that a decision could be made to expand the reserve past the 500-million-barrel mark at a later date. A larger-sized SPR "would be desirable," the FEA wrote, "if it is assumed that oil imports by 1985 will be significantly higher than 7.5 million [barrels per day]."[27] As American dependence on imported oil continued to increase in 1976 and 1977, a larger SPR would seem increasingly warranted. Indeed, within three months of the FEA's submission of the SPR plan to Congress, the Carter administration had moved to increase the size of the SPR to 1 billion barrels.

MOVING OFF THE DRAWING BOARD

A series of difficult technical, bureaucratic, and political setbacks plagued early efforts to build the SPR. The push to get oil into the ground as fast as possible led to the procurement of faulty and inappropriate equipment. All sorts of unanticipated problems emerged in the early years of SPR construction. The attendant bad publicity and delays quickly gave the SPR a reputation as an ill-starred program.

Such problems reflected the rush to apply a relatively untested technology on an unprecedented scale. The existing salt caverns were oddly shaped, with less storage space than anticipated. Much publicity was given to early reports that some of the first supplies of oil pumped into the salt domes had simply disappeared somewhere beneath the earth. Oversight procedures on the contracting process failed to stop increases in costs. Rumors spread that unscrupulous profiteers were filling the salt domes with inferior oil and even sludge. Heated political battles took place between local and federal officials over the FEA's use of eminent domain/condemnation powers to aquire properties. The plans to dispose of the brine produced in the leaching process in the Gulf of Mexico met fierce resistance from local fishermen and environmental groups. A blowout at the West Hackberry, Louisiana, site in September, 1978, caused an explosion and fire, killing one worker and seriously injuring another. Hurricanes and flooding hampered construction. The resulting delays and cost overruns opened the SPR program to criticism in the media and to added scrutiny in congressional hearings and investigations. The establishment of the Department of Energy in October, 1977, and its absorption of the FEA and the SPR office introduced further uncertainties.

As the SPR program struggled to get off the drawing board, world events reminded Americans just why the new program was needed. The Iranian revolution of 1979 reduced world crude oil supplies. This encouraged panic purchasing that increased oil prices more than 150 percent from 1979 to 1981, bringing severe economic dislocations to the major energy-consuming nations. Amid runaway inflation, gasoline shortages and rising fuel prices spread throughout the nation, renewing the debate over energy policies. One immediate response to the second oil shock was the Carter administration's order that the DOE suspend oil purchases for the SPR in 1979 and 1980, which brought still another setback for the program.[28]

Officials within the DOE concluded that the new energy crisis called for fresh analysis from the council. On June 3, 1980, DOE deputy secretary John C. Sawhill wrote to council chairman C. H. Murphy, Jr., requesting that the NPC produce a new report on how to respond to oil supply disruptions. "The Nation," Sawhill noted in his letter, "continues to depend on imported crude oil and petroleum products to satisfy its energy needs," and associated with that dependence was "high risk to the Nation's well-being and security" in the event of another oil supply disruption in the upcoming decade. Recognizing the valuable role of the council's previous reports on the SPR, Sawhill explained that "to prepare for the 1980s, a similar effort is required." Specifically, the DOE wanted the council to examine the ability of the nation's supply and distribution systems to operate under constrained conditions. In response, the council revamped and reformed its Emergency Preparedness Committee, which—in addition to the traditional representation of executives from the oil and gas industry—came to include academics, scientists, and representatives from labor unions, the League of Women Voters, and the Rand Corporation.[29]

The committee completed its report, *Emergency Preparedness for Interruption of Petroleum Imports into the United States,* in April, 1981. The introduction made clear to any remaining skeptics that the redefinition of national security was complete. It noted that oil supply disruptions reduced economic activity, produced price increases that did broad harm to the nation's economic well-being, and had "serious foreign policy implications." The report then listed the objectives of plans to manage oil import disruptions. At the top of the list was "the protection of national security and the foreign policy interests of the United States." The report went on to say that responses to import disruptions "should be designed to buy time and take pressure off top level government decision-makers to allow them to focus on critical foreign policy and national security issues which may accompany major interruptions of petroleum supplies."[30] The SPR was first and foremost an insurance policy purchased by the nation to protect against the threat that manipulation of oil supplies posed to national security.

The report offered a flexible approach for dealing with disruptions of oil imports that was "neither totally free-market oriented nor does it call for government intervention until the need is apparent." The council's recommendations for the "government's overall strategy . . . should be to rely to the maximum extent on market mechanisms." For "very severe energy disruptions," however, the report advocated that the government have available "a variety of emergency standby options."[31]

The report looked at disruptions ranging from 1 MMB/D to 3 MMB/D or more. The government's response would be greater the more dire the emergency. For disruptions up to 1 MMB/D the council recommended that the government rely totally on market mechanisms, including voluntary actions by suppliers and consumers to reduce consumption, interfuel substitution, and use of surplus private inventories. For disruptions up to 2 MMB/D the council advocated government actions such as mandatory interfuel substitution for utilities, temporary relaxation of environmental standards to allow refineries to process higher-sulfur crude oils, state and federal actions to facilitate emergency domestic petroleum production, mandatory lowered speed limits, commercial thermostat management, and the sale of SPR oil in private markets.

To the consternation of some NPC members, the report recommended that for disruptions of 2 to 2.5 MMB/D some standby allocation measures might be necessary to prevent shortages. The council's report conceded that "it is recognized that these measures are both fundamentally flawed" and "unsatisfactory." It also acknowledged that any mandatory oil distribution program would "act as a disincentive to private stockpiling" and require a massive bureaucracy, and that it might build "constituencies against its deactivation." The report did not specifically recommend consumption taxes and import fees but recognized that they might be appropriate in some scenarios. Yet while conceding that some government allocation of oil might be desirable in extreme cases, the report specifically recommended against a reimposition of price controls. Only in the case of "severe disruptions" of more than 2 or 3 MMB/D did the council advocate the use of the SPR, possibly in conjunction with crude oil sharing, a limited system of priority user designations, and product distribution guidelines. Other stronger government measures, such as consumption (gasoline) taxes, (oil) import fees, and rationing, were seen as requiring more study before meriting serious consideration.[32]

The report discussed how a small governmental energy emergency preparedness committee might function during a crisis. It recommended that an advisory body of officials from the energy industries and other groups, as required under the Federal Advisory Committee Act of 1972, be created to help counsel the government during a crisis.

Perhaps the most important recommendation in the 1981 report on emergency preparedness was that the SPR should be "more readily available" in crises of "varying sizes." The second oil shock encouraged rethinking of the proper use of the reserve, moving away from the "last resort/rainy day" policy and toward the policy of "early use." By 1980 some government and industry officials began to think that the SPR might be used early in a crisis to avert the kind of panic seen in 1979–81. Somewhat contradicting a recommendation (earlier in the same report) that the SPR should be drawn down only in "severe energy supply disruptions," the report also recommended that the SPR be "used in even smaller interruptions." Such early use of the SPR, however, was to be limited to SPR reserves above 200 million barrels. Stocks below this level "should be held in the reserve for vital defense, health, and safety needs."[33]

This early use recommendation, the report admitted, "represents a change" from the council's recommendation in the 1975 petroleum storage report that the reserve be used only as a last resort. That change "reflects a recognition of the need to try to both minimize the harmful effects on consumers of very severe interruptions, as well as cushion the significant impacts which may be unnecessarily experienced in [the] early months of even smaller interruptions, when the full effect of the cutoff hits the United States but before emergency supply/demand management measures have become fully effective." Increasingly energy market analysts in the private and public sectors came to think that the "proper signal" to send to the market was the early and public use of the reserve.[34]

This oil would enter the market through sales at competitive auction, rather than through allocation authorities, ensuring the most efficient utilization of SPR oil. Thus oil from the reserve would be made available early in a crisis, but the market, rather than the government, would determine the price and allocation of SPR oil. The DOE could still reject offers deemed to be too low. This recommendation brought quick action: On December 1, 1982, President Reagan transmitted to Congress the fourth amendment to the FEA's 1976 SPR plan, which provided that the principal method of distributing SPR oil would be through competitive sales, with sales going to those offering the highest prices.

Emergency Preparedness stressed that the market was superior to government in allocating and pricing of oil and petroleum products. But, ironically, a large government-owned reserve was needed to safeguard against severe disruptions of the market. The central role of the SPR was to dampen the incentive of foreign producers to withhold oil supplies in an effort to influence international relations. If successful, the SPR would provide a valuable cushion around the "normal" workings of the market, allowing it to function efficiently without the devastation of oil shocks produced by outside political forces largely beyond the control of the American government.[35]

FINE-TUNING FOR A REAL WORLD CRISIS

Events in the Middle East in the 1980s tested the assumptions of such emergency planning exercises. In May, 1984, the forty-four-month-old war between Iran and Iraq spilled out into the Persian Gulf, as oil tankers under the flag of third-party nations came under fire from both sides. In response President Reagan pledged that the United States would not allow any nation to block commerce in the Persian Gulf–Strait of Hormuz area, through which 20 percent of the noncommunist oil supply flowed in tankers. While the Persian Gulf crisis of 1984 did not pose the same level of threat to U.S. energy security as had the energy crises of the 1970s, it brought the issue of energy security back to the forefront of political debate.

For the first time the SPR held sufficient oil to be of practical use in meeting temporary shortages. In the first four years of the Reagan administration a series of contracts for oil purchases from Mexico and the resumption of open-market purchases had enabled the DOE to quadruple the amount of oil in the SPR, from just over 100 million barrels at the end of 1980 to roughly 400 million barrels by mid-1984. In a crisis, DOE officials estimated, the reserve could be drawn down at a rate of 2 MMB/D for a ninety-day period.

Despite the fact that the SPR now had considerable oil in the ground, questions remained about the program's drawdown and distribution capacity, as well as procedures to be used to sell oil from the reserve. The SPR had recently lost use of the Seaway and Texoma pipeline systems, which had been converted by their private owners to the transmission of natural gas for the private market. One SPR official acknowledged that "the questions have evolved from 'Can you get the oil out of the ground?' to 'Can you distribute it?'" One of the program's harshest critics declared that "the potential distribution problems are very serious," such that "even the administration has decided something has to be done about them. . . . With proper planning, the reserve can limit the price hikes that are sure to occur during a disruption. . . . But if we can't get the oil to the refineries and into the marketplace, the benefits are lost." Others in Congress voiced similar skepticism, and even the U.S. Chamber of Commerce questioned the viability of the DOE's drawdown and distribution plans.[36]

Energy analysts and industry officials had different concerns. Some feared that the DOE might wait too late to draw down the SPR in the event of an oil shortfall. Others voiced concern that the SPR might not be used in a timely manner in reaction to a "relatively minor supply disruption" or a "sub-crisis," which was similar to what was going on in the Persian Gulf at that moment. Amid such questions about the SPR, the Reagan administration came to emphasize a new outlook on using the SPR.[37]

Throughout the first Reagan administration, officials had stated that the SPR would be used only as a last resort, echoing the position of DOE officials throughout the reserve's history. But the potential energy crisis in summer, 1984, forced the Reagan administration to rethink the last-resort policy. In May, 1984, DOE secretary Donald Hodel announced that in a true emergency, "my inclination would be to use [the reserve] sooner rather than later" to supplement the increased production that the market could bring. A supply interruption that could not be made up from stepped-up production would be offset by selling oil from the reserve "up to the level of the interruption." Hodel also maintained that the SPR, with 400 million barrels in storage, could supply up to 2.1 million barrels of oil per day for six months. He promised that in the event of a crisis the administration would act quickly, even before consulting with U.S. allies, to initiate the complicated process of tapping the reserve so as to avert panic in the marketplace.[38]

Meanwhile, on November 7, 1983, Hodel had written council chairman Robert A. Mosbacher requesting that the council undertake a study on the SPR's drawdown and distribution capabilities. Such a study, Hodel wrote, should take into account the type of oil in storage, sources of supply, industry capabilities to distribute SPR oil from the storage sites to refineries, and "any other aspect of the Government/industry relationship wherein the Council believes changes in our current plans for SPR distribution and composition are warranted." The NPC accepted this request and in December, 1984, published *The Strategic Petroleum Reserve: A Report on the Capability to Distribute Oil.*[39]

Although the report's detailed analysis of SPR operations proved valuable, one of its most significant statements was "the Council believes that the Strategic Petroleum Reserve is a valuable national asset, capable of being drawn down and distributed in the event of a national emergency."[40] The program had traveled a rocky road since initial congressional debates on its creation a decade earlier. Although far from a finished work, the SPR could now be relied upon for use in future emergencies.

The 1984 report offered practical suggestions about how to improve the SPR's performance. It recommended that with the loss of the Texoma and Seaway pipelines, the DOE should shift at least 100 million barrels of SPR oil from the Texoma complex sites (West Hackberry, Sulphur Mines, and Big Hill) to the Capline complex sites (Weeks Island, Bayou Choctaw, and Saint James). The report recommended the completion of new pipelines, marine docks, and ballast water treatment facilities at each of the three complexes so that distribution capacity would match drawdown capability. It added that the DOE should restrict sale of SPR oil to a list of experienced oil purchasers, marketers, and traders, with contracts more in line with (or similar to) industry contacts. The report also recommended an increase in proportion of sweet crude in the SPR from its planned 35 percent to 45 percent. While rejecting this call for increased supplies of sweet crude, the DOE accepted all the other major recommendations in the NPC's report.

At least as important as the council's practical advice for improving SPR operations was the increased credibility that the report accorded the SPR within the industry. The SPR's public image had taken a beating in the decade since its authorization, and the report helped reassure both industry and government that the reserve could be used effectively in a crisis. As part of the study process the NPC sent industry inspectors to SPR sites to examine drawdown procedures and maintenance practices as well as the quality of crude oil in storage. What they found stood in stark contrast to the SPR's image as a program mired in troubles. The publication of the NPC report's optimistic findings helped to alter perceptions of the SPR as a failed program.[41]

The acid test came when Iraq invaded Kuwait in 1990, abruptly removing from world markets approximately 4.5 million barrels of oil (about 7 percent of world production). This produced a shortage on the same scale as those in 1973 and 1979, and crude prices leaped from roughly eighteen dollars per barrel to more than twenty-eight dollars per barrel in the three days following the invasion. Although crude prices quickly fell to twenty-five dollars a barrel, gasoline prices rose sharply across the nation, depending upon local supply conditions. There was, however, a major difference between the shortage in 1990 and those of the 1970s: This time the SPR held more than 580 million barrels of oil.[42]

Once again the government turned to the council for aid and advice in a time of crisis. Before the invasion, in September, 1989, DOE secretary James D. Watkins had requested that the council study how the industry might assist government in the event of a future energy supply crisis. In his request letter to council chairman Lodwrick M. Cook, Watkins asked the council to "recommend an organizational structure of an oil-related National Defense Executive Reserve (NDER) or its equivalent for use in a severe national security emergency," which might range from multiple earthquakes to mobilization for war. Noting that there might be antitrust constraints against the development of an NDER, Watkins advised the council to assume that such issues had been resolved satisfactorily and that the administration was promoting an amendment to the Defense Production Act of 1950 for such a purpose. Watkins noted that the last NPC study on emergency preparedness, completed in 1981, was limited to petroleum import interruption emergencies and that "previous NPC studies on emergency preparedness for mobilization and war are over 20 years old." A new study was a "high priority" of the DOE.[43]

The Iraqi invasion of Kuwait made this new study a high priority indeed. In August, 1990, the DOE again looked to the council for advice. The DOE's Energy Information Administration (EIA) had been producing daily reports describing the potential disruption of world oil flow and identifying areas of potential excess capacity. Bush administration officials very much wanted forecasts from industry insiders as to the short-term petroleum outlook on the world market. Thus, in October Secretary Watkins once again requested that the NPC assess the factors that might affect the short-term supply and demand of oil. These included the availability of crude, the overall refining capacity, the regulatory impact upon mothballed refineries, the levels of petroleum product exports and imports, private inventories, and the potential use of the SPR.

Concluding that the EIA's projections were sound, the NPC did not want to put forth another set of numbers whose slight differences might produce needless debate and conflict. It therefore agreed to make recommendations based largely on the EIA's projections. For this effort the council recalled many members of the committee that had produced *Petroleum Storage & Transportation* in 1989. This new Emergency Preparedness Committee, like the one of the early 1980s, had a diverse membership, with union representatives and DOE officials joining the traditional mix of executives from major, independent, natural gas, and oil-field service companies. The committee set to work quickly and produced two reports by January 23, 1991. *Short-Term Petroleum Outlook—An Examination of Issues and Projections* reported on the immediate crisis in response to Secretary Watkins's October 19 request letter. *Industry Assistance to Government: Methods for Providing Petroleum Industry Expertise during Emergencies* (which was discussed in chapter 2) was a response to Watkins's September 20 request letter.

Short-Term Petroleum Outlook stressed the free market approach that had prevailed in the 1980s. It concluded, for example, that further shortages would yield temporary rises in prices, especially in the event of hoarding. But government price controls, the report argued, would be counterproductive. Allowing prices to rise in the short term would dampen demand, encouraging conservation; it would also provide incentives for increased domestic production. "Government controls," the NPC committee wrote, "are not the answer to problems, because these stop the rebalancing mechanism and create artificial supply/demand balances." The report continued: "Past experience has demonstrated that unfettered market behavior is the most efficient allocator of limited resources. Artificially constraining prices tends to discourage conservation, slows the flow of needed supplies, and can lead to runouts. In the extreme, the longer-term effect can be reduced by industry investment." The principal role of industry is "to maintain continuity of product supply for consumers," and the "principal role of government is to minimize hardships." The U.S. economy, according to the report, is part of the "world petroleum supply system" that is driven by "free-market economics," and the United States could not "insulate itself from the world market."[44]

The council concluded that barring significant further supply disruptions, U.S. and world refining and transporting capabilities could meet current demands. Because world crude oil production was at full capacity at the end of

1990, additional supplies could come only from the SPR and from similar oil stockpiles belonging to the other IEA member nations. Thus, if hostilities in the Middle East created additional supply disruptions, the U.S. government should draw down the SPR, hopefully in conjunction with other IEA drawdowns so that American SPR oil alone would not make up for the shortfall alone. But if necessary, the council advised, the United States should draw down its SPR unilaterally.

The NPC recommended that volumes of SPR oil "be offered immediately if there is an outbreak of hostilities or other events that could disrupt the flow of oil from the Middle East." Such an action, according to the report, "would be a clear signal to U.S. and world markets of the intent of the U.S. government to make stocks available to maintain continuity of supply." The report also recommended that the United States and other IEA nations with oil stockpiles should not wait to see a physical shortage before making and announcing the decision to use their reserves. An "early commitment to draw down the SPR" would "calm petroleum markets." In light of the psychology of past crises, the early public announcement of the intention to use the SPR might prove just as important as the actual early use of oil from the reserve.[45]

The report advised that an SPR drawdown should include "the largest possible volume" of oil. There was little risk that SPR oil drawn down too soon or in an amount too large would glut the oil market, because companies would not bid for oil they did not want. It followed, therefore, that the drawdown might be smaller than originally planned but would be large enough to meet energy demands not satisfied by the market.

The report recommended vigorous efforts to obtain a blanket waiver of requirements under the Jones Act, or Merchant Marine Act. Such action would facilitate the prompt distribution of SPR oil, especially coastwise to the Northeast, which by the 1990s depended upon imports to meet 90 percent of its crude oil needs. Amendments to the Jones Act (originally passed in 1920) required that domestic maritime oil be shipped in U.S.-flagged tankers. While waivers to the act would widen the number of potential ships that could transport SPR oil to include foreign-flagged vessels, the council recognized that a general waiver might be politically sensitive. The Bush administration had already pledged to grant such waivers on a case-by-case basis in response to disruptions that forced SPR use.[46]

If the supply shortfall became too large for the SPR and IEA stockpiles to offset, the council argued, then additional government actions might be required to augment domestic supply, such as lifting environmental constraints on refineries. The NPC examined other possible government actions, including encouraging fuel-switching from oil to natural gas where possible among businesses, utilities, and consumers and providing financial assistance to help low-income households pay their energy bills. All the recommended actions that the U.S. government might take—SPR drawdowns, temporary suspension of environmental standards, Jones Act waivers, energy assistance to the poor—"should be undertaken to the extent possible within the framework of market prices and unrestrained product movements, both import and export."[47]

Short-Term Petroleum Outlook criticized government efforts to "jaw-bone" the industry into controlling its own prices in fall and winter, 1990–91. President Bush and members of Congress had been exhorting the industry to keep prices in check since the crisis began in August, 1990. The report stated that "the NPC is not questioning the prerogative of elected officials to seek to influence industry actions." Without naming names, the council was critical of the political pressures brought to bear on oil companies to influence them into restraining prices. "American industry," the report stated, "has traditionally complied with the requests of national leaders to make supply, manufacturing, logistical, pricing, or other decisions that may not be compatible with its interests or market conditions." But the report argued that "the consequences of jaw-boning should be recognized—it will likely exacerbate supply problems and delay the rebalancing of supply and demand."[48]

The NPC emphasized the need for "a uniform statutory and regulatory environment in lieu of a patchwork of state regulations and controls," which might limit the timely distribution of supplies in an emergency. It advised against closing the petroleum futures markets because "they have become highly integrated with the dynamic global oil markets," providing for price discovery and risk reduction.[49]

President Bush ultimately accepted and implemented two major recommendations of *Short-Term Petroleum Outlook:* immediate and public SPR use in the event of a shooting war in the Middle East; and a blanket waiver from the Jones Act requirements to facilitate shipment and transportation of SPR oil to where it was needed most. Thus, when the president ordered air strikes against Iraq on the evening of January 16, 1991, the framework for using the SPR as part of a collective IEA effort was in place.

Within hours of ordering the air strikes, the president issued a finding that events in the Persian Gulf had resulted in a potential national energy supply shortage constituting a "severe energy supply interruption," as defined in Section 3(8), and required under Section 161(d) of the 1975 EPCA. He then authorized Secretary Watkins to draw down and distribute SPR oil at such a rate as the secretary might determine. Adhering to the IEA plan, Watkins directed the DOE to withdraw 33.75 million barrels, equivalent to a draw-down of 1.125 MMB/D over a thirty-day period. This was part of a collective IEA action that included drawdowns by thirteen other nations to minimize world oil market disruptions caused by the Middle East conflict. In a state-ment to the media the Bush administration described its action as a "precau-tionary measure . . . taken in concert with the IEA, [and] designed to promote stability in world oil markets."[50]

Industry demand for SPR oil was strong. By January 28, 1991, the DOE had received bids from twenty-six companies for 45 million barrels of SPR crude, despite the fact that just under 34 million barrels had been offered. Watkins declared that "the response clearly shows that there is great interest in SPR oil, and shows that the system works." By January 30 the DOE had accepted bids from thirteen companies offering the highest prices for SPR oil. The National Petroleum Council's 1984 study on the SPR had voiced concern that the policy of opening up the bidding on SPR oil to "any firm, organiza-tion, or individual [that] can submit an offer" would result in inexperienced firms or organizations entering the fray. This might cause unnecessary confusion at a time requiring decisive action. But the companies selected by the DOE were all well-established energy firms, and they collectively agreed to purchase 17.3 million barrels of SPR oil, or just over half the 33.75 million barrels that had been originally offered. By March 31 the DOE had success-fully sold and delivered the 17 million barrels of SPR oil ordered drawn down by the president.[51]

On January 17, 1991, the day after President Bush announced both the allied air strikes and the SPR drawdown, posted prices plunged from their per-barrel range of thirty-three dollars to thirty-five dollars down to a range of eighteen dollars to twenty dollars a barrel, just slightly below what they had been before the crisis began. Observers disagreed about the cause of these sharp declines in price. Some felt that the use of the SPR had encouraged the normalization of crude oil prices; others dismissed the effect of the SPR, argu-ing instead that other factors, notably the early success of the air war, were more important. Few doubted, however, that the SPR played a significant role as a symbol that the United States had a measure of control over its own energy supply.

In the decade since the use of oil from the SPR during Desert Storm, the United States did not face a similar oil supply emergency, yet the debate over uses of the SPR continued. In 1996 sales from the reserve were used to help pay for the decommissioning of the Weeks Island, Louisiana, storage site.

Then in 1996 and 1997 the government sold almost $450 million worth of oil from the SPR in a controversial move to reduce the federal budget deficit. During the closing days of the heated presidential campaign of 2000, even more intense controversy greeted the decision to draw on the SPR in an effort to dampen price increases in oil products. This decision spurred a broad national debate on the proper uses of the SPR, raising again the central question: What sort of emergency justified the use of the nation's "insurance policy" against oil supply disruptions? By that time the SPR contained about 570 million barrels of oil acquired and stored by the public at a cost of about $20 billion. Inevitably, such an expense was a lightning rod for political debate in times of oil shortages or sharp rises in oil prices.[52]

Given the NPC's historical involvement in the SPR's evolution, it seems certain that the council will be asked to study future issues concerning management and use of the SPR. The Strategic Petroleum Reserve program offers the best example of the National Petroleum Council's influence upon national energy policy. Its reports helped shape debates on the SPR's size and location, as well as its storage medium, the type of oil stored, and the source of its funding. After the creation of the reserve, the council continued to advise the Department of Energy on the reserve's effective operation before taking an active part in planning for its use during Desert Storm. Many in the council and in the petroleum industry have remained wary of the potential impact this government-owned program could have on oil markets' efficiency during times of normal fluctuations in supply and demand. But few doubt its value in protecting the nation's military and economic security against extreme disruptions in foreign supply similar to the Arab oil embargo of the early 1970s.

CHAPTER 5

Seeking a Balance between Energy and Environment

IN THE 1960s POLLUTION CONTROL emerged as a major issue in all phases of the petroleum industry. In subsequent decades the NPC conducted a number of studies on the impact environmental laws were having on oil and gas industry operations. Its reports gradually gained credibility with government officials struggling to define a sustainable balance between energy and environmental policies. As numerous competing interests sought to shape environmental regulations in highly contentious political debates, the NPC became a respected voice of industry on this vital set of issues.

This was no easy task given the deep divisions on energy/environment within government, business, and the society as a whole. In its role as adviser to the Department of the Interior and then the Department of Energy, the NPC reported to federal agencies most concerned with the energy side of this equation. But another powerful federal agency, the Environmental Protection Agency (EPA), had primary responsibilities for enforcing environmental regulations. Structural and philosophical tensions between government agencies most concerned with energy and those most concerned with environment made the quest for balance highly political—and often confusing.

EPA officials and environmental interest groups generally had markedly different values and worldviews than those of industry representatives in the NPC. Political clashes over policy were heated and divisive. As the debate moved from issue to issue in subsequent decades, the NPC steadily put forward an argument for balance in energy/environmental policies. In practice, this meant consideration for costs as well as benefits in designing pollution controls. In theory, it generally meant support for incentive-based regulations that set societal goals but allowed industry some leeway in achieving them. Obviously, on environmental issues the definition of *balance* differed dramatically among competing interests. The NPC served a useful function in debates over environmental regulations by presenting the point of view of those responsible for satisfying the nation's energy needs.

Although the NPC's general arguments seemed to gain greater public support over time, the command-and-control regulations put in place during the first wave of federal environmental laws in the late 1960s and early 1970s proved difficult to reform. These laws had been shaped by the political climate in an era of strong demands for pollution control. In response to public pressures to act quickly and decisively on this set of issues, Congress passed a series of laws that put forward strict new standards on air and water emissions enforced by heavy fines. Such command-and-control regulations generally focused on industrial pollution and reflected the attitude of the times: Clean up quickly, regardless of costs, or face severe consequences. At the same time the new requirement for environmental impact statements forced all major construction projects through an environmental planning process open to public input and designed to anticipate potential environmental impacts before construction permits could be obtained. Such new laws had profound implications for the energy industries.

The intense political conflicts over environmental issues in the late 1960s and 1970s marked a great divide in the history of the National Petroleum Council. During its first twenty-five years the NPC had worked with officials in a relatively friendly DOI on national security issues. Its recommendations seldom were at odds with prevailing public opinions. This changed in the 1970s, when issues raised by energy and environmental controversies became much more divisive and NPC reports faced more aggressive challenges from well-organized groups with different points of view.

Amid the resulting political tensions the NPC continued to produce useful reports on an array of environmental issues. These reports did not succeed in altering the basic command-and-control approach of regulators, but they gradually helped to change the tone and then the agenda of the debates over the costs and benefits of environmental regulations. At times NPC members must have felt as if they were beating their heads against an unyielding wall of political opposition. But they continued to study environmental issues and make recommendations for environmental policies that paid greater attention to the societal need for energy.

The NPC became one industry voice pointing out the costs of complying with the new wave of environmental regulations. Its dispassionate, data-rich reports put forward practical methods to improve command-and-control regulations and ultimately to replace them with more flexible approaches that might achieve the same goals more efficiently. The NPC earned credibility by applying sophisticated analytical data to study the long-term impacts on industry of different approaches to pollution control. In the changing political climate in America in the 1980s and after, the NPC's long-voiced plea for more balanced, more efficient environmental policies found an increasingly sympathetic audience.

THE NPC AND THE NEW WAVE OF ENVIRONMENTAL REGULATIONS IN THE 1970S

Such a balanced approach was not the order of the day in the late 1960s, when the NPC first grappled with the issues raised by a rising tide of concern about pollution. The nation had long delayed confronting the serious environmental problems brought by sustained industrial expansion. Oil was a visible symbol of industrialization, and the petroleum industry responded to the obvious sources of pollution from its operations with a series of companywide and industrywide initiatives dating from the 1920s. But when broad segments of an increasingly wealthy American society began to demand a cleaner environment, traditional approaches to pollution control were deemed inadequate.

Unfortunately for the oil industry, it was singled out for political attacks in the early years of the movement toward much stricter environmental regulations. The symbol of "Big Oil" as an environmental villain in this era was the Santa Barbara (California) oil spill. In January, 1969, an offshore oil well in the Santa Barbara Channel blew out, producing a large oil spill that heightened public concerns about oil-related pollution. In response to this and other concerns Congress passed the National Environmental Policy Act of 1969 and slowed the rate of offshore oil leasing. The petroleum industry found itself in the path of a hurricane of political demands for stricter environmental regulations.

Within three months of the spill the assistant secretary of the interior, Hollis M. Dole, wrote to NPC chairman Jack Abernathy seeking the council's help in studying oil-related pollution. Citing growing national concern about environmental pollution, Dole wrote that "it would be extremely useful and timely if the oil industry could present comments on the proper role of the industry in formulating or cooperating in correcting actions." He believed that the National Petroleum Council study process provided the proper forum for the petroleum industry to present its views on the prevention or alleviation of pollution. He felt that such a report would indicate the industry's willingness to cooperate with government efforts in pollution abatement. Dole specifically requested that the council discuss major disasters such as tanker accidents and offshore well blowouts, as well as saltwater flooding, waste oils, storage, and pipeline operations. Finally, he wanted the council to analyze the impact of pollution control efforts on the supply and cost of petroleum products. He added that "this part of the study should include a careful analysis of regulations on raw material development, environmental controls and direct specifications on product properties."[1]

The NPC's Agenda Committee evaluated Dole's request in April, 1969. It was reluctant to undertake a comprehensive look at the issue—or to turn down the DOI's request. One member acknowledged, "I don't think any of us would decline to prepare such a report." Another member suggested that the American Petroleum Institute "be pulled into it in some way to get you a report much more quickly and certainly it would be a tremendously comprehensive thing, because they have been on this for the last three or four years or so."[2]

Still others raised more specific questions. Longtime council member Bruce Brown focused on the request's reference to pollution by fuels. He asked, "Do we or do we not go into all of the law and technology of whether you desulphurize all gasoline and take tetraethyl lead out of it? I think he means to include it, but I hope he says no." Others on the committee questioned the importance of such matters to the Department of the Interior, since at that time air quality was under the jurisdiction of the Department of Health, Education, and Welfare (HEW). Some asked whether the proper role of an industry advisory committee was to tell consumers what type of vehicles to drive or indicate the cost of various approaches to reducing pollution by petroleum fuels. Chairman Abernathy noted the reluctance on the petroleum industry's part to address the auto industry's problems, and he doubted whether the NPC had the expertise to do so.[3]

To nudge the Agenda Committee into action, Dole reminded them of the NPC's special relationship with his department and its advisory and fact-finding responsibilities. Department of the Interior officials prodded the council to do a comprehensive study that would encompass all the subjects in the request letter. "When we start throwing out fuels . . . because HEW has some responsibility and then because API has some responsibility, we wind up with really doing nothing, and that was not our intent. We wanted a whole over-view of this situation so the Secretary can then pick up one document and get an attitude and opinion and finding of the industry." Interior officials hoped that this would include some discussion of technical options in dealing with the pollution caused by fuels as well as the environmental impacts of direct operations of the oil and gas industries.[4]

Despite misgivings, the Agenda Committee accepted the study request, but with significant qualifications. The council committee handling the as-signment would operate under a general mandate with authority to impose limitations on matters to be studied. In accepting, the NPC also reiterated its hope that its study committee would work in close coordination with other groups in the petroleum industry examining problems involved in air and water pollution.[5]

The council established a twenty-eight-person Committee on Environ-mental Conservation chaired by William W. Keller (chairman of the board of Phillips Petroleum Company) and a coordinating subcommittee chaired by Leo A. McReynolds (director of research, Petroleum Products and Environ-mental Conservation, Phillips). Government cochairs of the respective com-mittees were Gene P. Morrell (deputy assistant secretary of mineral resources, DOI) and Dr. Wilson W. Laird (director of the Office of Oil and Gas, DOI). Keeler told the council as a whole in January, 1970, that his committee hoped to put "pollution of our environment in perspective. We felt that in doing this, national objectives to meet growing requirements for energy and na-tional objectives for achieving environmental quality should be placed in proper relationship." The committee focused on economic aspects of environmental conservation. Its report addressed the environmental impact of industry op-erations as well as the particularly complex environmental problems associ-ated with petroleum-product utilization. A twenty-three-person coordinating subcommittee took responsibility for writing the interdisciplinary report.[6]

In June, 1970, the council issued an interim report entitled *Current Key Issues Relating to Environmental Conservation—The Oil and Gas Industries*. While defending the petroleum industry's past efforts to promote "conserva-tion of the environment," this report struck a cautious tone. It noted that a highly industrialized society could not exist without the intensive utilization of natural resources. Balance was necessary between the interests of the envi-ronment and other interests. The report read:

> It is a fundamental responsibility of government, after consultation
> with the private sector, to determine reasonable standards of environmental

quality that are to be maintained and, where remedial action is required, the period of time within which those standards are to be reached. In determining such standards and the time required to reach them, government should carefully take into account the cost-benefit factor and its impact upon the economy. Since environmental circumstances differ dramatically from place to place, these standards cannot and should not be expected to be reached in unreasonably short time-periods nor will they be attained uniformly throughout this country or internationally.[7]

The report stressed the necessity of developing essential offshore petroleum resources and emphasized the industry's record in minimizing accidents and oil spills. It cautioned that reductions in allowable sulfur content below 1 percent for residual fuels would reduce their supply. It suggested that the reduction of sulfur from stack gases was a more effective means of reducing emissions of sulfur dioxide. The NPC opposed federal approval or licensing of motor fuels under the 1967 Clean Air Act amendments, arguing that governmental involvement in the composition of motor fuel should be approached with great caution. The report noted that the "interrelationship between variables in vehicle design and fuel composition, as they affect emissions, are highly complex and to be treated effectively must be approached as a total system."[8]

Six months after the publication of this interim report, the NPC issued the first volume of a more comprehensive study entitled *Environmental Conservation—The Oil and Gas Industries*. Volume 1, published in June, 1971, put forward ideas about the environmental responsibilities of the oil and gas industries. It commented on general law and regulatory policy, the economics of environmental conservation, and the specific environmental concerns for air, water, and land pollution. Volume 2, released in February, 1972, was a comprehensive 406-page treatise on the technical aspects of operations of the oil and gas industries and the economic, legal, and scientific facets of environmental quality for the operations and products of the petroleum industry. These two volumes argued that the benefits and costs of environmental quality needed to be balanced with the energy requirements of a modern society. Positive results in such an endeavor could best be achieved by flexible regulation that prescribed workable standards and then allowed the private sector to determine the means to meet them. The public should recognize the high costs involved, and those costs should be paid by society as a whole. Government might need to loosen antitrust constraints so that people of goodwill in industry and government could cooperate to improve environmental quality.[9]

The principles first enunciated by the NPC in *Environmental Conservation* comprise what might be labeled a "traditional industrialist" approach to pollution control. They reflected the historical experience and philosophical bent of men who had lived their lives in the petroleum industry and who assumed that managers of private companies were best situated to fashion effective responses to pollution. At the time *Environmental Conservation* was published, however, these principles found little public sympathy. The prevailing sentiment was that industrialists had failed to solve the problems created by pollution in the decades before the 1960s and that stronger public initiatives would be required to force them to do so in the 1970s.

Environmental Conservation closely examined the economics of pollution control. It emphasized that the "cost benefit factor to society and the impact of that factor upon our economy should be taken into account" and that the costs associated with environmental conservation and control must be borne by society at large. The council supported flexible regulation "where environmental quality does not meet prescribed standards, but the constantly moving limits of technology and economics should be taken into account in setting realistic and stable timetables for achievement of the desired quality." It inveighed against the use of economic penalties to obtain environmental compliance; it opposed regulations prescribing the lead content of gasoline as inappropriate and unnecessary, noting that low-lead and no-lead gasolines were already available. Further restrictions on the use of lead in fuel, according to the council, would result in "significant technical and economic effects on the production of gasoline," since lead alkyd additives were the most economical method to increase the octane level of gasoline.[10]

The report defended the past practices of the industry, citing its substantial expenditures and investments in pollution control equipment and engineering, and emphasizing the role of petroleum products in raising living standards. While acknowledging that emissions from vehicles contributed significantly to air pollution, the NPC asserted that the most cost-effective solution to auto-related pollution was the further development of emission control technology, not additional restrictions on fuel content. Continuing this argument, the report stated that only about one-fifth of the sulfur dioxide emissions in the United States resulted from the use of petroleum products. It cited substantial progress made by industry, including reducing the sulfur content of lighter liquid petroleum fuels by 50 percent and suggested that further advances in stack control technology would allow consumers to use high-sulfur fuels.[11]

The threat of oil spills remained a sensitive question, and the report directly addressed this issue. It anticipated that spills could be minimized but not eliminated. The report recommended improvements in standard industry practices to minimize spills, as well as corporate contingency plans to cope with them. The avoidance of major tanker spills, the report went on, required the continuing attention and cooperation of industry and government. It added that more sophisticated environmental control equipment should be developed so that oil refineries could continue to reduce pollution.[12]

In December, 1972, the NPC published *U.S. Energy Outlook—A Summary Report,* which reinforced its call for balance between environmental goals and energy requirements. The report urged the use of environmental standards compatible with other broad national goals such as "full employment, reduction of poverty, further improvement in average living standards, and the assurance of energy supplies at all times for health, comfort and national security." It reiterated key points from *Environmental Conservation,* focusing on the need to minimize delays associated with oil and gas exploration and development as well as the necessity of granting the private sector the widest possible latitude in methods and technology used in achieving environmental standards.[13]

These initial NPC reports on environmental issues must be understood as the response of an industry under siege. In the early years of the environmental movement there was little public sympathy for the petroleum industry when it called for cost-effective, flexible regulations.

At the same time, some industry leaders in this era of transition—having not yet fully accepted the idea of strong, permanent new powers of government over pollution—fought losing battles against needed changes. Most Americans voiced little concern about the long-term impact of strict new regulations on the industry, which they assumed had both the technical wherewithal and the investment capital to meet strict new environmental standards and remain productive and profitable. In this climate *Environmental Conservation* was an industry lament that fell on deaf ears outside the industry. Only after increased awareness of the long-term costs of environmental regulations and their impact on the availability and cost of energy would the public become more sympathetic to the views of the petroleum industry.

ENVIRONMENTAL CONSERVATION REVISITED, TEN YEARS AFTER

Environmental Conservation established the parameters of the industry's initial response to the environmental movement. But subsequent events raised a series of new environmental issues while altering the approach taken toward others. The energy crises of the 1970s changed the context of the debate on environmental quality by offering a sobering reminder that abundant supplies of inexpensive energy could no longer be taken for granted. Amid the swirl of competing demands on environmental, energy, and economic issues, the NPC's earlier call for balance took on new meaning.

One clear example of the impact of these changes was evident in the regulation of leaded gasoline, which had been a controversial environmental issue in the early 1970s. By the end of the decade the debate on leaded gasoline was muted. The 1970 Clean Air Act (CAA) amendments had mandated phased reductions in the use of leaded gasoline, which could not be used with the catalytic converters required under the act. By 1981 lead use in gasoline had decreased some 75 percent, and it continued to decline until being banned by law in the late 1980s.[14]

Environmental Conservation had predicted the market-driven development of unleaded gasoline. General distribution began in July, 1974, and accelerated following widespread adoption of catalytic exhaust emissions controls after 1975. But the report had underestimated the vexing adjustments required to produce unleaded gasoline, which required complex and costly changes in refineries to increase the octane levels of gasoline blending components.[15] The switch to unleaded gasoline encouraged the growth in refinery capacity in the 1970s while also reducing the gasoline yield from each barrel of crude oil compared to what had been achieved with lead.[16] These changes in refining contributed to problems that the NPC would later be called on to study.

The petroleum industry had to adapt to many other major changes in the 1970s, most notably the uncertainties caused by OPEC pricing, the demands for conservation embodied in the corporate average fuel economy (CAFE) standards, and the rise and fall of enthusiasm for synthetic fuels. Never far from view in political debates over all energy-related issues in these tumultuous years were environmental issues. Implicit in the call for a balanced approach to energy/environment was the knowledge that these two concerns were often the flip sides of the same coin. In the long term neither could be effectively addressed without consideration for the other.

The Carter administration acknowledged this reality in 1980 when it called on the NPC to revisit its previous study on environmental conservation. Citing the existence of extensive new regulations in the decade since the 1971 study, Secretary of Energy Charles W. Duncan, Jr., requested the update. He noted that "significant technological advances in the oil and gas industry have occurred since 1971" and that these "advances not only increase economic efficiency but mitigate environmental hazards as well." At the same time Duncan requested a study on Arctic oil and gas and an update of the NPC's reports *Emergency Preparedness for Interruption of Petroleum Imports into the United States* (1974) and *Petroleum Storage for National Security* (1975). The Iranian revolution of 1978–79, supply interruptions, and a dramatic rise in oil prices reinforced the need for these studies. In May, 1980, the DOE's deputy assistant secretary, R. Dobie Langenkamp, discussed the proposed environmental study with the NPC's Agenda Committee. He clearly labeled it as the one the council could exclude if it wanted to undertake only two studies. Langenkamp emphasized, however, that the DOE relied heavily on NPC studies and that the department considered an update of *Environmental Conservation* important enough to include as a potential third study.[17]

The Agenda Committee's discussion of this request displayed little of the reluctance shown eleven years earlier. All present appreciated the value of the council's earlier effort in developing a comprehensive treatment of the issue. The committee recognized that the recent efforts of the API and EPA advisory committees on the subject were narrow examinations of a "particular situation rather than being broad" and that they were "nothing really comprehensive." Committee members pointed out that the environmental problems of acid rain and synthetic fuels, not discussed in the earlier report, were now major concerns for the petroleum industry. The Energy Department wanted the council to examine environmental requirements imposed by other government agencies, such as drilling mud specifications set by the EPA, since "nobody in the department [Energy] is really paying much attention to it though EPA is." The Agenda Committee accepted a charge to update *Environmental Conservation* and decided that the environmental aspects of the Arctic oil and gas study should be coordinated with it.[18]

Despite reservations about the ability to staff all of its ongoing studies, the NPC planned a major effort. The NPC appointed Alton W. Whitehouse, Jr. (chairman and CEO of the Standard Oil Company [Ohio]), as chair of the new Committee on Environmental Conservation. Chairing the coordinating subcommittee was Donald L. Cawein (director of engineering health and environmental affairs of Sohio). Task groups on air quality, water quality, land use, hazardous wastes, and synthetic fuels were formed. The same groups also coordinated the Arctic oil and gas study's environmental protection task group. At its initial meeting the coordinating subcommittee focused on the secretary of energy and Agenda Committee's charge for an analysis of the "environmental problems that are most serious and the impact of current environmental control regulations on the availability and cost of petroleum products and natural gas, and the appropriateness of a careful examination of the synthetic fuel issue." It also set a schedule for completion of a draft report for the full committee's consideration by October, 1981.[19]

At the initial meeting of the Committee on Environmental Conservation it was decided that the study would use a three-pronged approach. First, it would examine the environmental impacts of changes in technology in the petroleum industry since 1971. Second, it would look at "the impact that we have seen and can project, of government regulations on the oil and gas industries related to the environment" as it affected the future availability of petroleum products. Finally, Chairman Whitehouse wanted to examine the petroleum industry of the future and "try to provide perspective on environmental problems that we think are in the forefront or will be in the forefront of this industry." He had in mind a ten-year frame of reference, looking at the likely problems of the 1980s.[20]

Changes in the NPC since 1971 ensured that the study process for the update would differ from that of the original report. The new report would be conducted under the provisions of the Federal Advisory Committee Act of 1972, which mandated public access to the deliberative process. Notice of meetings would be published in advance in the *Federal Register,* and the public would be invited to attend. All working papers would be available for public inspection and copying, with transcripts available from full committee meetings and minutes provided for task group meetings.

The expansion of council membership in 1974 also affected the update. Ruth Clausen, the government cochair of the Committee on Environmental Conservation and assistant secretary for environment of the DOE, had been a public member of the council when she was national president of the League of Women Voters. The Committee on Environmental Conservation and the representatives on the Arctic oil and gas environmental task group included representatives of environmental organizations such as the National Wildlife Federation.[21] The task group on Arctic oil and gas held extensive hearings in Alaska and encouraged the involvement of local stakeholders. The task group on air quality included representatives of General Motors and the Edison Institute. At the final meeting of the NPC Committee on Environmental Conservation on March 9, 1982, Chairman Whitehouse and industry participants noted the widespread participation of representatives from environmental groups and others and their significant contributions to the final product.[22]

The NPC issued *Environmental Conservation—The Oil and Gas Industries: An Overview* in 1981, followed by the full report the next year. The report began by discussing dramatic changes in the petroleum industry's operating environment during the decade since the council's earlier study. Its discussion reflected the political uncertainty and supply crisis of the late 1970s and early 1980s. The council stated that the dramatic changes in the supply/demand balance in the decade of the 1970s created new interest in energy security and that achieving energy security required balancing environmental concerns against the need to develop domestic energy supplies. The report projected that during the remainder of the twentieth century the United States would increasingly emphasize the development of nonoil and nongas sources, such as coal, nuclear, and synthetic fuels. It cited substantial progress in environmental conservation in the 1970s, concluding that concerns perceived as arising from the industry in the 1970s "are now vastly diminished because pollution sources are under effective control." Finally, the council called for a reexamination of many environmental regulations in place in 1980, since they had been written in response to conditions in the 1960s and 1970s and "may place unnecessary constraints on domestic energy development."[23]

The updated report reflected the political milieu of the early years of Ronald Reagan's presidency, when regulatory reform was in vogue. The council identified six significant environmental issues that needed to be "resolved promptly as the nation seeks in the 1980s to balance the goals of energy supply and security with the goals of environmental quality." These issues were listed as follows: (1) access to federal lands for resource development; (2) delay and uncertainty caused by the complexity of regulatory requirements, including permitting procedures, the number of government authorities involved, and the opportunities for legal intervention by third parties; (3) siting of energy facilities, determined by natural resource location; (4) incorporation of scientifically acceptable techniques in setting air and water standards; (5) siting and operation of facilities for hazardous wastes; and (6) the ecological and public health effects of, and control strategies for, the synfuels industry.[24]

The report also discussed several issues "whose causes are not clearly defined and which are affected by many factors and industries, of which the petroleum industry is only one factor"; these included acid rain, CO_2 "greenhouse" effects, groundwater contamination, and indoor pollution.[25] These issues had not been examined directly in the more general 1971 report, which was written before many of the specific concerns cited in the 1981 report had arisen. Such problems, in particular acid rain and the greenhouse effect, were not yet understood well enough to allow for the design of effective long-term control strategies.

The NPC advised the DOE that most of the environmental impacts of the petroleum industry's routine practices were known and that during the previous decade the industry had made significant progress in controlling them. According to the report, the industry's operations accounted for only small or fractional percentages of the nation's emissions of carbon monoxide (CO), total suspended particulates (TSP), sulfur dioxide (SO_2), nitrogen oxide (NO_x), and volatile organic compounds (VOC). The industry's refining sector had made significant reductions in air emissions per barrel in all of these except VOC. Refining operations had achieved a 91 percent reduction in discharge of conventional water pollutants between 1967 and 1979. The report noted that new technologies had reduced the environmental impacts of the industry's operations. For example, the industry had made significant improvements in the treatment and disposal of its wastes.

The report examined the impact of several major oil spills in the 1970s. After conceding that such spills near shore could have dramatic short-term impacts, it concluded that "accidental releases of oil and hazardous substances from conventional and routine petroleum industry operations usually did not constitute an irreversible or serious long term environmental hazard." It acknowledged that gasoline leaks from service station underground tanks and piping occurred throughout the industry and had the potential for serious harm to people, property, and the environment. As a general matter, the report stated that groundwater contamination could create serious local problems and that further "definition of the extent and degree of the risk is required."[26]

One of the most controversial issues addressed in the report was the potential environmental impact of the synthetic fuels industry. In those days of high oil prices plans were under way for the creation of a vast new industry to create liquid fuel from coal and tar sands. Government subsidies passed in 1979 had encouraged many oil companies to enter this challenging new endeavor, and environmental groups strongly protested the potential impact of synfuels development on air and water quality. The report argued that a large synfuels industry would not pose a major threat to the environment. It noted the need for further evaluation as the industry entered the developmental stage but said that many aspects of the developing synfuels industry were common to conventional mining and refining technologies and did not present insurmountable problems.[27]

Environmental Conservation went on to discuss the "environmental legislative, regulatory, and administrative actions that adversely affect the cost or availability of petroleum products, natural gas or synfuels." This discussion was organized around the general categories of land use, air quality, water quality, and hazardous waste. Also examined were delays in petroleum development due to failures to provide for adequate offshore government land leasing, as well as cumbersome and arbitrary procedures involved in leasing onshore property. The council cited Coastal Zone Management consistency reviews, designation of marine sanctuaries, and operation of the Endangered Species Act as preventing or delaying resource development.[28]

The report's discussion of air quality issues included a detailed critique of the impact of the Clean Air Act (CAA) amendments of 1970 on petroleum industry operations. The CAA provided a mechanism for evaluation of U.S. compliance with existing air quality standards. Its designation of "attainment and nonattainment areas" for certain pollutants had a major impact on further industrial development, especially in those areas that had not attained mandated levels of air quality. The CAA also included provisions for exceptions or "offsets." The council's report suggested that the system of attainment and nonattainment classification areas, and an insufficient supply of offsets in some nonattainment areas, inhibited economic growth. It voiced fears that such regulation could ultimately ban construction of new refining and transportation facilities or modification of existing facilities. The NPC criticized the lack of EPA guidance in determination of "Best Available Control Technology" and "Lowest Achievable Emission Rate" under the CAA. It also noted that divisions of authority among federal, state, local, and industry officials over the level of controls caused delays in processing and permitting. The report criticized monitoring and data gathering regulatory requirements as excessive, costly, and time-consuming. In addition it found that modeling requirements for air quality were expensive and time-consuming and that the results were only predictions that were usually too conservative. Such results often resulted in delays and restrictions on new and modified sources that, in the opinion of the NPC, "may be unnecessary to protect air quality or achieve environmental benefits."[29]

The council also criticized restrictions on the use and composition of petroleum products. The report noted that automotive exhaust emissions restrictions, "particularly those that prevent the use of alkyd lead compounds in automotive fuels, reduce the amount of transportation fuel that can be obtained from a given quantity of crude oil." The NPC cautioned that natural sources of photochemical oxidant precursors, hydrocarbons, and NO_x contributed to ozone formation and complicated an effective control strategy. It urged the inclusion of cost-effectiveness in evaluating the moving target of improved automobile emissions controls.[30]

The NPC continued its comprehensive critique of environmental regulations by citing unreasonable delays in the issuing of offshore exploratory drilling
permits. It charged that the EPA placed unrealistic limits on wastewater discharges, and it faulted the agency's tardiness in issuing petroleum effluent
guidelines. The council criticized hazardous waste policy on the general
grounds that the existing scheme of regulation "has not been based on the
degree of hazard presented to human health and the environment by the
specific waste being stored." The NPC found that technical and societal problems concerning siting hazardous waste management facilities could hamper
the nation's long-term ability to dispose of such wastes.[31]

In pulling together its conclusions about costs, *Environmental Conservation* referred to an API study that estimated that environmental protection
for about 70 percent of petroleum industry refining capacity had cost about
$21 billion from 1971 through 1980. It cited another survey that projected
capital expenditures by the conventional petroleum industry for environmental
protection at $57 billion (constant $1979) for the 1970–90 period and annual
operating costs of about $6 billion (again in constant $1979) per year by the
latter half of the 1980s. Although groups outside the industry disputed such
industry calculations of environmental costs, these high numbers made the
point that pollution control was far from free. While recognizing that expenditures to protect the environment were necessary costs of doing business, the
report stressed the need for realistic, cost-effective policies based on valid studies
subject to peer review.

The council concluded by repeating its earlier call for a better balance
between environmental protection, energy development, and security. It noted
that in addition to easily quantifiable costs, "costs of delay" created by the
permitting process needed to be calculated. Steps to improve the permitting
process were needed to facilitate domestic oil and gas resource development.[32]

Taken as a whole, the updated version of *Environmental Conservation* was
much more combative than the original. By 1981 the industry had real costs
of environmental regulations to analyze, not the projected costs that had dominated discussion in 1971. Written in the heady days of high prices and the
election of a president perceived to be a friend of the industry, the updated
report offered a prolonged and stinging critique of command-and-control
regulations. Optimistic that regulatory reforms were on the horizon, the NPC
in its report aggressively identified the costs of current regulations while pointing the way for change.

THE NPC AND THE OIL POLLUTION ACT OF 1990

The next major environmental study of the National Petroleum Council went forward in the early 1990s, a much less optimistic era for those seeking reforms of command-and-control regulations. The sense from the 1980s that regulatory change was in the air vanished quickly in the wake of the *Exxon Valdez* oil spill. Congress had debated stricter controls on oil spills since the 1970s, and the much-publicized 240,000-barrel spill in Prince William Sound, Alaska, in March, 1989, brought these debates to a head. As had been the case after the Santa Barbara oil spill in 1969, public outcry over the *Exxon Valdez* disaster persuaded Congress to pass a new round of command-and-control regulations, complete with expensive new pollution control requirements, a short timetable for compliance, and heavy penalties for noncompliance.[33]

As passed in August, 1990, the Oil Pollution Act (OPA) placed strict new demands on tankers. To try to minimize the possibility of future oil spills, the act phased out the use of large tankers with single hulls in American waters by 2010. To try to minimize the impact of spills that did occur, it imposed new financial liabilities on shippers of petroleum. It prescribed a new prevention, response, liability, and compensation scheme for oil pollution from vessels, offshore facilities, pipelines, and certain onshore facilities, based on the principle that the polluter pays. The OPA established a strict, comprehensive liability system backed by "financial responsibility requirements to ensure that those responsible for an oil spill would have accessible financial resources to enable them to pay for cleanup and damages." Under the provisions of this law, parties responsible for offshore facilities had to show evidence of financial responsibility up to $150 million, more than four times the $35 million required under prior legislation.[34]

OPA 1990 was not the first law regulating oil spills, but it marked a clear departure in cost and coverage. Earlier regulations had placed limits on the liability for damage done by oil spills, but the new law greatly increased those limits and widened the legal definition of what constituted an offshore facility subject to the law.[35] To prevent the federal or state government from being a de facto guarantor of last resort for offshore cleanup and damages, the OPA required that operators of offshore facilities maintain evidence of financial responsibility of $150 million through insurance, surety bond, guarantee, letter of credit, qualification for self-insurance, or other evidence of financial responsibility. The legislation, however, also stated, "Any claim for which liability is established . . . may be asserted directly against any guarantor providing evidence of financial responsibility for a responsible party liable." This provision blurred the distinction between commercial insurance, which insurers had been traditionally willing to extend for offshore facilities, and guarantees of financial responsibility. Furthermore, OPA did not preempt the possibility of more extensive state requirements.[36]

The enhanced financial requirements of OPA would also be applied to the Interior Department's Minerals Management Service (MMS) expanded definition of "offshore" facilities. MMS concluded that the financial responsibility provisions of OPA applied to "facilities in, on, or under navigable waters of the U.S. and any facilities subject to the jurisdiction of the U.S. in, on, or under other waters." The increased financial requirements of OPA would be applied to a broad definition of offshore facilities that included many supporting onshore operations.[37]

During the comment period on the MMS's proposed interpretation of the new regulations, Secretary of Energy Hazel O'Leary requested that the NPC "consider the impacts the financial responsibility proposal may have on domestic energy exploration, development and production, as well as recommendations on ways the goals of the legislation could be met while minimizing adverse economic impacts, if any, on the domestic petroleum industry." She wanted the council to report to her by December 1, 1993, which was less than eight weeks away. On October 20, 1993, the council considered and accepted the study request. It established a committee on the Oil Pollution Act and appointed as chair H. Leighton Steward (president of Louisiana Land & Exploration Company) and as cochair Jack S. Siegel (acting assistant secretary, Fossil Energy, DOE). A subcommittee was also established, chaired by Robert D. Armstrong (Louisiana Land & Exploration) and cochaired by Donald A. Junkett of DOE.[38]

The MMS set a revised deadline of December 24, 1993, for comments on its proposal, and the council's OPA committee wanted to meet Secretary O'Leary's timetable and submit its recommendations by the first week of December. The OPA study would not make use of extensive quantitative analysis as had been the case in the NPC's recently completed refining and natural gas studies. Rather, it required the council to mount a more qualitative analysis of the proposed implementation of OPA within a short period of time.

Meeting in New Orleans on November 3, 1993, the OPA committee made important decisions about the scope of the study, which would be done in two phases. An interim report completed before the secretary's December deadline would show the dramatic effects of MMS proposals on the oil industry and the country as a whole, not just on producing states. A later report would provide more details and analysis. The proposal by MMS was only an advanced notice of proposed rule making; more specific rules had yet to be proposed. Without this two-pronged approach the possibility existed that after the NPC published its analysis to meet Secretary O'Leary's deadline MMS could consider public comments and substantially alter the thrust of its implementation of OPA when it later proposed specific rules. If such a scenario occurred, the NPC's advice and recommendations would be directed at mooted MMS interpretations and contribute little to a refocused debate.[39]

The OPA committee ratified subcommittee decisions about the scope of an interim report, including introduction and background, risk assessment, impact on the parties, state and federal revenues, and a section on solutions. A substantial effort would be made to involve federal agencies other than the DOE, state governments, environmental groups, and financial institutions in the NPC process. In a wide-ranging discussion committee members expressed the view that Secretary O'Leary's letter did not call for the council to confine its analysis solely to the impact of OPA and the MMS proposals on exploration, development, and production. The committee undertook a broad discussion of the difficulties created by the OPA and the MMS proceeding.[40]

The NPC's work continued at the subcommittee's November meetings in Washington, D.C., as the MMS conducted hearings on its pending rules. William Cook of the MMS reported to the OPA subcommittee about these hearings, discussing the degree of flexibility that the MMS believed it had in interpreting OPA's requirements. Several participants noted that the MMS interpretation would include virtually all terminals and refineries under OPA's provisions. Rough drafts of various sections of the interim report were discussed at the meeting. One draft developed hypothetical insurance requirements, both high and low cost, for offshore producers of various sizes under OPA. Others examined the impact of OPA on the oil service sector and operators and the secondary impacts that could arise from declines in activity on the outer continental shelf.[41]

In December, 1993, the council issued *The Oil Pollution Act of 1990—An Interim Report.* After discussing the legal background and the history of regulation, it compared the record of spills from offshore facilities (nine spills, 69,957 barrels in eighteen years) and spills from tankers (ninety-two spills, 1,883,708 barrels in eighteen years). These numbers suggested that the risk of a catastrophic spill from offshore facilities, as opposed to tankers, was minimal. The interim report noted that the MSS's expansive definition of "offshore facility" would affect 98 percent of the crude oil and 95 percent of natural gas produced from onshore and state-water wells. The council concluded that few of the approximately twenty-five hundred independents who produced 60 percent of Louisiana's production could qualify as self-insured or afford $150 million in Certificate of Financial Responsibility (COFR) insurance, even if that coverage were commercially available. With offshore production accounting for 17 percent of U.S. crude oil and 28 percent of U.S. natural gas production, the OPA might ultimately increase American dependence on imported oil.[42]

The council believed that the insurance industry would continue to provide coverage for offshore pollution but that it would not allow such policies to be used as guarantees of financial responsibility. Insurers were particularly concerned about OPA provisions that made guarantors directly responsible for damages and costs and prevented them from asserting certain legal defenses. Also troubling was the OPA's deliberate lack of preemption of state laws that could result in liability in excess of its $150 million provisions. The interim report voiced the petroleum and insurance industries' concerns about some of the new liability provisions in the OPA, especially the Natural Resource Damage Assessment (NRDA), which was intended to recover environmental damages on behalf of the public.

The NPC found that such liabilities might prove unpredictable and "potentially insurmountable." These were not damages associated with the cleanup or restoration of the environment to its "pre-spill" state, but were "a desire to compensate the public in economic terms for their concern about the environmental consequences of a spill." The NPC expressed concerns about certain valuation techniques for claims for "the diminution in value of natural resources pending restoration." It noted that economists had defined these damages as the "actual lost use values" or losses to those members of the public who actually used the resources, such as hikers and sport fishers. The council characterized lost resource value, or "nonuse value," as "the public's benefit deriving from the knowledge of the mere existence of a natural resource, separate from any actual uses such as recreational activities or resource extraction that the resource might invite and support." The report expressed fear that calculation of such benefits' value using hypothetical constructs might greatly inflate potential liability under the OPA.[43]

The council offered succinct solutions to these problems. The MMS should narrow the scope of its regulations to conform to commercial realities, follow the statutory language and intent, and specifically differentiate between onshore and offshore facilities. The NPC wanted final regulations that would recognize the distinction between insurers and guarantors, who make a distinct promise of payment or a legal guarantee. The interim report argued for more flexible mechanisms for financial responsibility, including calibration of levels of responsibility to the degree of risk posed by facilities and operations; a de minimus rule; state financial responsibility programs to be accepted as part of federal obligations under OPA; and allowance of arrangements whereby a number of parties could aggregate revenue (for self-insurance) or insurance coverage. The NPC asked Secretary O'Leary to work with the MMS to promulgate regulations that met OPA and energy policy goals without imposing unreasonable costs; to work with the president and the National Economic Council to create a risk-based approach to financial responsibility under OPA; and to continue "to participate in the natural resource damage assessment rulemakings to avoid unpredictable and potentially bankrupting liability on oil and gas operators."[44]

The council's OPA committee met in December, 1993, to discuss issuance of the interim report and set the stage for phase two of the study. Tom Fry, director of the MMS, addressed the meeting on the status of the rule-making process and the criticisms voiced by those drafting the NPC report. He defended his agency's approach while assuring committee members that it had used the mechanism of an advance notice "to seek advice and counsel from anyone involved." Fry noted increased congressional interest in the proceeding and stated that the MMS would "wait to see what action Congress wants to take in this matter." He also reported that the agency had begun examining what type of legislation the administration might propose to mitigate some impacts projected in the NPC's interim report.[45]

The committee was heartened by the frank remarks of Director Fry and his statement that rules would not be finalized until 1995. Some members of the committee cited the OPA as an unfortunate example of what was likely to occur when Congress hurriedly legislated in response to public agitation over a specific incident, rather than analyzing issues in a more thorough and detached manner.[46]

Despite these concerns, the committee went ahead with plans for phase two of the study. Robert Armstrong, chair of the subcommittee, thought that the report should include reactions to comments on the interim report, including those from Director Fry and Secretary O'Leary. The phase two report, he felt, should stay within the general context of the MMS proceeding, but legislation introduced in the intervening period should be analyzed in the section on solutions. He added that the committee need not wait for an MMS notice of proposed rules but should inform O'Leary that the NPC would submit supplemental views if proposed rules were subsequently published.[47]

The NPC subcommittee on OPA met in March, 1994, to determine the direction and writing assignments for the phase two report. It discussed two legislative initiatives that proposed to grant the Department of the Interior discretion in implementing the financial responsibility provisions of the OPA; recognize insurers as indemnifiers, not guarantors; and structure a regulation regarding de minimus activities. The MMS now informed the subcommittee that it was unlikely any proposed rule-making would be issued in 1994. Subcommittee Chair Armstrong asked Director Fry's advice on what the NPC should be doing in phase two of its study, and Fry replied that the NPC should provide further financial analysis and additional legal reasoning to support its positions.[48]

The final report reflected the impact of developments since issuance of the interim report and the NPC's dialogue with the MMS. In July, 1994, the NPC released *The Oil Pollution Act of 1990—Issues and Solutions,* which contained extensive discussion of OPA requirements and of MMS's interpretation of them. The report's chapter on solutions reiterated the interim report's analysis and recommendations that the MMS clarify that OPA's financial responsibility requirements only applied to (1) facilities in the territorial seas and the outer continental shelf, and (2) lessees, permittees, or holders of right of easement under existing laws. The council argued that the language of the OPA and relevant case law allowed the MMS enough flexibility to craft a liability/financial responsibility regime with requirements less than the $150 million specified by the MMS. Furthermore, it suggested a de minimus rule that would exempt from financial responsibility requirements those facilities with worst-case discharge volumes of 250 barrels or less; allow petitions for exemption for those with worst-case discharge volumes between 250 and 1,000 barrels; exempt dry natural gas from the requirements; exempt facilities handling condensate of 1,000 barrels or less; and limit to $35 million financial responsibility for worst-case discharges of more than 1,000 barrels of condensate from natural gas pipelines.[49]

The report reiterated that the MMS should specify that an insurer is not a guarantor. It also recommended that the MSS structure its self-insurance criteria to allow inclusion of pollution liability insurance, third-party reserve evaluations in net worth calculations, and membership in newly formed mutual funding mechanisms. Finally, the council said that the MMS should allow offshore facilities meeting a state's financial responsibility requirements to credit that amount toward the federal requirements and encourage states to administer OPA proof of financial responsibility requirements.[50]

The NPC report helped focus congressional attention on difficulties presented by the OPA. The MMS did not have the authority to make major changes in the law, but in October, 1996, Congress did so with the passage of the Coast Guard Reauthorization Act of 1996, which included several revisions recommended in the 1993 and 1994 NPC reports. The new law limited liability requirements to $35 million but gave the MMS authority to increase them to $150 million if circumstances warranted. A de minimus provision of one thousand barrels of oil was included in the statute, and jurisdiction was specified from the coastline outward, including bays and estuaries connected to the open sea. Finally, the legislation clarified the distinction between insurers and guarantors by allowing suits against the guarantor only when the injured party was the federal government or the party who spilled the oil was bankrupt. All of these changes gave evidence that the NPC's study had made a significant impact on lawmakers and regulators alike.

The passage of the Oil Pollution Act of 1990 followed a pattern all too familiar to industry. A widely reported environmental catastrophe fed intense political demands to take action and punish villains, and a strong new command-and-control regulation passed with too little concern for long-term costs or alternative methods of achieving the admirable goals of minimizing the occurrence and impact of future oil spills. But the NPC's role in helping shape the new law's implementation in the years immediately after its passage illustrated that some change had taken place in the politics of environmental regulations. The NPC's analysis of the new regulation's potential impact was one loud voice in an industry chorus calling for a reexamination of the law with an eye toward creating a more effective set of regulations somewhat more informed by the costs of implementation.

THE REFINING INDUSTRY AND THE 1990 CLEAN AIR ACT AMENDMENTS

Along with strict new regulations on tankers, the 1990s also brought demanding new regulations on the operations of refineries. By the 1990s American petroleum refining had been especially hard hit by economic changes and environmental legislation. Since its inception the NPC had undertaken periodic studies of crude oil supplies and product specifications for domestic refineries. The council also examined the more general economic, environmental, governmental, technological, and international factors affecting the ability of the domestic refining industry to respond to demands for petroleum products.[51] Through these reports the NPC had provided government with an extensive data base on refining. Given this background, the council was the obvious choice to examine the state of this vital sector of the industry in the early 1990s.

One key issue was the impact on refining of the 1990 CAA amendments, which imposed stringent new controls on refineries as stationary sources and required demanding changes in the products they produced.[52] In an effort to attain previously defined standards for carbon monoxide and ozone, the 1990 CAA amendments mandated major changes in the composition of motor fuels over a relatively short period. Beginning in winter, 1992–93, motor fuels in all CO nonattainment areas were required to have a minimum oxygen content of 2.7 percent for a minimum of four winter months. Beginning October 1, 1993, standards for sulfur in diesel fuel had to be met; sales of leaded gasoline were prohibited after 1995. The legislation also required reformulated gasoline (RFG) for nine of the most severe ozone nonattainment areas (all large metropolitan areas) by the beginning of 1995. State governors in other nonattainment areas could "opt-in" to the program, and EPA could delay the effective date of such opt-ins if domestic RFG production were inadequate. Fuel composition requirements (minimum oxygen, maximum benzene, no heavy metals, and no increase in NO_x) were specified, beginning in 1995, and minimum performance standards for "pool average" RFG were set for 1995, with a more stringent standard for 2000. Standards for volatile organic compounds (VOC) were in effect only for the high ozone season, but the standards for toxic air pollutants (TAP) were in effect for the entire year. Within one year of enactment of the CAA amendments (November 15, 1991), the EPA was to promulgate regulations for RFG to be used in gasoline-fueled vehicles. The statute mandated the greatest reduction in VOC and TAP emissions achievable considering the costs, any health and environmental impacts related to air and nonair quality, and energy requirements.[53]

These amendments had far-reaching implications for domestic refiners. The cost of compliance for refineries as stationary sources would be substantial, posing difficulties for a sector with profits in decline. RFG requirements would decrease the flexibility of the refining industry when it operated at or near capacity and faced further increases in product demand. Enforcement of the legislation also would shape the nation's petroleum logistic system. The existing product specification system administered by the EPA allowed effective utilization of the petroleum refining and logistical system. Possible EPA-mandated requirements for absolute batch segregation under the CAA's regional and seasonal requirements, along with promotion and increased use of alternative fuels, could require basic changes in the shipment and storage of refined products.[54]

During the 1990 legislative debates on the Clean Air Act amendments, the petroleum industry and government policy makers expressed fears about the short-term and long-term ability of the refining sector to meet projected requirements. Such concerns dovetailed with traditional uneasiness about imports (and the possibility that future imports would require additional processing to comply with CAA amendments). In a June 25, 1990, letter to NPC chairman Lodwrick Cook, Secretary of Energy James D. Watkins requested that the National Petroleum Council assess "the effects of these changing conditions on the U.S. refining industry, the ability of that industry to respond to these changes in a timely manner, regulatory and other factors that impede the construction of new capacity, and the potential economic impacts of this response to American consumers."[55]

At a meeting of the NPC's Agenda Committee in July, 1990, representatives of the DOE, headed by Linda Stuntz (deputy undersecretary for policy, planning, and analysis), discussed the problems presented to the petroleum industry, especially the refining sector, by proposed CAA amendments under consideration by Congress. They also noted that recent oil spill liability legislation (Oil Pollution Act of 1990) could have dramatic impacts on the operation of domestic refiners.

Stuntz expressed concern that since people in the United States seemed incapable of considering construction of "greenfield" refinery capacity, they were placing many demands on the refining sector. She admitted, "I don't get a lot of sense that anybody has great confidence that we know exactly anymore what is the refinery capacity. . . . We're running at what appears to be peak capacity utilization to most people. I don't know whether that is true or not."[56] She voiced fears that the inadequacies of the domestic refining industry might result in American dependence on imported petroleum products, rather than crude oil. Most of those present believed that the Clean Air Act amendments then pending in Congress would reduce the flexibility of domestic refiners and that a potential increase in imports was a legitimate concern.[57]

The NPC's last refining study had been completed in 1986 using 1984 data. Several committee members expressed regret that such a study had not been undertaken two years earlier, when it might have influenced congressional debates on CAA amendments. They believed that the public did not understand the strains created in the petroleum industry by environmental requirements. They noted, however, that the EPA would have flexibility in implementing the final legislation and that an NPC report might have a major impact on that administrative process. Stuntz agreed that any action by the council probably would not influence legislative debates but might affect the EPA's implementation of new legislation. There had been no credible study on the costs of environmental regulation on facilities and fuels and its impact on product supply, and the NPC could fill this void. Ray Hunt, vice chairman of the council, suggested that a fast-track NPC study completed in six to nine months could have immediate impact on the EPA's implementation of the new amendments. The study could be followed by a more comprehensive analysis of the refining industry and the long-term effects of CAA amendments. The NPC Agenda Committee accepted the study request.[58]

In September, 1990, leaders in the refining industry met with the NPC to discuss the upcoming study. This discussion launched the council's effort to analyze the impact of the Clean Air Amendments on refining. The subsequent study marked a departure for the NPC, which had never before conducted such a detailed and timely analysis of the potential impact a specific piece of environmental legislation could have on a particular segment of the industry.

The first step in the study was to survey changes in the refining industry since the 1986 report. This step was followed by assessments of the industry's capability to produce the quantity and quality of products required in the 1990s and the first decade of the next century; the investment requirements for meeting new environmental legislation and regulation of refinery products and refineries themselves; the impacts of the 1990 CAA amendments; and the capability of the U.S. engineering and construction industry to provide facilities required by the refining industry to meet these challenges. The report included extensive quantitative analyses of the potential impacts of these requirements on refining over the next two decades.[59]

To supply timely information to those charged with implementing the CAA amendments, the refinery discussion group decided to conduct the study in two phases. Phase one would focus on the implementation of the CAA's formula for gasoline by using a questionnaire to assess the availability of gasoline to meet the new CAA requirements for CO and ozone nonattainment areas. This would provide Secretary Watkins with information about oxygenate supply and the volume of CAA-conforming and conventional gasoline in the immediate future. Phase one would be completed in approximately six months, with a target delivery date of spring, 1991. The more extensive analytical effort of phase two would begin concurrently with phase one. The complex econometric modeling and surveying required by phase two ultimately required twenty-five months to complete.[60]

The NPC Committee on Refining, under the chairmanship of Kenneth T. Derr (chairman and CEO of Chevron) and government cochair Linda Stuntz, met on November 12, 1990. It approved the bifurcated approach, with a four-to-six-month study on the impact of short-term mandates of CAA amendments and a two-year examination of the full range of environmental initiatives facing refiners, in the context of a comprehensive industry study.[61]

A coordinating subcommittee supervised phase one of the study. Since time constraints prevented the use of a questionnaire for phase one assessments, interviews with five to six people from each firm represented on the NPC Committee on Refining were used instead. McKinsey & Company conducted these interviews, releasing only aggregate or unidentifiable results. The scenario was that the year was 1996 and that the refining and gasoline supply industry had met CAA goals. Committee members hoped that this would facilitate a positive approach and avoid participant digressions on factors that could prevent CAA goals from being met. More than one hundred in-depth interviews with representatives from oil, engineering, and construction companies took place early in 1991.[62]

At its first meeting the coordinating subcommittee began to define the parameters of the broader phase two study. Volunteers were requested for four task groups. Chairman John H. Matkin said that decisions would soon have to be made concerning which years to use for displaying data. He emphasized the importance of early creation of a group to integrate various aspects of the analysis. It would be necessary to determine what laws and regulations would be in place, conduct a phase two survey, and determine how many different possible scenarios should be developed. A decision on whether or not to use a consulting firm to conduct the survey would have to be made quickly.[63]

As the interview process in phase one neared completion, government and industry representatives involved in the study discussed how the information being gathered could influence the EPA's implementation of CAA amendments. Since release of the phase one report was scheduled for June, some study participants expressed concern that the report would be unavailable during the EPA's ongoing negotiated rule-making process. The openness of the NPC study process was a distinct advantage here; information from all NPC meetings was available to everyone, including those in all branches of government and industry involved in the ongoing regulation negotiation process at the EPA.[64]

Phase two activity accelerated. At a February, 1991, meeting of the coordinating subcommittee, each task group assessed its progress and needs. Use of consulting and accounting firms for data collection and coalition, econometric computer modeling, and analyses of specific subject areas (i.e., trends in environmental regulation) had become an increasingly necessary part of NPC studies. The use of accounting firms protected the confidentiality of surveys and avoided disclosure of identifiable, proprietary information from participating firms.

Refinery facilities and the study's task groups needed such surveys. The task group on product quality needed process modeling to address the implications of proposed product specifications under CAA amendments. The task group on supply, demand, and logistics required the use of economic modeling to integrate data using a logistical model. Its chair, W. R. Finger, a veteran of many NPC studies, believed that the refining industry, if unimpaired by regulatory constraints, could and should focus on several levels of future demands. In addition, a subgroup of this task group needed to analyze developing world supply, demand, facility information, and trends in foreign environmental regulation.[65]

Extensive use of contractors in conducting these studies reflected general staff cutbacks, especially in the areas of industry analysis and corporate planning, within the oil and gas industries in the 1980s. Such cuts affected operations of industry advisory groups such as the NPC in several ways. The council's budget represented only a small fraction of the total costs of a study, since industry participants were volunteers paid by their employers while participating in NPC business. The council's staff and operations also reflected industry changes; fewer employees having specialized expertise resulted in greater reliance on outside contractors. These changes forced the NPC to rely more heavily on council staff and industry participants to interpret information generated by contractors assigned to specialized tasks. Thus, expenditures for consultants were becoming an increasingly large part of the cost of the NPC studies.[66]

By April, 1991, the coordinating subcommittee had finished collecting interview data for the phase one report. McKinsey & Company believed that the study's "looking back" approach generated a good qualitative analysis of the refining industry's ability to respond to CAA amendments' short-term mandates. A more quantitative analysis of the legislation's post-1995 economic impact would be a major objective of phase two.[67]

The NPC released its report from phase one, *Petroleum Refining in the 1990s—Meeting the Challenges of the Clean Air Act,* in June, 1991. It presented the aggregate opinions of the twenty firms represented on the NPC Committee on Refining about the refining industry's ability to meet the requirements of CAA amendments and EPA regulations. The study assumed that total gasoline demand in the United States and in nonattainment areas would remain constant, that there would be no opt-ins or opt-outs in the program, that no additional regulation or legislation would occur through 1995, and that the permitting process operated in a normal fashion. Under such assumptions, the surveys indicated that the EPA would have to take several key steps to enable industry to comply with the CAA. These steps included early clarification of the waiver process for 1992 oxygenates, delayed opt-ins for 1995 oxygenates, simplified certification requirements for 1995 RFG, simple systems of compliance monitoring, early and careful assessments of environmental benefit/cost ratios for fuel and other air quality improvements in the post-1995 period, and best efforts to expedite the permitting process. Many respondents expressed concern about the post-1995 environment. They feared that compliance with the CAA would require additional investment, technical risks, and poor cost-effectiveness and that uncertainties created by the act "contributed to unfavorable industry conditions, thus magnifying the compliance challenge and leaving little margin of error in their decision making."[68]

Many refiners had serious concerns about the 1992 oxygenate requirements in the CAA's fuels section. The facilities to produce oxygenates (such as methyl tertiary butyl ether [MTBE] and ethanol) were believed to be insufficient to meet government mandates. In addition the location of production facilities on the Gulf Coast and in midwestern corn-belt regions was far from several key markets. Phase one predicted a 15 to 50 percent shortfall in supply. The NPC report called for the EPA to exercise its waiver power under the CAA to balance oxygenate supply and demand for winter, 1992–93. In contrast, the surveyed refiners were cautiously optimistic about industry prospects for meeting the 1995 oxygenate requirements.[69] The industry interviewees thought that their success in meeting the 1995 RFG requirements depended on the EPA's management of opt-ins and the actions of state and local governments. Also essential in meeting the CAA's timetable would be simple RFG certification and compliance programs based on a straightforward emissions model with fuel compliance determined at point of manufacture, point of blend, or import location.[70]

Phase one of the refining study embodied a significant departure in the NPC's study of environmental regulations' impact. Previous studies had taken retrospective views to analyze costs; this study came at a time when information generated could still be used to explore the implications of regulatory choices in enforcing a new law. The CAA had been passed without the benefit of a thorough study of its impact on industry. But its implementation would be carried out with detailed information about the potential impact of different approaches on the petroleum industry.

As phase one ended, work on phase two moved forward. The spring, 1991, meetings of the coordinating subcommittee were used to provide updates on the EPA's regulation negotiation process. By July the various task groups began to interview consultants to assist in their work while making decisions about the study's parameters.[71] The subcommittee and the task group on supply, demand, and logistics determined that future years to be examined would be 1995, 2000, and 2010. The task group on refinery facilities identified a slate of potential regulations and their impacts for further analysis. They made plans to develop a survey in conjunction with other task groups. After reviewing a list of questions developed by DOE's Policy, Planning and Analysis Office and the Energy Information Administration, the coordinating subcommittee held a session at Keystone, Colorado, in June, 1991, to identify key issues.[72]

The coordinating subcommittee met almost monthly to provide consistency among the task groups. It assigned and prioritized issues for them and examined some "cross cutting" issues such as alternative fuels on an ad hoc basis. The subcommittee eventually developed a report outline, and it later coordinated the preparation of the report. A "summit" dinner was held in San Francisco on September 17, 1991, to assess the progress of the study. Results included a decision to take an extra month for analysis of the refinery survey questionnaire to ensure that only information not available elsewhere would be collected and that only data necessary to the study would be requested. By now study participants recognized that the six-month push to produce phase one had put the second phase two to three months behind schedule.[73]

By April, 1992, the survey had been completed, preparing the way for the study's critical analytical stage to begin. Once survey data had been accumulated, models had been run, and results had been analyzed, the actual writing of the report could begin. Participants anticipated presenting the report to the council's membership in early 1993.[74] Wanting to keep options open for as long as possible to get industry consensus on various proposals, the EPA was reluctant to choose a model. The NPC made a decision to use the preliminary EPA model and then to make comparison runs with other models when they became available. Ultimately the EPA's revised and final complex emissions model for its phase two RFG was similar to its earlier version and the NPC's assumptions for the purposes of the refinery study.[75]

Drafting of the report began in October, 1992. Some of the preliminary observations diverged sharply from widely held industry assumptions and elements of the NPC's 1986 refining study. The task group on supply, demand, and logistics concluded that the domestic refining industry would look much the same in the future as it did in 1992. Imports would not be a major threat because of cost increases foreign refiners faced to meet growth in local demand and local environmental regulations. In contrast to the fears raised by phase one of the study, preliminary analysis of phase two data suggested that 1995 oxygenate supplies would be adequate.[76] The task group on refinery facilities reviewed initial estimates of future environmental regulation costs, and it appeared that the cost of facility regulations (stationary source) would probably exceed the costs necessary to comply with product quality regulation.[77]

MEETING REQUIREMENTS FOR
CLEANER FUELS AND REFINERIES

After approval by the council as a whole, the NPC released *U.S. Petroleum Refining—Meeting Requirements for Cleaner Fuels and Refineries* on August 30, 1993. The report addressed the complex and interrelated problems of a mature sector of the petroleum industry and the major impacts of the most comprehensive air quality legislation on refinery operations and products in more than a decade. A broad range of issues had been vetted in an open, public process involving a wide spectrum of industry, government, and stakeholders. In his transmittal letter to DOE secretary Hazel O'Leary, NPC chairman Ray Hunt characterized the report as "a stark yet comprehensive portrayal of the U.S. petroleum refining industry over the next twenty years." Hunt noted that during the 1980s the refining sector earned a modest profit of 2.5¢ per gallon and realized a return on investment of 8.8 percent. Also during this period 120 refineries shut down. He added that in 1991 and 1992 the decline in refinery profits had accelerated. The cost of environmental compliance in supplying consumers with light petroleum products was projected to increase by 6¢ and 10¢ per gallon in 1995 and 2000 respectively. Investments in the 1990s to meet the environmental requirements for refineries and refined products were projected to be $37 billion, a figure greater than the 1993 book value ($31 billion) of all domestic refineries. Historical cash flows would be insufficient to recover such costs. Hunt observed that many refiners expected that their facilities would be underutilized. He also noted that formidable barriers existed to closing refineries, because of environmental cleanup costs.[78]

Chairman Hunt discussed the implications of the report's three demand cases on imports and refinery utilization. He noted that in the increased demand case, the domestic refining industry would be fully utilized and increased imports would be needed to satisfy demand. But in the declining demand case, imports would decline and domestic refiners would face underutilization. The latter case could be magnified by CAA enforcement regulations that might disrupt the gasoline distribution system. Hunt noted that foreign refiners had lower embedded environmental costs than U.S. refiners did, but that over time foreign refiners would experience costs equal to domestic refiners. Hunt raised a note of caution, however, stating that if the United States pursued a more vigorous environmental agenda or foreign requirements were less stringent or later than assumed by the report, the ability of domestic refiners to compete and recover increased CAA environmental costs would be compromised.[79]

Hunt advised Secretary O'Leary to take the lead in implementing three broad recommendations supported by the report's quantitative and qualitative data. His recommendations included: (1) that the CAA be implemented through "cost-effective reformulated gasoline regulations that are fully compatible with the existing distribution system"; (2) that a constructive partnership process involving interested stakeholders could create cost-effective solutions to societal concerns related to the industry; and (3) that policy makers recognize that the cost of regulation is reflected in the marketplace, where it affects the long-term viability of the industry.[80]

Several years of intensive study had produced a comprehensive analysis of the impact a specific law, the Clean Air Act Amendments of 1990, would have on a particular segment of the industry—refining. The NPC, through its members, had looked at the inner workings of the refining industry to examine the impact of different strategies for implementing the CAA's new regulations. The NPC report moved far beyond the general call for cost-effective, flexible regulations by suggesting how this goal might be achieved. In this sense the report made an important contribution to policy makers with the responsibility to implement a new set of regulations that had far-reaching impacts on a vital sector of the American economy.

Those impacts ultimately proved difficult for the refining industry to absorb. Throughout the 1990s U.S. refiners struggled to manage the demanding transition to cleaner gasoline in an era of low margins and ongoing consolidation. In December, 1997, Federico Peña, the secretary of energy, met with the NPC coordinating subcommittee to discuss growing concern about the American refining industry's long-term health. Preliminary talks led to a formal request from Peña to council chairman Joe B. Foster in June, 1998, to update the NPC's landmark 1993 refining study.[81]

A year later a new secretary of energy, Bill Richardson, approved the establishment of a new NPC study committee on refining chaired by Lee Raymond (chairman and CEO of Exxon Corporation). The request letter noted that "petroleum product deliverability and the viability of U.S. refineries are critical to United States energy security and the personal mobility by its citizens." The ultimate goal of the new study would be to "assist the Department of Energy and the Environmental Protection Agency to better understand the potential implications of future environmental and other public policy initiatives."[82]

To justify updating the massive 1993 report only six years after its publication, Secretary Richardson pointed to ongoing changes in refining. Since 1993 "new forces have raised concerns about the future of domestic refining," he reported, and refinery output had become "less flexible than in the past." Added regulatory requirements, reduced product inventories, and greater demand threatened to increase the volatility of markets for petroleum products vital to the smooth functioning of the American economy. Such conditions raised a new fear: Was the United States entering an era when adequate domestic refining capacity could no longer be taken for granted?[83]

The new study began with several planning assumptions. First, the primary issues to be analyzed were near-term, with the work focused on the coming decade. With much data available from the NPC's 1993 refining report and other sources, the new study could be completed by June, 2000. The committee decided to focus on four pending changes in environmental rules that posed immediate difficulties for refiners. These included: (1) reducing the sulfur content of gasoline to thirty parts per million (ppm); (2) making similar reductions in the sulfur content of on-highway diesel fuel; (3) eliminating the oxygenate MTBE from gasoline; and (4) reducing the "drivability index" (a measure of gasoline's volatility) of gasoline. As the study went forward, a variety of initiatives in all of these areas by the EPA lent a sense of urgency to NPC efforts.[84]

The common thread linking these issues was the nation's efforts to produce and use cleaner fuels, which had become a crucial element in the clean air policies of the 1990s. Throughout the decade refining had shouldered a heavy load in the nation's quest for cleaner air through cleaner fuels, with large capital investments in new equipment. The NPC, through this study—which came to be subtitled "Assuring the Adequacy and Affordability of Cleaner Fuels"—sought to put concrete numbers on the potential costs that the proposed new wave of changes in cleaner fuels would entail. In so doing, the NPC sought to educate regulators about the consequences of their choices while making the point that anything worth doing was worth doing efficiently.

Sharp reductions in the sulfur content of both gasoline and diesel fuel would require expensive modifications of existing refineries. The NPC's advanced accounting of the range of these costs was higher than the EPA's preliminary estimates. The council estimated that reducing the sulfur content in gasoline to thirty parts per million by the years 2004 to 2006 as proposed by the EPA might cost as much as $8 billion. For diesel fuels to reach the same standard by the 2007 and 2008 automobile model years might add another $4 billion to the refiners' price tag for cleaner air. The council's report suggested that industry probably could complete the required refining process changes in the time frame proposed by the EPA. But it noted the importance of good regulatory choices in implementing change. Most obviously, regulators should avoid asking refiners to meet the new standards for gasoline and diesel fuel simultaneously. Such "overlap" would mean that "engineering and construction resources will likely be inadequate during peak periods, resulting in implementation delays, higher costs, and failure to meet regulatory timetables."[85]

The same sort of regulatory care was needed in guiding reductions of MTBE in gasoline during the same general time period. As an additive that seemed capable of meeting new air standards while maintaining acceptable octane levels, MTBE had emerged in the early 1990s as the oxygenate of choice for much of the oil industry in meeting the demands of CAA amendments for cleaner burning gasoline. After a period of rapid expansion of MTBE production and the modification of refineries to make use of the additive, however, debates had arisen about the potential impact on groundwater of the manufacture, distribution, and use of MTBE. By the late 1990s MTBE had become a sort of poster child for the discussion of unintended consequences in regulation. Amid much controversy environmental regulators began to debate the merits of removing the additive from gasoline. As the debate went forward, the NPC took a sobering look at the potential impact of this choice on refiners.

Sharp MTBE reductions in gasoline would be less expensive, but no less difficult, than reductions in sulfur content. Indeed, *U.S. Petroleum Refining: Assuring the Adequacy and Affordability of Cleaner Fuels,* published in June, 2000, argued that the final cost of removing MTBE would be "highly dependent upon the specific requirements" selected by regulators. Would oxygenate requirements in general be altered as MTBE was removed? Would the other primary oxygenate of the 1990s, ethanol, need to be expanded dramatically? Would refineries be required to remove MTBE at the same time they removed sulfur? Each regulatory choice came with its own set of costs. Lacking the power to dictate what it considered the best choices to the EPA, the NPC focused instead on educating regulators about the potential costs of the various choices under consideration.

In analyzing such costs the council returned to a theme it had developed consistently for more than twenty-five years. Effective, sustainable regulation required a careful definition of goals and an efficient strategy for achieving them. Yes, large investments in refining and distribution would be required to meet the proposed changes in cleaner burning fuels, and the industry would be "significantly challenged." But the council remained cautiously optimistic that industry could meet the challenge, at least if government regulators efficiently managed the process of change. "With timely permits, proper sequencing of fuel quality changes with minimum overlap, and sufficient lead times to respond to each major specification change," the report stated, "the NPC believes that the domestic refining industry can be expected to satisfy product demand under the more stringent product specification requirements studied."[86]

CONCLUSIONS

In 2000, as in 1970, the National Petroleum Council stressed the need for efficient government regulation that minimized costs and confusion within the petroleum industry while pursuing the benefits of pollution control policies. But the council's emphasis and tone had shifted noticeably over the years. Gone was the confrontational stance of the early years of the environmental movement, when an industry under siege had challenged the authority and at times even the legitimacy of environmental regulators. The NPC and its industry had moved from despair over the initial command-and-control statutes in the 1970s, to optimism over the prospects for regulatory reform in the 1980s, to a focus on cooperation in the interest of regulatory efficiency in the 1990s. As the nation entered the twenty-first century, the industry embraced the broad goals of cleaner air and water, and it sought to gain a more influential voice on the critical questions raised by implementation: What were the best ways to protect and improve air and water quality? How could this be done at the least cost, so that environmental improvements could be affordable and thus sustainable? And, finally, the old question remained: What was the best available balance between energy and environmental policies?

Such questions did not, of course, have definitive answers. For years the industry had protested the high costs of meeting air and water standards, only to roll up its sleeves and meet the new standards while continuing to supply the nation with ample energy. Its own record of past success at times undermined its arguments over the need to factor in costs as well as benefits in framing environmental policy. But the industry understood the harsh realities of the new competitive environment in refining, as well as other phases of the industry. And it sought to convince others that it was past time to fashion more efficient approaches. As the reports of the 1990s illustrated, careful implementation of environmental policies could reduce the costs of pollution controls without necessarily reducing their effectiveness.

Environmental issues remained politically loaded, and the voice of industry presented through the NPC was still heard with skepticism by many environmental groups and government officials. But over the nearly three decades since the initial wave of command-and-control regulations, the society and its political leaders had become somewhat more willing to consider the costs of pollution control. The NPC was one among numerous organizations that presented an increasingly sophisticated vision of what might be called "economic environmentalism," which includes the pursuit of a cost-effective, sustainable approach to environmental quality that recognizes the need for energy and economic growth. Certainly the political battle for such an approach was far from won. But by presenting to government in a nonconfrontational format basic data on the economic and technological impacts of environmental regulation on the energy industries, the council served a productive role in the ongoing societal debates over pollution controls.

The National Petroleum Council's reports on these controversial issues proved the council's value to government officials as an organization that could gather from the petroleum industry timely information needed to frame effective public policies on energy-related issues. From its earliest reports the NPC has recognized that it would have legitimacy only if it presented trustworthy information drawn from an array of experts on energy. As a voice drawn largely from industry, the NPC consistently reminded government officials to respect market forces. The council argued for public policies that achieved broad societal goals while remaining aware of the impacts of these policies on the workings of the engine of growth.

The recommendations in NPC reports often were lost in the intense political lobbying on environmental issues; they were often unheeded by environmental agencies in a federal government paralyzed by the division of authority on energy and environmental issues. But despite such problems in having its voice heard and heeded, the National Petroleum Council consistently produced thorough reports on environmental issues of great import to the energy industry and to the larger society.

CHAPTER 6

Charting the Ascent
of Natural Gas

NATURAL GAS BECAME AN IMPORTANT topic
for the National Petroleum Council only after the deregulation of the industry beginning in 1978. During the previous era of price regulation in natural gas, the council focused its efforts on oil. As Congress debated the passage of some form of gas deregulation in the 1970s, the council began to find a stronger voice on conditions in the industry. After the passage of the landmark Natural Gas Policy Act of 1978 (NGPA), the NPC produced a detailed report on the prospects for unconventional gas that reflected the prevailing pessimism about the fate of more conventional supplies. Then as the industry gradually became more market-oriented in the 1980s and 1990s, the NPC undertook several important studies of the movement toward freer competition. Its landmark study on conditions in the industry in the early 1990s gave the council a ringside seat from which to observe the "market revolution" then surging through natural gas and other related sectors of the world energy economy. After the pace of change in the industry accelerated in the 1990s, in 1999 the NPC conducted a follow-up study on conditions in the industry and published another major report on natural gas supply and demand. These two reports helped government officials and people in all segments of the natural gas business see more clearly how this vital industry was being transformed by competitive forces.

THE NPC AND NATURAL GAS: THE EARLY YEARS

The council had not originally taken much interest in natural gas. Just seven of the original eighty-five appointments to the NPC were from natural gas companies, with only one from a local gas distribution company. Such figures did not change dramatically in the first thirty years of the NPC's existence, during which a highly regulated gas industry developed along lines far different from the market-oriented oil industry. In these years the Federal Power Commission (FPC), an independent regulatory agency not housed in the Department of the Interior, defined natural gas policies in case-by-case decisions on rates charged by producers and on the location and financing of pipelines. In fulfilling its duties, the FPC did not make use of the services of the National Petroleum Council. Some of the council's early reports on oil nonetheless dealt with gas as a secondary issue. In such reports the NPC generally noted the problems of regulation but did not call for deregulation. For the first twenty-five years of the NPC's existence, natural gas simply was not central to its mission within the DOI.

This situation reflected the fact that the Department of the Interior held little direct responsibility for the industry. Various state and federal agencies regulated the different sectors, and separate segments of the natural gas industry had their own trade associations. Gas transmission companies addressed common concerns through the Interstate Natural Gas Association of America (INGAA); the local distribution companies found some common voice in the American Gas Association (AGA); and producers, including most of the major oil companies as well as independents, had no shared voice until the creation of the Natural Gas Supply Association. Unlike the oil industry, the natural gas industry remained segmented by regulation, with no vertically integrated companies active in all major sectors. There was no established forum for the industry as a whole to address public policy issues, including the regulation of wellhead prices.

The regulatory system ensured that the natural gas industry differed fundamentally from the market-oriented oil industry. In the decades after World War II the Federal Power Commission managed many phases of the industry's expansion. After the controversial *Phillips Petroleum Company* v. *Wisconsin* decision by the Supreme Court in 1954 directed the FPC to regulate gas prices at the wellhead, the process of setting gas rates administratively became a central concern of gas producers and transporters. In this era before deregulation the FPC had power to approve the price of natural gas and the route and financing of new pipelines. In this sense the FPC became the major "customer" of the giant gas transmission companies, which devoted considerable managerial and legal resources to the quest for favorable rulings by the commission. Laws passed in the 1930s blocked these interstate pipeline companies from owning local distribution companies, which had long been regulated as public utilities, with rates and services subject to control by state and local commissions. The regulatory system at both the federal and state levels had strong political incentives to keep consumers happy by keeping the price of natural gas low, and demand for this excellent fuel spiraled upward in America's postwar boom, which witnessed the rapid construction of a massive new gas pipeline grid.

In these years of price regulation by the FPC, the National Petroleum Council generally studied natural gas only as a by-product of oil-related studies. In its 1949 report, *A National Oil Policy for the United States,* the NPC noted the increased use of natural gas and cited with alarm arguments for interpretations of the Natural Gas Act to include "control over the production and gathering of gas and the price charged by producers and gatherers." The report expressed NPC opposition to federal control "directly or indirectly [of] the production, gathering, and processing of gas or its price prior to its delivery into the main line of an interstate carrier, or to control the local distribution of gas." It contained arguments that controls over the end uses of natural gas ultimately would require similar mandates over the end uses of other forms of energy and that unspecified "pressure groups" might use federal regulation to retard the growth of the gas industry. These conclusions, which reflected the general sentiment of the oil and gas industries, proved no match for political and legal arguments. In 1954 in the *Phillips* case, the U.S. Supreme Court imposed price regulations by the FPC.[1]

More than a decade later, the NPC included a section on the regulation of wellhead prices of interstate natural gas in *Petroleum Policies for the United States* (1966). The report attacked the FPC's efforts to enforce the *Phillips* decision. Arguing that "no regulatory definition of standards can take the place of clearly defined legislative standards," it called for legislation to remove "Federal regulatory confusion and uncertainty as to what prices producers can count on receiving from sales of gas to interstate pipelines." While warning that federal policies were hurting the natural gas industry, the report stopped short of a direct call for deregulation.[2]

This report reflected a dilemma facing natural gas companies in the 1960s. While opposing FPC-directed price regulation in principle, those in the industry had to find practical ways to survive and, if possible, prosper under the existing system. As long as the FPC retained the power to regulate prices, sellers and shippers of natural gas had no choice but to fight for reasonable rates before the FPC while lobbying for deregulation. Regulated prices held low in the interest of consumers encouraged mounting shortages by feeding a growing demand for natural gas while failing to provide adequate incentives for new exploration. As gas increasingly flowed into unregulated intrastate markets that allowed higher returns for producers, shortages in interstate markets grew, forcing curtailments to interstate natural gas customers.[3]

Against this backdrop, in January, 1970, the secretary of the interior asked the NPC to undertake what became the comprehensive report *U.S. Energy Outlook.* Both the oil and natural gas industries had reached critical cross-roads. The existing oil import quota program was no longer sustainable, since domestic oil supply could not keep pace with soaring demand. At the same time federal price regulation and surging demand for natural gas had created a political economy of shortage. But when the NPC's Agenda Committee discussed the secretary's request, it made little note of the pressing issues raised by gas shortages, focusing instead on oil-related issues.[4]

The composition of the committees, subcommittees, and task groups that produced *U.S. Energy Outlook* reflected oil's dominance of council member-ship and concerns. Most of the members of the Committee on U.S. Energy Outlook were from large integrated producers of oil and gas. Only one, Howard Boyd (chairman of El Paso Natural Gas Company), came from a major natu-ral gas transmission company. The important coordinating subcommittee was similarly constituted, with one representative and a special assistant from El Paso. The task group on oil supply's gas subcommittee was also staffed by representatives from El Paso. The task group on gas demand was chaired by a senior vice president of one of the largest gas distribution companies, Colum-bia Gas Systems Service Corp., and included representatives of all segments of the natural gas industry.[5]

U.S. Energy Outlook established four supply cases for natural gas with varia-tions of drilling and finding rates and assumptions about when production of reserves from Alaska's North Slope would be marketed. Production in 1960 of 13 trillion cubic feet (TCF) had increased to 22.3 TCF in 1970. The report projected a range of U.S. conventional natural gas production in 1985 of between 14.9 and 30.6 TCF, depending on differences in future trends in technology, discovery rates, and public policies. According to the report, to sustain production at 14.9 TCF in 1985, natural gas prices would have to more than double, increasing from 17.1¢ per thousand cubic feet (MCF) in 1970 to 38.7¢/MCF in 1985. Higher production rates required higher prices. The re-port also projected a dramatic increase in demand for natural gas through

1985. Under two intermediate NPC scenarios, domestic demand for natural gas increased from 22 TCF in 1970 to more than 41 TCF in 1985, if not constrained by supply. Domestic production, however, was projected to be between only 20.4 and 26.5 TCF in 1985.[6]

Based on an intermediate demand scenario and the four supply cases, the NPC concluded that imports of Canadian gas and expensive liquefied natural gas (LNG) would be needed to satisfy demand. It projected that such imports would grow to between 5.9 and 6.6 TCF in 1985, or 15 to 29 percent of total U.S. gas supplies. Imports might rise even higher if they were not constrained by Canadian policies and the capacity to build more LNG facilities, such as tankers. These expensive imports could be "rolled in" with cheaper domestic, regulated interstate gas to reduce the effects of price increases on end users.[7]

U.S. Energy Outlook did not treat natural gas as a critical part of the nation's energy future. Although the council noted with approval the FPC's efforts to increase the regulated price of natural gas, it attacked the illogic of federal natural gas policy. According to the report, gas was priced below the energy equivalent of alternative fuels, and government regulation of wellhead prices had dampened incentives to explore and produce natural gas. While recommending "permitting market forces to work" and ending "counter-productive regulation of natural gas prices and de facto, arbitrary allocation of supplies," the NPC did not include an outright call for deregulation through legislative action.[8]

In the years after the publication of *U.S. Energy Outlook,* curtailments of natural gas grew from 2.4 TCF in 1974 to 3.7 TCF in 1977. After several years of regular curtailments, many large industrial users converted to more reliable fuels such as coal and residual fuel oil.[9] On March 17, 1975, Jack W. Carlson, assistant secretary of the interior, requested that the NPC examine these curtailments, which were beginning to have a major impact on employment and industrial output in regions heavily dependent on natural gas. In conjunction with the administration's Emergency Advisory Committee on Natural Gas, Carlson wanted the NPC to conduct a study including "an assessment of the extent of the shortage, its likely impact on employment and industrial output, both for the Nation as a whole and for particular regions and industries," and including recommendations to reduce impacts in the short term and resolve the problem in the long term.[10]

Some members of the NPC's Agenda Committee objected to the proposed study, voicing concerns about potential legal problems if the study discussed the allocation of future natural gas supplies to customers. NPC vice chairman Collis Chandler expressed the general sentiments of the council when he stated that the long-range solution to the natural gas shortage was deregulation. After much hand-wringing the committee decided that the study request was not "proper or advisable," and Carlson withdrew it.[11] Thus at a critical time in the debate over the gas industry's future, the NPC had backed away from study of the tricky political and legal issues raised by debates over deregulation. The regulated gas industry was not the "natural" domain of an organization that focused on advising the secretary of the interior on oil-related issues.

In the mid-1970s the FPC responded to the new realities of shortages by allowing prices to rise and by implementing new approaches to regulation such as multitiered pricing.[12] Such regulatory reforms could not, however, deflect the mounting political debate over more fundamental change of the existing regulatory system. In the mid-1970s few voices defended the FPC's efforts to "fix" its approach to price regulation. Instead, a growing chorus loudly lobbied for legislation to alter the existing regulatory system. Strong, well-organized interests from across the political spectrum—ranging from a variety of competing interests within the oil and gas industries to consumer groups—struggled to shape a new approach for natural gas. In such a charged political environment the National Petroleum Council could not and did not play a leading role in defining public policy options. The issue was in the hands of Congress and its many constituencies, not the DOI or the NPC.

Congress finally acted in 1978 with the passage of the Natural Gas Policy Act (NGPA), which embodied elaborate compromises among competing interest groups, including the various sectors of the natural gas industry and their stakeholders. The new law established multiple categories and subcategories of natural gas and based ceiling prices on a projection of future crude oil energy (BTU) equivalent prices. It also regulated intrastate gas for the first time. In practice, the NGPA's choice of "phased deregulation" satisfied few. It introduced a protracted period of uncertainty and confusion as the natural gas industry moved haltingly toward greater reliance on market forces.[13]

Congress also responded to the shortages and curtailments of the 1970s by enacting the Powerplant and Industrial Fuel Use Act in 1978. Acting on the assumption that natural gas was a scarce "premium" fuel, this law blocked its use as the primary fuel in newly constructed utility power generation and limited its use in existing utility facilities to levels prevailing in 1974–76. Before Congress substantially repealed this law in 1990, it blocked the expanded use of natural gas for electric power generation.[14]

The National Petroleum Council played little role in debates leading up to 1978 passage of the two landmark laws that shaped the evolution of the gas industry for the next two decades. But as the FPC navigated the strange new waters of deregulation, it needed guidance from those more familiar with competitive markets. Along with individual companies, organizations such as the NPC were well positioned to monitor the transition away from regulation. In the decades after 1978 the Federal Energy Regulatory Commission (FERC), which in 1977 inherited most of the traditional gas-related functions of the FPC, gradually introduced more competition into the gas industry. During this difficult transition era the NPC produced several important studies describing conditions in the emerging marketplace for gas.

THE NPC AND UNCONVENTIONAL GAS

The Natural Gas Policy Act of 1978 set a new course for the natural gas industry that demanded more information on the sensitivity of gas supply to changes in price. Under the new law the price of previously discovered gas was not immediately deregulated, but much higher prices were allowed for categories of newly discovered gas supplies, including several "unconventional" sources not previously developed under low, regulated prices. As all energy prices surged upward in the late 1970s, unconventional gas became important to policy makers urgently seeking additional sources of domestic energy.

In 1978 Secretary of Energy James R. Schlesinger asked the NPC to study the recovery of natural gas from unconventional sources such as tight gas sands, deep geopressured zones, Devonian shale, and coal seams. The DOE wanted the council to assess the unconventional natural gas resource base and state-of-the-art recovery technology for unconventional gas sources. Schlesinger directed the council to include an analysis of the "outlook for costs and recovery of unconventional gas and . . . how government policy can improve the outlook."[15] To undertake the study the NPC established a twenty-six-person committee chaired by John Bookout (president and CEO of Shell Oil Company). Included were representatives of major oil companies active in natural gas technology, large gas transmission companies, independent oil and gas companies, and consumer and environmental groups, as well as six researchers from universities and science and technology companies.

The committee faced the difficult assignment of building data bases in relatively new areas. Although the higher energy prices of the 1970s in theory presented excellent prospects for the development of unconventional gas resources, the realities were by no means certain. Earlier evaluations of tight gas, the most promising of the new sources, indicated potential resources between 423 and 793 TCF. (Tight gas was characterized as natural gas in formations that had effective permeability of less than one millidarcy.) Gas from such formations had previously been noncommercial, and the council's study committee faced the dual task of estimating both the amount of tight gas potentially available and the price ranges that would call forth the production of this new supply. To analyze the uncertainties involved with tight gas development, the NPC used scenarios with eight price levels from $1.50 to $12.00 per million BTU (MMBTU), three discounted marginal real rates of return, and two different projections of rates of technological advance.[16]

In an extensive set of studies published in 1980, the council advised the secretary of energy that natural gas from coal seams, Devonian shale, and, especially, tight gas reservoirs could make significant contributions to future U.S. natural gas supplies—at least under certain "optimistic" assumptions made by the study participants.[17] After a thorough appraisal of 12 basins and extrapolation of conditions in 101 other basins, the NPC concluded that 924 TCF of tight gas was in place, 608 TCF of which was ultimately recoverable. The report concluded that the extent of recoverable gas depended about equally on the price of natural gas and the pace of technological development.[18]

Unconventional Gas Sources comprised five volumes with more than twelve hundred pages of text and appendixes. The council carefully qualified its projections of increased utilization of unconventional gas, stating that such results depended greatly on economic conditions such as price levels, incentives, and the rate of technological development. With energy prices soaring in 1980, projections that unconventional gas might soon contribute much-needed domestic energy at competitive prices seemed reasonable.

Energy prices plummeted in the mid-1980s, however, slowing the development of the new technology for tight gas recovery projected in 1980. But in its major natural gas report in 1992 the NPC found that "this has been more than offset by new stimulation fluids, better fracture techniques, cavity completion techniques, and significant advances in ability to detect, interpret, and selectively develop potentially productive intervals" that were not present in 1980. Such rapid advances in recovery technology partially offset the impact of lower natural gas prices.[19]

A comparison of the projections and assumptions in the 1980 and 1992 studies serves as a reminder that the council had no crystal ball for predicting future costs or technology. This was particularly true in areas such as unconventional gas, where there was relatively little data about historical costs or long-term trends in technology. In this situation the council could only make its best projection, using the most sophisticated methodology available and drawing on the opinions of leading experts in the industry. What had become evident to the NPC by 1992, however, was an important general conclusion: Technological innovations could expand production at price levels considered depressed little more than a decade earlier. Technology might be hard to analyze in a dynamic marketplace, but it was impossible to ignore.

FACTORS AFFECTING U.S. OIL AND GAS OUTLOOK

The deregulation of conventional sources of natural gas went forward in a confusing time of boom and bust that made projections of supply and demand difficult. In search of a broad context for understanding the ongoing transition in the natural gas industry, in September, 1985, Secretary of Energy John Herrington asked the NPC to undertake a study of "the factors affecting the Nation's supply and demand for oil and gas." He asked for a retrospective analysis of "the factors that generated the energy crises of the 1970s, the appropriateness of the government's response, the potential for a recurrence, and how future crises could be avoided or mitigated."[20] The study of history might yield a greater understanding of change over time in an industry clearly marked for more sweeping changes in the near future.

One clear change over time was the development of new tools for evaluating energy policies. The NPC's *U.S. Energy Outlook* had broken new ground in the early 1970s with its comprehensive analysis of energy supply and demand. But in considering the new request, the NPC's Agenda Committee recognized that such forecasts of energy supply and demand by government and private sources were now commonplace. Rather than working from "the ground up," as had been the case with *U.S. Energy Outlook,* the NPC planned to use existing studies as starting points for its analysis.[21]

The council began with two energy price trends provided by the DOE's Energy Information Administration. The upper price trend started at eighteen dollars per barrel of oil in 1986 and incorporated real price growth of 5 percent per year, reaching thirty-six dollars per barrel in 2000. The lower price trend began at twelve dollars in 1986, had 4 percent real price growth, and reached twenty-one dollars per barrel in 2000. To project future supply and demand, a survey incorporating these two assumptions was sent to fifty-two representatives from industry, utility, government, consulting firms, and the financial community. The NPC received twenty-eight usable responses. It also undertook another survey of the near-term outlook for oil and gas drilling, using more than one thousand responses to a survey sent to members of the Independent Petroleum Association of America and the Society of Independent Professional Earth Scientists.[22]

By the time the NPC Committee on Oil and Gas Outlook had its first meeting in April, 1986, the price of crude oil had declined to twelve dollars per barrel from a high of thirty-two dollars a barrel just six months before. The committee feared that this unprecedented decline might lead to dismantling of much of the domestic petroleum industry's exploration and development sector. Faced with this prospect, the committee chose to produce an interim report discussing the effects of this price decline on the industry and the economic and strategic security of the United States.[23]

Issued in October, 1986, the interim report focused on oil-related matters but also included discussion of trends in natural gas. Dramatic increases in net imports of oil from politically volatile regions were projected. In the report the NPC noted that price instability in the oil and gas industries was particularly damaging because of the long lead times necessary for capital investments and returns. The NPC survey of the natural gas industry painted a bleak future for domestic supply. Even at the higher price trend these surveys projected that domestic consumption would stabilize at approximately 17 TCF through 2000 but that domestic production would decline from 16.4 TCF in 1985 to 14.5 TCF in 2000. Under the lower price trend domestic consumption would fall to 15 TCF in 2000, with production declining to 12.4 TCF. Under the higher price trend only small amounts of imported oil would displace unsatisfied gas demand by 2000, but in the lower price case unsatisfied gas demand of 1 TCF would be filled by imported oil. The interim report projected that the "gas bubble"—the name given to the existing surplus supply of gas—would end by the late 1980s with lower price trend assumptions and in the early 1990s under the higher price trend assumptions. According to the report, once the bubble "burst," anticipation was that natural gas prices would need "to rise slightly above the low sulfur residual fuel oil price to reduce potential demand, through fuel switching."[24]

When the NPC issued its final report and "policy options" in *Factors Affecting U.S. Oil & Gas Outlook* in February, 1987, crude oil prices had inched upward from their low levels of the previous year. This report acknowledged that although "all constituencies may not agree about what specific policy options for avoiding or mitigating vulnerability to future energy crises may be best, it is clear that there are basic guidelines that should apply to government policies. The industry believes that past lessons strongly suggest the need for stability and predictability in government actions." It outlined policies directed at reducing the United States' growing dependence on imported crude oil and products and at reducing the possibility of an energy crisis.[25]

Of the five broad policy options the NPC recommended to stimulate domestic oil and gas supplies, only one targeted natural gas. Easier access to federal lands on more favorable lease terms was endorsed. In the report the NPC examined the option of removing tax disincentives and using incentives to stimulate oil and gas production. Recommendations included using import fees to stabilize the price of domestic oil "at a level that will reduce consumption and stimulate domestic oil and gas production; [and] promote research and development to increase recovery of domestic oil and gas." The final recommendation was to "decontrol natural gas prices and markets by repeal of NGPA price controls on old gas, NGPA incremental pricing provisions [not currently in force, but these provided the basis for possible future discrimination between natural gas and boiler fuel], and the Fuel Use Act."[26]

The report discussed options to lessen dependence on imported oil by reducing oil and gas demand, noting that the oil price shocks of the 1970s had significantly lowered demand. These included suppressing demand through increases in consumption or excise taxes, creating incentives and mandates to continue energy conservation, and encouraging greater use of alternative fuels for oil and gas. It suggested four policy options to reduce the likelihood of energy crises and/or mitigate their impact: the diversification of U.S. sources of oil imports; the pursuit of diplomatic policies that promote greater stability in the Middle East and Africa; expansion of the use of the Strategic Petroleum Reserve; and the development of fiscal and monetary policies that could be used to mitigate the macroeconomic impacts of oil price shocks or supply disruptions.[27]

The council also looked at the impact of price decontrol, focusing on proven reserves. Citing DOE projections that decontrol would increase proven reserves by 30 to 34 TCF, the council argued that this would increase production by approximately 1.5 TCF annually, displacing 750,000 barrels a day of crude oil imports. It acknowledged that in areas of the country heavily reliant on "old" gas, decontrol would harm consumers in the short term. Noting projections of future electric generation demand, the NPC argued that combined-cycle power plants fired primarily by natural gas "would be attractive options for a portion of this capacity."[28]

The memory of shortages in the 1970s shaped the NPC's analysis of natural gas in the 1987 report. The council downplayed the large potential reserves of natural gas discussed in *U.S. Energy Outlook* (approximately 1,050 TCF) and the smaller, more recent estimates of the United States Geological Survey

(USGS) of approximately 750 TCF, including Alaska. The new report discounted these numbers by as much as 30 percent. According to the council, "the United States has very few low cost [oil and] gas reserves yet to be discovered and developed," and remaining resources were medium to high cost. Furthermore, the council expressed concern that "the impact of new technology tends . . . to be felt rather slowly." Given these factors, natural gas would remain a premium, high-cost fuel once the "bubble" had vanished.[29]

The council's reluctance to break with established paradigms was seen in its focus on proven reserves and its analysis of the ability of natural gas to displace other fuels. After concluding that natural gas was "an extensive domestic resource, efficient, cost effective, and environmentally desirable," concern was expressed in the report that the removal of restrictions on the use of natural gas to generate electricity would cause gas to displace domestic coal. Implicit was the council's assumption that natural gas and domestic oil should be reserved for higher priority uses, such as displacing imported oil. The psychology of shortage continued to hamper market-oriented thinking about natural gas.[30]

But despite such assumptions bred by regulation, phased decontrol was gradually creating a freer, more diverse, and complex market for natural gas. After declining since 1972, natural gas demand had bottomed out in 1985 and then slowly increased. It was becoming apparent that natural gas would continue to play an important role in energy supply, and with more stringent environmental requirements on the horizon, that role could be expected to expand in the future.

Late in the Reagan administration and during the transition to the Bush administration (1988–89), serious consideration was given to the idea of a separate agency and assistant secretary at DOE for natural gas matters, as well as a separate "natural gas council" to replicate the functions of the NPC. But the desire to avoid duplicate advisory committee functions encouraged the expansion of natural gas representation within the NPC, rather than the creation of new organizations. In an era of "downsizing" in the petroleum industry, many found it difficult to rationalize separate advisory committee memberships for oil and gas.[31] Likewise, in an era of "cutting bureaucracy," many in government remained skeptical of the creation of a new government agency for natural gas. The council's involvement in natural gas matters had been increasing since publication of *Unconventional Gas Sources* in 1980, and the completion of several monumental NPC studies of natural gas in the 1990s muted the debate over a separate advisory committee for natural gas.

A NEW LOOK AT NATURAL GAS

As the FERC gradually allowed more competition into the industry, market forces began to pull natural gas in directions not earlier predicted. For much of the 1980s many assumed that natural gas was an industry in decline, with a future as a relatively high priced specialty fuel but not as an expanding contributor to the nation's energy supply. Such observers felt that the gas bubble would soon disappear and that higher prices would be needed to call forth adequate replacements for gas being consumed, much less to expand supplies. But a different reality slowly emerged as new technology and creative management transformed the natural gas industry, making it more competitive and thus more unpredictable.

Expansion of the NPC in 1990 reflected the growing importance of natural gas. In May of that year Secretary of Energy James D. Watkins increased the size of the NPC from 125 members to 152 while appointing 40 new members to the council. More than half of the new members were appointed "specifically for their expertise in natural gas matters," according to the DOE. Watkins said that "the expanded Council will be capable of giving the Energy Department and the government, as a whole, greater representation from this key segment of the energy industry." The new appointees came from all sectors of the natural gas industry, including for the first time significant representation from local distribution companies.[32]

These new members provided the personnel needed for a major new report on natural gas. In a letter dated June 25, 1990, Secretary Watkins asked the NPC to undertake two major studies. This request resulted in publication of *The Potential for Natural Gas in the United States* in 1992 and *U.S. Petroleum Refining—Meeting Requirements for Cleaner Fuels and Refineries* in 1993. He asked for a gas study that would be "a comprehensive analysis of the potential for natural gas to make a larger contribution, not only to our national energy supply, but also to the President's environmental goals," and that the NPC consider the "technical, economic and regulatory constraints to expanding production, distribution and the use of natural gas." The NPC was to evaluate gas reserves (including undiscovered and unconventional gas reserves), the nature of future gas markets, exports and imports, and "potential barriers that could impede the deliverability of gas to the most economic, efficient and environmentally sound end-uses."[33] The old world of natural gas was changing, and Watkins sought the NPC's assistance in understanding the new world on the horizon.

Secretary Watkins had been considering a comprehensive natural gas study for at least a year, and members of the council's Agenda Committee asked for an explanation of the timing of the request. His deputies responded that the economic and environmental advantages of gas had been widely discussed in the process of developing the National Energy Strategy (NES) and amendments to the Clean Air Act. They reiterated the administration's unwillingness to mandate the use of one fuel over another but concluded that this approach might not be realistic given the evolving requirements of the CAA and other environmental legislation. The DOE was much concerned with the capacity of the industry to meet growing demand.[34]

The discussion then shifted to the elements necessary for a comprehensive study. NPC executive director Marshall Nichols reminded those present that study task groups usually evaluated public and private studies and made adjustments so that NPC studies did not have to start from scratch. William Finger voiced reservations about such an approach, reminding those present that the NPC's use of EIA price projections in *Factors Affecting U.S. Oil & Gas Outlook* (1987) had not resulted in "a very high comfort level." The wording of the study request allowed the NPC to proceed in a different manner than it had in earlier studies. Because the study presupposed the need to use more natural gas in the future, primarily for environmental reasons, the NPC could focus on identifying constraints to increased use of natural gas and recommending how to remove them.[35]

The NPC's Committee on Natural Gas ultimately set the parameters and timetable for the study.[36] Frank Richardson (president and CEO of Shell Oil Company) became chairman of the NPC's Committee on Natural Gas, with James G. Randolph (DOE assistant secretary for fossil energy) serving as government cochairman. Lawrence L. Smith (vice president for production, Shell Oil Company) was cochair of a coordinating subcommittee along with Michael R. McElwrath of the DOE as the initial government cochairman.[37] Because of the many divisions within the industry and the complexity of the issues, the NPC Committee on Natural Gas was large (forty-two members) and diverse. It included representatives from eight integrated oil companies, eleven independent producers, eleven distribution companies, three transmission companies, and seven in other categories, such as consultants. A similar balance characterized the coordinating subcommittee and the various task groups. About two hundred people ultimately worked on the study, including more than one-third of the NPC's members and numerous special assistants.[38] The National Petroleum Council brought together the people and data needed for the difficult task of peering into the future of an emerging competitive gas industry.

An informal meeting of the proposed coordinating subcommittee of the NPC Committee on Natural Gas in Washington, D.C., on November 27, 1990, included discussion of the scope and organization of the study and setting timetables and preliminary work schedules. The subcommittee decided to take the study out forty years, with the twenty-year period from 1990 to 2010 addressed in detail and the period from 2010 to 2030 discussed in broad outline. While examining traditional residential, commercial, and industrial markets for natural gas, the study would also analyze the prospects for the expanded use of gas in transportation and power generation. The impact of new technology would be addressed as well.[39] A consensus developed against the publication of an interim report, since the thorough research and consensus building needed to produce a useful report could not be done quickly enough to justify the effort.

The NPC had studied the natural gas resource base in two recent studies: *Factors Affecting U.S. Oil & Gas Outlook* (1987) and *Petroleum Storage & Transportation* (1989). The subcommittee began its work by reviewing these and other studies to see if they could be modified for NPC use. The subcommittee noted the need for a methodology to address "gas producibility as a function of time, price, technological advances and government policies," as well as LNG imports and export and import possibilities with Mexico and Canada. The NPC's recent study on transportation and storage could be updated and used to evaluate gas transmission capabilities. But the prospect that a new study would show increases in demand for gas in excess of the 1989 study required a detailed analysis of the probable locations of new facilities.[40]

The coordinating subcommittee had to integrate into the study all issues that affected the future deliverability of natural gas, including demand, local distribution requirements, transportation and storage, and supply. One priority was to identify potential constraints on the expansion of the natural gas system and to evaluate "alternatives and trade-offs in removing barriers or living with constraints." The subcommittee envisioned the study as a set of self-contained scenarios that would develop tools for projecting the future for gas supply and demand under different assumptions.[41]

The subcommittee organized task groups on demand and distribution, source and supply, transmission and storage, and regulatory and policy issues. Committee members anticipated that at least eighteen months would be needed to complete the work, based on the complexity of the issues and experience in conducting similar studies in the past. They took note of the Agenda Committee's discussion of an alternative scenario that set various demand levels and then tested the system to determine if that level could be produced

and transported and at what price. The price then would be used to determine if the demand was justified.[42]

At the initial meeting of the subcommittee in Washington, D.C., on January 21–22, 1991, plans were made to develop natural gas demand growth scenarios with Data Resources, Inc. (DRI), to identify ways natural gas usage
could be increased. The base scenario assumed economic growth in the United
States and the world, the impact of demand management on U.S. energy
growth, interfuel competition, development of a largely unrestricted North
American market, and stringent environmental requirements. The "removal
of all constraints" also was included in the base scenario.[43] At its second meeting in February, 1991, the subcommittee proposed the creation of a "best
guess" case as a starting point for the analysis of supply and demand under
various conditions. This case, which became known as "Strawman," could be
revised after review by all the task groups and then used as a point of reference
for additional sensitivity analyses. This revised reference case would be available for use by June.[44]

In May, 1991, the task groups critiqued the first Strawman case and suggested important changes. The task group on source and supply voiced concern that the base case was at the low end of the supply range, despite its use
of high natural gas prices. It questioned whether an adequate contribution
had been attributed to new technology, an issue that ultimately would have a
major impact on the study's findings. Chairman William A. Smith of the task
group on transmission and storage said that the EIA model did not include
Canadian pipelines or have a good grasp of seasonal variations. He believed
that these issues and Mexican gas would have to be addressed outside the
framework of the model. The demand and distribution task group listed its
concerns about Strawman and announced that it had begun a series of scheduled meetings to discuss regional issues. The regulatory and policy task group
divided its work into five subgroups, including one established to study information about myths and misconceptions that dogged the natural gas industry.[45]

In June, 1991, the study's leaders decided that the Strawman scenario should
be supplemented by a scenario that assumed no real growth in world oil price;
this alternative quickly acquired the name "Scarecrow." This midsummer assessment by the subcommittee generated new initiatives. The subcommittee
approved a recommendation by the task group on regulatory and policy issues to organize a series of focus groups of natural gas consumers to provide
firsthand information on fuel choice decisions and perceptions of the natural
gas market. The task group subsequently refined the focus group concept to

ensure that it assisted in the identification of specific impediments to the increased use of natural gas.[46]

As the task groups moved forward, computer analyses of the Strawman base case and its revision, "Strawman II," yielded results that allowed for the development of "Strawman III," which integrated all aspects of Canadian gas and allowed the North American gas market to be modeled.[47] Strawman III was later modified to increase the annual impact of technological advances on drilling efficiency consistent with historical trends over forty years. The incorporation of a 4 percent annual reduction in drilling costs due to technological change produced projections of flat real drilling costs over the period covered by the study. Such modifications and new assumptions about tight gas resources and recovery led to projections that the market for natural gas would be constrained by demand at 27 TCF in 2010.[48]

The study as a whole reached a critical phase in August, 1991. Task group changes to the EIA model were due on August 13, and modifications to the original Strawman case could then be completed in a week. By the end of August the task groups submitted their lists of identified constraints to expanded natural gas usage and the recommended options for removing these constraints. Arrangements were made to hire a consultant to conduct the focus groups. In addition NPC staff planned a joint meeting of all gas study participants for October 13–16, 1991. This meeting would be used for consensus building, with presentations by all the task groups to give participants a fuller understanding of the study's scope.[49]

More than ninety study participants attended the three-day meeting, which served as a mid-course evaluation of the study. Participants discussed the assumptions of the reference case and the constraints and options identified while refining plans to complete the study. Each task group summarized its activities, including constraints and options identified, remaining issues, and plans for the future. During the second afternoon the task groups met simultaneously to access the comments and criticisms received and catalog agreement or disagreement on issues. On the final day each task group presented the results of the first two days of meetings. The subcommittee then attempted to reconcile differences and develop a plan and schedule for completion of the study.[50] The meeting produced a consensus on the latest refinements to the Strawman and Scarecrow reference cases, preparing the study to move into a new phase that would include reference-case documentation.[51]

Major conclusions that emerged at the meeting subsequently became the core of the study's findings. The meeting identified an emerging new "conventional wisdom" that projected an abundance of natural gas supplies at realistic, competitive prices well into the twenty-first century. The conclusion was reached that future gas markets would be demand-constrained, with the greatest potential new demand in the largely untapped market for power generation. The recognition that serious regulatory problems blocked the expanded use of natural gas was best symbolized by the observation that gas transactions required three times as many person hours to complete as did transactions in coal or oil.[52]

After the mid-course meeting, work continued on refinements to the Strawmen cases. To serve as a check on the "top down" approach of the Strawmen scenarios, the task group on demand and distribution analyzed demand in "a micro, bottom-up look at the natural gas market." Ten separate regional analyses were used to increase the comfort level of those study participants who remained concerned about the high demand numbers, based on the modeling assumptions about future advances in technology and its impact on supply.[53]

Such rigorous, overlapping analyses of conditions in the industry increased confidence in the study's ultimate findings. But the NPC staff realized that more than numbers would be required to boost consumer confidence in the long-term supply situation and in the reliability of the delivery system. Convincing industrial customers of the study's optimistic conclusions about the bright future for gas would be a difficult task.[54]

As a first step in this direction, in November, 1991, subcommittee members met with executives from seven electric utilities from different regions of the country. The discussion focused on the problems and the promise of natural gas as a power-generating fuel. These electric utility executives acknowledged that environmental pressures gave natural gas an advantage, but they felt that their industry would continue to rely primarily on coal, nuclear, hydro, and renewable energy plants, with gas used as a "swing on the peaks."[55] They noted that even if more kilowatt hours were generated from gas, the volume probably would not increase because of the increased efficiency of new plants. Finally, concern about the reliability of the gas transmission network increased with the distance from producing areas. These utilities added their support to the concept of some type of "gas reliability council" patterned after such groups in the nuclear energy industry.[56]

To help the industry understand the point of view of its potential customers, Benetek Energy Research conducted a series of "focus group" discussions that became an important part of the NPC study.[57] This exercise included meetings in December, 1991, with natural gas producers, state regulators, and electric utilities. Dominating the discussions were "hang overs" from the late 1970s shortages, including fears of imminent resource depletion and expectations that prices eventually would rise dramatically with the end of the "gas bubble."[58] Such "noneconomic" motivations of potential consumers could not be ignored if the industry hoped to increase the demand for natural gas.

Activity on all fronts increased as the study moved toward preliminary conclusions in late 1991. In December, 1991, the subcommittee approved revisions to the Scarecrow case, which now showed little growth in total U.S. energy consumption through 2010.[59] The ten regional demand trends and issues teams began their work. The regulatory and policy issues task group focused on an appropriate philosophy for future natural gas regulation. The staff of the NPC believed that an agreement on the principles would be simple. However, they feared that each segment of the industry might not control divisive "instincts and agents" created by industry fragmentation and the legacy of adversarial relationships in a regulated environment. In the view of the staff, such problems represented major uncertainties for the entire study, since further significant regulatory reform could be achieved only through a unified natural gas industry.[60]

Consensus on many issues grew as the study moved toward preliminary conclusions and recommendations. Computer analyses of modeling scenarios produced quantitative results, but the final report would require the interpretation of such numbers. Vigorous discussions among task groups and subgroups would be needed to build consensus on the report's recommendations; traditional factionalism in the industry and the "newness" of some of the findings posed barriers to the creation of a broad consensus. Yet it was becoming clear that the long study process had brought together representatives from all sectors of the industry and forced them to examine trends shaping their industry as a whole and to place their own concerns into the broader context suggested by these trends. The NPC's executive director, Marshall Nichols, recognized the importance of this process, and he wanted to ensure that if the study fell behind schedule, consensus building would not be subordinated to the analytical effort in the final stages.[61]

The various pieces of the report gradually came together. The coordinating subcommittee completed its review of the preliminary recommendations on March 12, 1992, reaching a general agreement subject to modification after completion of the study's analytical effort. By the beginning of April eight of the scheduled focus group interviews had been completed, but the regulatory and policy issues task group wanted to schedule additional focus groups for state consumer offices and environmental groups.[62] The task group on source and supply laid plans to begin testing sensitivity cases. Progress on the ten regional studies undertaken by the demand and distribution task group was uneven, and NPC staff members feared that coverage and completeness of the reports would not be uniform. Some subgroup leaders hired contractors at their own expense to assemble basic data. Ultimately the council accepted the regional reports as written and did not force their reconciliation with the main report of the demand and distribution task group.

The regulatory and policy issues task group had completed eleven of its fourteen scheduled focus group meetings. The contractor planned a summary report and reports on the individual sessions. The task group, however, wanted to prepare a separate report to analyze the contractor's findings and how the natural gas industry could best address misconceptions and respond to valid criticisms. Its "vision" statement began to take shape around a concept of a dramatically reduced role for government regulation, reliance on private contracts to define efficiency, and revision of standards for that regulatory touchstone, "the public interest." The task group on transmission and storage reviewed reports about pipeline and storage capacity of each region and how to integrate transportation model results into the EIA model. The coordinating subcommittee began a two-faceted review of all the task groups' recommendations. Initially the subcommittee crafted a "vision" of an ideal regulatory and economic environment using an inductive approach. Then it compared recommendations developed from the analytical work of the task groups with this hypothetical regulatory and economic environment.[63]

Conflicts surfaced as findings took shape. The transmission and storage task group (composed primarily of representatives of pipeline companies) planned to recommend open access on local distribution company (LDC) systems, a view supported by the regulatory and policy issues task group's vision of a deregulated market-based natural gas industry. However, representatives of LDCs in this task group and the coordinating subcommittee voiced strong doubts about such policies. Fearing that this issue might shatter the fragile coalition that had formed during the study, the council avoided directly addressing it. The report recommended instead that "regulatory policy should provide LDCs with the appropriate cost allocation, rate design, and pricing flexibility to enable LDCs to compete in the marketplace so that regulators do not have to promote or prohibit bypass of local systems."[64]

A second area of controversy involved projections of the demand for natural gas. In July the EIA reviewed the results for Strawman and Scarecrow, now referred to as case one and case two, respectively. Case one (the high-price case) projected gas consumption at 25 TCF at $3.50/MMBTU (constant $1995) in 2010, and case two (the low-price case) projected 21 TCF at $2.75/MMBTU. The EIA considered these results conservative with regard to electric generating demand, the most promising prospect for increased natural gas usage. Since gas demand was a critical and visible part of the study, such discrepancies had to be resolved.

The potential impact of environmental regulations on gas supply and demand was also open to debate. An environmental team formed from all the task groups compiled and reconciled the environmental aspects of the task group reports. Conflicts developed over whether the report should endorse special treatment of natural gas because it represented the best opportunity to address the apparently conflicting goals of environmental quality and economic efficiency. Upstream producers remained reluctant to endorse any approach that might get more local and environmental groups involved in their decision-making process. In its final recommendations the NPC sought to finesse this delicate issue with general language calling for a careful balance of environmental considerations and efficiency.[65]

A "Technology Cross-Cutting Team" compiled and evaluated the technology discussions and findings of each task group. Disagreements surfaced about increased federal funding for natural gas research, specifically for the Gas Research Institute (GRI). Some major producers believed that increased federal funding of gas research was a waste of taxpayers' money, since the private sector funded a sufficient level of research. Not wanting to take sides in the GRI funding debates, the NPC ultimately supported the primacy of private research but also called for increased funding of federal research.[66]

Task group meetings, report writing, and review of study results continued through August. After the coordinating subcommittee and all the task groups met to compare each other's findings and recommendations and to reconcile outstanding conflicts, on October 22, 1992, the NPC Committee on Natural Gas reviewed the completed draft report and approved it.[67] The executive summary highlighted the four "messages" in the report: (1) the resources are available and can be supplied at competitive costs; (2) the elements for a viable, long-term market in natural gas exist; (3) federal and state regulators need to take actions to facilitate such a market and let it function; and (4) the entire natural gas industry needs to undertake measures to address impediments to market success.[68] During November, 1992, council members received six volumes of data supporting the conclusions of the executive summary, and on December 17, 1992, the NPC membership met and approved the report.

A NEW PARADIGM FOR THE NATURAL GAS INDUSTRY

In his cover letter submitting the report to Secretary of Energy Watkins, Chairman Ray Hunt of the NPC outlined the most important findings in *The Potential for Natural Gas in the United States.* According to the report, natural gas had the potential to make "a significantly larger contribution to the nation's energy supply and its environmental goals" because it "(1) can be produced and delivered in volumes sufficient to meet expanding market needs at competitive prices; (2) is a clean-burning fuel, and can be used in a variety of applications to satisfy environmental requirements; and (3) is a secure, primarily domestic source of energy that can help improve the national balance of foreign trade." While acknowledging that much of the groundwork for a competitive and customer-oriented industry had already been laid, Hunt cautioned that the industry needed to work to change many perceptions inherited from its heavily regulated past. In particular, "the industry must pay more attention to meeting customer needs through greater efficiency and more competitive prices."[69]

The central conclusion of the report was that the "United States has a vast and diverse natural gas resource base and estimates of the recoverable portion continue to grow with production experience and technological advances." The NPC concluded that such trends were likely to continue through at least 2010. The source and supply task group estimated that the technically recoverable natural gas resource base in the lower forty-eight states was 1,295 TCF and that about 600 TCF of this was recoverable at wellhead prices of $2.50/MMBTU or less.[70] Such a projection sharply departed from previous estimates.

This high estimate of recoverable natural gas reserves had surprised some study participants, especially producers. Although the conventional wisdom about gas had been changing, it still reflected attitudes inherited from the 1970s, when the price of gas was tightly regulated and curtailments of gas supplies were commonplace. Despite the gas bubble and oversupply in the 1980s, even gas producers had come to assume the eventual return of conditions of scarcity. The fears of industry and customers alike reflected the heavy reliance on the relatively low figure of proven reserves. Previous estimates of proven reserves of 160 TCF, or less than a ten-year supply at current demand rates, had contributed to a mentality that gas supply could not expand to meet future growth in demand.[71]

The NPC report characterized proven reserves as finished inventory. The source and supply task group examined the major gas-producing regions basin by basin and the trends in proven reserves, reserve additions, and new fields. It determined that constant rates of reserve additions and new fields had generated no deterioration in the ratio of proven reserves to annual demand over the past fifteen years. In addition to proven reserves of 160 TCF, it projected 616 TCF of recoverable conventional resources as well as 519 TCF of nonconventional resources, primarily tight sands, coal-bed methane, and shales. Thus, the natural gas industry's recoverable reserves stood at an impressive 1,135 TCF, assuming increased access to restricted areas, sufficient prices, and continued advances in technology.[72]

The projected impact of technology on the natural gas resource base also surprised some study participants. The NPC's new study analyzed technology much more comprehensively than had been done in *Factors Affecting U.S. Oil & Gas Outlook* five years earlier. Historically, technological advances had reduced drilling costs by an average of 3 percent per year, and the rate of technological advance had accelerated in the 1980s. The projected reduction in drilling costs allowed more gas to be recovered without compensating increases in wellhead prices, thus allowing more costly natural gas to be recovered at constant prices in the future.

The NPC also provided new estimates of the impact of environmental regulations on natural gas supply. Sensitivity analysis on this issue assumed more stringent and less cost-effective regulatory requirements than those used in reference case one. This scenario reduced 2010 production by approximately 2 TCF, or about 10 percent.[73]

The report also assessed natural gas available in the North American market from outside the lower forty-eight states. Recoverable natural gas resources of Canada and Mexico were large. The NPC expected imports from Canada to rise and reach 3 TCF by 2010, or more than 10 percent of the U.S. market. The council projected that Mexico would continue to be an importer of U.S. gas during the next ten years but could become a net exporter if its internal conditions developed more favorably for its production of natural gas. The NPC concluded that Alaskan and northern frontier Canadian gas would be unavailable in 2010 under the price and demand levels used in the study. Finally, it projected that LNG imports from other sources would remain low.[74]

To tap the recoverable resource base, the costs (and therefore prices) would have to rise. In the study the council projected that if natural gas prices gradually rose to $3.50/MMBTU (the equivalent of $28 a barrel of oil in $1990), supply growth would increase with demand and reach 24 TCF in 2015. Thereafter the market became supply constrained. Conversely, at an average wellhead price of $1.50/MMBTU, a supply level could not even be maintained in the short term at 20 TCF prior to the year 2000. An intermediate average price of $2.50/MMBTU (the equivalent of $20 a barrel in $1990) sustained a supply of approximately 20 TCF through the year 2020, and then supplies declined rapidly.[75]

The task group on transmission and storage supplemented these findings by concluding that projected levels of natural gas resources would be deliverable. Though U.S. natural gas consumption peaked at 22.3 TCF in 1972, the transmission and storage system continued to expand because of long-term shifts in supply and demand. This task group found that the 1991 annual capacity of the system was 24 TCF and peak-day capacity was 120 billion cubic feet per day (BCF/D). These levels were substantially above 1991 annual consumption of 19.2 TCF and estimates of peak-day demand of 102 BCF/D. The NPC projected that changes in consumption and supply patterns for transmission and storage would continue through 2010. To adapt to these changes would require expenditures comparable to those made in the transportation and storage of natural gas in the preceding twenty years.[76]

The Potential for Natural Gas in the United States was the most comprehensive study of the gas industry to date. It took into account many technological and environmental considerations not integrated into earlier studies. Its conclusions, which reflected a consensus of all segments of the natural gas industry and its major stakeholders, represented a paradigm shift in thinking about natural gas. Even without accounting for technological change beyond 2010 or Canadian and Mexican supplies, the report concluded that with annual consumption of 25 TCF, a fifty-year supply existed. This figure allowed for substantial market growth in the next twenty-five to thirty years, corresponding to the planning time frames of electrical utilities. Such a large natural gas resource base had the potential to liberate thinking about natural gas from the mentality of the 1970s, with its focus on constraints to growth in production. It allowed a market-driven industry, commodity pricing of natural gas over the long term, and the potential to recapture industrial and utility markets lost in the 1970s and 1980s.[77]

The NPC also found that "the natural gas market is increasingly diverse, with new challenges and opportunities." The demand and distribution task force projected annual natural gas demand for the year 2010 of 25.0 quadrillion BTU (QBTU) in reference case one (equivalent to 24 TCF) and 21.3 QBTU (equivalent to 20 TCF) in case two. Current (1990) consumption was 19.0 QBTU. The residential and commercial markets formed the core of the natural gas industry and continued to do so in either reference case; 55 percent of all single-family homes in the United States used natural gas. However, the council noted that in those areas where future growth was significant, conservation and efficiency improvements, along with vigorous competition from electric heat pumps, limited increases in consumption under either case.[78]

Promising prospects for growth existed in industrial and electric utility markets. While price competition from other fuels promised to be intense in industrial markets, significant opportunities existed for gas in emissions control, waste recycling, and waste remediation. Additionally, natural gas was attractive because conversion of industrial coal boilers to natural gas or cofiring created tradable allowances under the 1990 Clean Air Act amendments.[79]

Electric power generation was potentially the fastest growing market for natural gas, but the NPC noted substantial obstacles to growth. Constrained by the Fuel Use Act of 1978, natural gas use had dropped by half in the electric-generation market between 1972 and 1990. Even after the repeal of portions of the Fuel Use Act, other barriers to increased use of natural gas remained, including aggressive competition from other energy sources. Fears of interruption of gas services remained as a legacy from the shortages and curtailments of the 1970s and 1980s. Finally, use of natural gas by vehicles represented a small but promising market, especially for commercial and government fleets in ozone nonattainment areas under the 1990 Clean Air Act amendments and the Energy Policy Act of 1992. The NPC's reference cases estimated consumption at 140 BCF per year by 2010, but under more optimistic scenarios that projection tripled.[80]

Several important conclusions of the NPC study came out of its regulatory and policy issues task group but reflected the work of the entire study. The council stated that "reliance on competitive market forces has improved the gas industry's ability to serve customer needs in a diverse and expanding market place." Analysis of the inner workings of the emerging natural gas market had been no easy matter. Deregulation had affected each segment of the industry in different ways at different times. At the time of the report's publication in 1992, it was still not clear when or even if deregulation would produce a unified industry with truly competitive markets. Despite great advances in the deregulation of wellhead prices and open access to pipelines, segments of the industry remained regulated.[81]

The local distribution companies were in a particularly difficult situation. These firms remained comprehensively regulated by state regulatory commissions, many of which subjected LDCs to some type of natural gas procurement reviews that analyzed, after the fact, the wisdom of terms under which firms purchase natural gas. LDCs expressed concern about slow state regulatory acceptance of the options now available in the interstate natural gas market. State regulators had to be "convinced that long-term contracts, futures, options, and other diverse contract arrangements can be effective risk management tools, rather than highly speculative 'gambles,' as they had been perceived," according to the NPC. Finally, participants in the gas study cited regulatory uncertainty as a major constraint on industry growth. The NPC believed that it was crucial for the evolving regulatory regime to allow all sectors of the industry to match risk tolerance with costs and obligations. It concluded that regulation should support and encourage moves toward contract-defined relationships between parties, emphasizing that "gas providers and consumers must be allowed to be accountable for their contractual decisions in the marketplace, not in regulatory decisions."[82]

The report concluded with practical suggestions for improvements in reliability, customer orientation and marketing, and behavioral issues. It noted that the long-term impacts of regulation and the underestimates of supplies had suppressed demand and fostered oversupply. Market forces would eventually reverse the situation, but restrictions on access to federal land and the impact of environmental restrictions on producer activity reinforced old concerns about scarcity. Furthermore, in the views of industrial and power-generation customers, the history of past curtailments had fostered the perception that natural gas was an unreliable fuel.[83]

The natural gas industry had not been sufficiently customer-oriented, according to the report. Rather, natural gas had been handled as a commodity that passed through various distribution channels pursuant to comprehensive regulatory requirements, that is, "Gas was marketed by taking orders." All segments of the industry needed to develop more marketing savvy, particularly in regard to "behavioral issues" that affected all segments of the industry. Many natural gas customers thought that the regulated segments of the industry had no incentive to become more efficient because regulation muted or eliminated market incentives and rewarded what customers characterized as "regulatory game-playing." Such disputes led to the perception that the industry was unable to work together to satisfy customer needs.[84]

Noting that a competitive natural gas industry was developing, the NPC called for regulatory policies that enhanced the number and quality of choices available to buyers and sellers of natural gas without "unnecessarily interfering in the consequences of those choices." The report, in identifying regulatory constraints to increasing natural gas usage, called the regulatory process unpredictable and slow and accused it of lacking coordination between state and federal processes, distorting business decision making, causing industry fragmentation, limiting consumer choice, treating natural gas as a scarce commodity, and using rate making to promote social policy, thereby distorting natural gas markets. The NPC argued that "efficiency improvements, innovations, and new value-added services are more likely to develop in a competitive market than in one that is regulated" and concluded that regulators could hasten the transition to competition by being "clear about the goals of regulatory change, and mak[ing] an effort to articulate the objectives with clarity to avoid uncertainty." Regulators and policy makers, however, would be challenged to practice restraint in periods of price and supply volatility, according to the report.[85]

Noting the importance of advances in technology in mitigating cost increases and ensuring reasonably priced natural gas supplies, the council supported a primary role for private investment, with a supplementary role for government. The majority of private investments in the industry had been successfully directed toward increasing supply and reducing costs, but regulated companies (especially LDCs) were subject to rate-of-return regimes that provided small rewards to firms for adoption, rapid development, or commercialization of new technologies. This constrained the development of much needed new gas end-use technologies, which, according to the NPC, needed much greater funding. The council also noted the relative underfunding of gas technology by the federal government compared to that of other energy sources. According to the report, increased end use of natural gas had the potential to contribute dramatically to U.S. environmental goals, but environmental regulations and limitations on the exploration, production, transportation, and storage of natural gas had the potential to limit the industry's ability to increase production.[86]

The NPC recommended that the federal government reexamine its natural gas research effort, giving serious consideration to raising the level of federal funding for gas-related research and development to $250 million. Also the council called for the DOE to initiate a review of the impact that cost-based regulatory regimes had on end-use commercialization efforts. For its recommendations addressing environmental regulation and access, the NPC returned to its old theme of balance. It wanted federal regulations reevaluated in view of the net environmental benefits of natural gas.[87]

The optimistic projections of gas supply in *The Potential for Natural Gas in the United States* were based on the assumption that a deregulated market would continue to develop. This scenario would require an emphasis on the principles of competitive markets and consumer choice, through contractual relationships, while recognizing a continued, though greatly reduced role for regulation. The report recommended deference to market forces where reasonable choices were available, such as the elimination of FERC's traditional tests for new pipelines and reliance on allocation of risk through contract. It called on regulators to refrain from restricting service choices. In those limited areas where regulation continued to be necessary, the council advocated rate making based on incentives, not profit ceilings. The report encouraged state regulators to consider unbundling of LDC and intrastate pipeline services, to explore options to traditional service obligations, and to distinguish between captive and noncaptive customers. The report recommended the deregulation of gas procurement, giving buyers equal access to competitive supplies. It called for reexamination of regulations on gathering systems at the state level and the end of such regulations where sufficient competition was found to exist.[88]

The council called for state regulators to seek ways to increase efficiency, improve productivity, and reduce costs while avoiding cross-subsidies among types of services and classes of customers. Uncertainty about rates and access to transportation could be reduced if the regulatory system allowed parties to have knowledge and confidence in rates and terms at the time transactions occurred, without the prospect of subsequent regulatory revisions. Important elements of such a system included determination of rate treatment of new facilities before construction, the policy that rate changes are not allowed to have retroactive impact, timely and efficient regulatory proceedings, and scrutiny of statutes to remove impediments to "informed choices and educated risk assumptions by natural gas sellers, transporters, and customers."[89]

The council also focused on the natural gas industry itself. It cautioned that "regulators and other policy makers are poised to help the competitive natural gas market work, but it is the responsibility of industry to make it work and perform to the benefit of the consumer, the environment, and the nation." The NPC concluded that the natural gas resource base was not a limiting factor, that gas could be delivered at competitive prices, and that significant opportunities existed to increase gas consumption in markets, especially industrial and power generation.[90]

The industry urgently needed to address directly the reliability question, since it represented the largest constraint to the increased use of gas by industrial and power-generation customers. The NPC recommended the creation of a natural gas reliability council to improve reliability and customer confidence. It endorsed a previous study for such an organization done by the Natural Gas Council, a group of eighteen gas industry executives from all segments and presidents of four gas trade associations and the GRI. Other suggested actions included use of the NPC report to bolster confidence in industry reliability; coordination of maintenance and downtime by transmission companies and LDCs to minimize disruptions; and encouragement of producers to seek maximum discretion, under state conservation programs, to manage production to match changes in natural gas markets.[91]

The NPC report emphasized the need for the gas industry to commit itself to customers if it wanted to increase its share of the energy market. It recommended that the industry work with customers to install facilities necessary for their needs, especially in markets where major opportunities existed, notably electric power generation, natural gas vehicles, and gas cooling. Efforts were needed to make contracting for gas simpler and less subject to subsequent regulatory revision, to decrease regulatory compliance costs, and to find better ways to communicate the availability of transmission and storage capacity. In light of historical divisions within the gas industry, the council asked the "leaders of all segments of the natural gas industry to commit to a concerted, ongoing, and consistent effort that focuses on the unique attributes of natural gas and its ability to deliver superior value to customers."[92]

Given the importance of technology in expanding the gas resource base, the NPC encouraged each segment of the industry to make technical innovation a top priority. The industry should invest aggressively in its own programs and willingly participate with government in jointly funded programs. The council also wanted the industry to take a much more active role in increasing public awareness of the benefits of natural gas and develop "new and innovative strategies for dealing with environmental issues." These included new methodologies of cost-benefit analysis, better information gathering on natural gas and the environment, and improvement of the integration of environmental issues into strategic business planning and decision-making processes.[93]

Taken as a whole, *The Potential for Natural Gas in the United States* provided a comprehensive analysis of the bright prospects for a deregulated natural gas industry. The transition to a market-oriented industry was under way, but difficulties remained because of the culture and assumptions developed over a long era of regulation. The central message of the study was clear: If the nation had the will to finish the process of deregulation, it would reap great rewards in the form of increased supplies of a reliable, clean source of energy.

The National Petroleum Council was a logical bearer of this message. Although the NPC had slighted natural gas during the decades of tight regulation, its historical commitment to competition in the oil-related studies made it an experienced, authoritative voice for a free market in natural gas. Indeed, in this particular study the NPC went beyond its traditional role of studying conditions. By bringing together in the study process most segments of an industry long segmented by regulation, the NPC facilitated the continued evolution of a more market-oriented industry. By presenting a comprehensive view of a rapidly evolving, new competitive industry, the NPC's landmark study hastened its evolution.

The industry's sustained expansion in the mid-1990s quickly called into question even the most optimistic projections from the NPC's 1992 report. Indeed, as the ink on the report dried, the pace of change accelerated in the dynamic natural gas industry. Restructuring of many aspects of the industry quickened, as fast-moving companies responded to the market opportunities opened by deregulation. New products and services sprang up. New ways of thinking about old problems produced forays by innovative gas companies into closely related markets such as electricity. The application of new technologies encouraged the growth of gas supplies, improvements in transmission and distribution, and new end uses for natural gas. And as the American economy boomed in the 1990s, natural gas demand surged beyond the best-case scenario put forward in the council's 1992 study.

Against this backdrop, in May, 1998, Secretary of Energy Federico Peña approached the NPC about the prospects of a new study of trends in the natural gas industry. Peña's request letter asked the council to "reassess its 1992 study" in light of "evolving market conditions." Such conditions included "five years of sustained growth in the use of natural gas," as well as "two major forces that are beginning to take shape, which will profoundly affect energy choices in the future—the restructuring of electricity markets and growing concerns about the potentially adverse consequences that using higher carbon-content fuels may have on global climate change and regional air quality."[94] As both the fastest-growing fuel of the 1990s and the cleanest-burning fossil fuel in an era of heightened concern about air pollution, natural gas seemed poised for a period of rapid expansion. Secretary Peña turned to the National Petroleum Council for help in understanding what the future might hold for an industry becoming increasingly important to the nation's energy future.

The council quickly responded by organizing a study committee chaired by Peter Bijur (chairman and CEO of Texaco). The committee created three task groups: demand, supply, and transmission and distribution. Acknowledging that far-reaching changes in the 1990s promised an era of faster growth in natural gas demand, the task groups organized their efforts "to test supply and distribution systems against significantly increased demand."[95] In his letter approving the establishment of the new Committee on Natural Gas, the new secretary of energy, Bill Richardson, phrased the same goal in different language, stating that government officials needed to "be confident that industry has the capability to meet the significant increases in natural gas demand forecasted for the twenty-first century."[96]

The study focused on the period from 1998 to 2010, with a less detailed view of the years from 2011 to 2015 and a more general discussion of the long-term sustainability of natural gas supplies. Conclusions about future trends were built from the ground up, using detailed analyses of specific sources of supply and demand to construct more general projections. The task groups looked closely at the adequacy of future supplies, the potential sources of future demand, and the expansion capacity of existing infrastructure to handle the projected rapid growth in demand projected for the coming decades.

The demand task group began with an overview of conditions in 1998, when natural gas accounted for about one-quarter of the nation's energy use. After examining trends in all sectors of the economy that consumed large amounts of natural gas, the task group concluded that demand would continue to grow, increasing from about 22 TCF in 1998 to about 29 TCF by 2010. Electric generation would be the focus of growth, accounting for about half the projected 32 percent increase in demand. The task group acknowledged that this estimate of rapid growth might rise even higher if environmental regulations further increased the demand for clean-burning gas. Extending ongoing trends into the future required careful thought about which market conditions might change and which might remain roughly the same. Any such projection of future demand required a series of simplifying assumptions, such as the study's projection that no new nuclear power plants would be added by 2010. All involved understood that change was seldom predictable with precision; the best that could be done was to think rigorously and systematically about existing conditions and then try to understand the basic outlines of future changes. By any accounting, if trends were not completely disrupted by unforeseen events, natural gas demand was moving onward and upward in the coming decade.[97]

Could supply keep pace? This was the key question facing the supply task group. The group analyzed the prospects for increased production throughout North America, with special emphasis on Canada, the Gulf of Mexico deepwater areas, and the Rockies. It identified supplies adequate to keep pace with booming demand if conditions were right for rapid development. Particularly important would be the loosening of restrictions on access to federal lands, a healthy oil and gas industry capable of generating more than $650 billion in investment for exploration and production, and additional investments in much-needed research and development.[98]

Other large expenditures would be required to expand the natural gas transmission and distribution system to transport additional supplies of gas. In the era before deregulation such expansion of infrastructure had been financed primarily by giant transmission companies and large regional utility companies. These regulated companies could fold the costs of such development into ever-expanding rate bases, with a comfortable rate of return guaranteed by regulators. But as the transmission and distribution task group noted, the new age of competition had dramatically altered the old system; with the opportunities of deregulation came the risks of taking on the large investments required for new infrastructure. It was unclear who would have the incentive to assume such risks in the future.[99]

The findings of the three task groups supported a variety of recommendations. In contrast to the detailed analyses put forward in the task group reports, these recommendations were stated in relatively general terms. The report endorsed the cooperative creation of a balanced strategy for the responsible development of natural gas in the context of a realistic overall national energy policy. It requested a "drive" to develop the new technology that had been and would continue to be essential to the growth in gas supplies. Careful planning would be needed to ensure the orderly expansion of infrastructure and human resources needed by sustained expansion. Finally, the report urged the industry to take advantage of the opportunities opened by new competition to design innovative new services and products.[100]

While the broad thrust of the NPC's 1999 gas report did not differ sharply from that of the 1992 report, revisions aimed to reflect the impact of change brought by the market revolution in natural gas. Given the vast changes in motion in the 1990s, neither report could expect to be definitive; neither could hope to make precise predictions of the future. Indeed, as had been demonstrated initially in the early 1970s by *U.S. Energy Outlook*—the NPC's landmark effort to forecast energy trends—all projections in the uncertain and ever-changing world of energy had to be taken as best guesses. But the value of such reports went far beyond the concreteness and accuracy of the numbers with which they projected future conditions. Equally important was the deliberative process that produced these numbers. In times of rapid change systematic, detailed analyses of conditions by specialists from every part of an industry offered useful insights into the focus, direction, and pace of change. Such analyses helped point an industry toward future possibilities and identify barriers to potential expansion.

For the first twenty-five years of its existence the National Petroleum Council seldom focused its energies on natural gas. In the 1990s it made up for lost time by producing comprehensive reports on the industry in a critical period of its evolution. As the market revolution in natural gas continues in the future, spilling over into other energy markets such as electricity, the NPC will no doubt continue to study the resulting changes. These changes promise to be among the energy industry's most significant in the first decades of the twenty-first century.

CHAPTER 7

Future Issues for the National Petroleum Council

IN THE MORE THAN FIFTY YEARS since its founding, the National Petroleum Council has fulfilled a critical function: supplying government officials with detailed, accurate information about fundamental conditions within the petroleum industry. At times when energy issues have not been at the top of the political agenda, the basic constituency for the NPC's reports has been a relatively small group of energy specialists in government agencies and in Congress. At other times, especially when shortages or national security concerns have made petroleum-related issues more visible politically, the council's reports have found larger audiences. But at all times since 1946 the NPC has been counted upon for credible, useful data about an industry vital to the health and national security of the nation.

Each generation faced its own particular challenges, grappling with new dimensions to traditional issues as well as emerging new issues facing the petroleum industry. Thus national defense, which originally meant preparedness for the next shooting war, was transformed by events into broader concerns including reliance on imported oil, energy security, the need for a Strategic Petroleum Reserve, and protection of the industry against terrorism. New issues were called forth by changing times, notably environment/energy trade-offs in the 1960s and 1970s and deregulation of natural gas in the next two decades. Each new secretary of the interior and secretary of energy has discovered the value of the NPC in understanding the petroleum industry's changing conditions.

FUTURE ISSUES

As Hazel O'Leary took over as secretary of energy during President Bill Clinton's first term, she turned to the NPC for assistance in thinking through the key energy-related issues that might face policy makers in the future. In December, 1994, she requested that the council "identify the issues and policies that will most likely shape the industry over the next twenty-five years, and advise me on the most constructive and realistic resolution of these issues with respect to the future vitality of both the industry and the economy."[1] Thus was born what came to be called *Future Issues,* an ambitious report that peered twenty-five years into the future, identified potential problems, and provided a context for thinking creatively about solutions.

The difficulties in predicting how changes in foreign policy, economics, and technology might affect energy in future decades made projecting key trends a tricky business. To find the best way to move forward, the chair of the NPC, H. Laurance Fuller (chairman and CEO of Amoco), appointed a Committee on Future Issues cochaired by Philip Carroll (president and CEO of Shell Oil Company) and William H. White (deputy secretary of energy). By relying heavily on independent third parties to compile much of the data and conduct the opinion surveys needed for the report, this committee moved a step away from standard council procedures in the past. In the process they found a creative way to address the critically important task of identifying central future concerns and suggesting ways to address them.

The NPC selected Arthur D. Little, Inc., to help in identifying future issues. The methodology employed included both extensive interviews with 45 opinion leaders from inside and outside the industry and a series of three workshops with a total of 46 other individuals. Participants in both parts of the exercise were chosen from a list of 250 names identified by the Coordinating Subcommittee on Future Issues.

Selected were energy and environmental specialists from a variety of backgrounds, including all phases of the petroleum industry, customers, public interest and environmental groups, governmental policy makers and regulators, and industry observers. These individuals were interviewed with questions covering change over time in the industry since 1970, opinions about trends in the future, and speculation about the significant issues that might be expected to arise in the twenty-five years before the year 2020. The preliminary results of these interviews became a starting point for the workshops, which consisted of three small groups (fourteen to sixteen people) organized by the following categories: government policy makers and regulators, public interest and environmental organizations, and industry custom-ers and observers. These groups analyzed the survey results and discussed their implications before working to identify and prioritize future issues as well as specific policies and actions needed to address them. Members of the subcommittee observed the workshops but, by design, did not participate in them. The interviews and workshops gave the NPC a creative new tool with which to reach into the industry, including its stakeholders, to generate a body of data about prevailing opinions and projections of these opinions into the future.[2]

Over the course of about seven months this process generated a broad consensus on key issues facing the oil and gas industries and appropriate ac-tions in anticipation of these future issues. The conclusions tended to be stated in general terms, as was to be expected from an effort to gaze into the future. The results, as published in *Future Issues* in August, 1995, provided a useful point of departure for understanding the broad trends shaping the future of the industry. In so doing they implicitly posed a historical question: What might the NPC be called upon to do in the future compared to what it has done in its past?

The report began with an overview of the petroleum industry's role in the national economy compiled by the Charles River Associates, a consulting group based in Cambridge, Massachusetts. These compiled statistics showed that petroleum makes a healthy contribution to the nation's output, account-ing for almost 5 percent of the U.S. economy's gross output. The industry's impact on employment was less substantial; the 1.5 million jobs in petroleum made up only 1.5 percent of the national total. But this number understated the industry's impact, since scientists and engineers in petroleum accounted for more than 8 percent of the total workforce, a much higher percentage than those professions' presence in most industries. The report demonstrated clearly that petroleum was a vital sector of the American economy with im-pact far beyond strictly economic measures.

Before identifying key future issues, the report recounted a brief "view of the past" that placed current concerns in historical perspective. This overview of events since 1970 focused on "the massive changes in energy markets." To illustrate the fundamental impact of energy crises since 1970, the boom and bust in energy prices, and the deregulation of natural gas, the NPC compared projections on energy conditions from *U.S. Energy Outlook* to actual condi-tions in 1985, the year used in that earlier report as a benchmark for predicting "future" conditions. Obviously, new conditions had greatly altered assump-tions of supply and demand, which had failed to rise to even the "low" scenario used in 1970. To extend such general statistical measures into the future, the NPC used statistics projected by the Energy Information Administration.[3]

These numbers reminded readers of a disturbing fact of life for the American petroleum industry: Domestic oil production had never rebounded from the decline noted in reports beginning in the late 1960s. Despite higher oil prices that temporarily provided incentive to explore for petroleum in the United States, oil production had slipped down to 6.9 million barrels per day (MMB/D) in 1993. History had resolved the heated debates on domestic production levels within the NPC in the early 1970s in favor of those who saw little prospect for increased domestic production. Unfortunately, time had proven them correct, and there seemed little prospect for reversing this decline. Indeed, the EIA estimated that domestic production would continue to slip in the future, falling to 5.4 MMB/D in 2010. Inevitably this suggested that the level of oil imports required to bridge the gap between oil supply and demand in the United States would rise sharply. This harsh reality provided the backdrop against which participants in the interviews and workshops identified crucial "future issues."[4]

The surveys and workshops came to a consensus that in the future four broad sets of issues faced the industry. These were energy security, which included declining U.S. production and supply security and availability; industry-government interface, which focused on global competitiveness and the role of government in markets; environment, notably the impact of oil and gas products and operations on environmental quality, global climate change, and sustainable development; and industry image, which focused on the industry's need to find ways to increase stakeholders' understanding of petroleum-related issues. These were broad issues meant to delineate general areas of concern, not sharply defined issues driven by more specific public policy consideration, as had been the case with most NPC reports in the past. But peering into the future was, of necessity, a search for understanding of general trends, not of specific events.

The list of future issues suggested that one reason to study the past was, simply put, that history is not over. Trends from the past continue to shape current and future choices. Most future issues had strong roots in the NPC's past. Energy security and industry-government relations have been core concerns of the NPC since its founding in 1946. Environment became an important issue for the NPC in the 1960s and 1970s. Though seldom directly addressed by the council, industry image had been a nagging concern to many in the industry since the days of John D. Rockefeller, and this concern was magnified by an anti-oil backlash during the 1970s energy crises. The interviews and workshops used to generate the future issues list included a brief look back at the past, and the list reflected the importance of trends extending from the past into the future.

What made *Future Issues* more than simply an exercise in historical prediction was the prism through which long-term trends were passed during the study. That prism was the perspective of a group of energy and environmental experts seeking to come to grips with far-reaching changes all around them in the 1990s. The participants in the study brought to their task the realization that the petroleum industry had become more competitive, more international, and more subject to environmental considerations. Looking at the impact of such forces on long-term trends in the industry, they produced a document that used past realities and present concerns to produce a thoughtful vision of the future.

The first issue discussed, national energy security, had always been a primary concern of the NPC. From its origins in the mobilization for World War II and then through the cold war, the energy crises of the 1970s, and the Persian Gulf War the council had been called on repeatedly to help government understand the close ties between energy supply and national and economic security. It had assumed an important role in the evolution of the Strategic Petroleum Reserve, the nation's primary security against cutoffs of foreign oil supplies. The basic concern remained the same: What were the military and economic implications of the growing use of imported oil to fill the nation's energy needs? This issue had remained at the forefront of NPC activities since its founding; not surprisingly, *Future Issues* confirmed that it would remain there through 2020.

But the report's discussion of energy security placed the historical debate in a new context. For one thing, it was clearer than ever in the mid-1990s that domestic oil production was destined to supply a shrinking percentage of the nation's energy needs. Thus, of necessity, to meet growing U.S. and world demand, supplies of oil would increasingly come from sources outside the United States. Future U.S. policy should pay increased attention to several issues: improving coordination of international efforts to plan for supply disruptions through the International Energy Agency and ensuring that new imports came from diverse sources. The industry had moved from focusing on policies that decreased U.S. dependence on imported oil to policies that addressed the vulnerabilities occasioned by an inevitable dependence. In light of growing internationalization of the petroleum industry and its impact, the report acknowledged that future U.S. military presence in the Middle East would be required even if the nation successfully reduced its imports from this volatile area. World energy markets would grow increasingly intertwined, the Middle East would remain central to world oil supply, and the United States military would remain the primary "police officer" in the area. This was a hard-edged look at the realities of international energy security. Past events were projected into a future in which the key certainty about international oil supplies was their uncertainty.[5]

The second set of issues discussed in *Future Issues*—the interface between industry and government—also had deep roots in the history of the NPC. Indeed, the council had been created to foster cooperation between the Department of the Interior and the petroleum industry. The structure of government remained an impediment to close cooperation, since energy-related functions at the federal government level remained dispersed in various agencies. The creation of the DOE in 1977 had rationalized many of these functions and placed them in a single department, but all sorts of divisions of authority remained, including that between energy and environmental policy makers and inevitable disconnects between the executive and legislative branches. Such organizational problems within government traditionally had plagued business-government cooperation on energy-related issues. Despite the inefficient structure of government authority over energy-related issues, the NPC had found a secure historical identity as a provider of information to the DOE. But other government officials were not necessarily as responsive to the NPC's reports as were energy specialists within the DOE. All over Washington public policy choices with far-reaching impacts on oil and gas production and use were made with little systematic analysis of their impact on the consuming public or the petroleum industry and with little understanding of their implications for other public policies in related areas.

Those involved in the *Future Issues* study saw the need to rationalize government powers to avoid future problems. They looked around the changing world of the 1990s and concluded that the nation would pay higher prices for government inefficiencies in coming decades. In an increasingly intertwined international economy, government's unwieldy structure could no longer be considered strictly a domestic concern. Its impact on the global competitiveness of U.S. companies would become a serious problem as these companies competed head-on with companies from other nations with more efficient governments. All over the world governments were busy redefining their roles in the economy, with emphasis on moving toward more market-oriented approaches to business-government relations. But the U.S. government had been slow to reexamine its traditional command-and-control approach with "more flexible goal-based regulation" that often "provides incentives to solve problems more innovatively and cost-effectively."[6]

The "future debates over the role of government in the energy industry and energy markets" would shape a broad range of important public policy choices. Included were "the continued deregulation of natural gas to the end consumer; access to resources in the United States; taxation and royalties for domestic production; and the government role in research, development, and dissemination of technology."[7] Other items on the list covered a range of regulatory issues from pipeline-permitting processes to regulation of financial instruments for energy markets. But the general implications of the report were clear: The rationalization of the structure of government powers and the move toward use of less coercive, more market-oriented policies would enhance the productivity of the American economy and increase the competitiveness of American companies in global markets.

A final set of issues highlighted in the report concerned the environment. Since at least the early 1970s, environmental issues had been a kind of recurring nightmare for the petroleum industry and even for many government officials whose specialty was energy. The wave of environmental regulation that first crested in the 1970s had never been integrated with existing policies on energy supply and demand. In essence, energy and environmental policies were made and enforced by different groups in government, and these groups generally remained at odds over the proper balance between the two sets of competing demands. Because energy production and use were so closely related with many identifiable environmental problems, the need for cooperation between the two groups was critical to the creation of successful long-term policies in both areas. But as those involved in the *Future Issues* study were painfully aware, on these vital issues there had long been more conflict than cooperation, more name-calling than coalition building.

The National Petroleum Council had labored long and hard on environmental issues, but its regular calls for more efficient and balanced approaches had found smaller audiences in government agencies focused on environment rather than energy. This symbolized the great divide in energy/environmental policy making: What sounded like the voice of the marketplace at the DOE sounded more like the self-pleading of polluters at the EPA. A pattern of conflict had become embedded in the structure and policies of government, and the societal costs of such conflict grew with the passage of time. From the perspective of the petroleum industry, this conflict was easy to summarize but quite difficult to resolve. Environmental policies had too often pursued pollution control without sufficient regard for costs. As the energy shortages of the 1970s became a distant memory and fuel supplies once again became relatively cheap and plentiful, supply-side issues resonated less and less in the halls of government. With the training and pride of engineers, many in the oil industry felt that they could design more efficient, flexible approaches that produced the desired reductions in pollution at a lower long-term cost to society. And they deeply resented the tendency of many environmentalists to dismiss their ideas as self-serving and harmful to the environment.

At issue were two fundamental questions. What level of regulation was needed to balance the costs and benefits of environmental initiatives? What was the best available type of regulation? The NPC had put forward strong views in a variety of past reports, and the discussion in *Future Issues* echoed many of these. A better balance was needed to take into account more fully the nation's need for energy. Market-conforming regulations should be used instead of rigid and confrontational command-and-control systems of the past. The petroleum industry should not be treated as an enemy of the people, but rather as an important part of any practical means of finding a sustainable balance between the inevitable energy/environmental policy trade-offs. Since the future undoubtedly held difficult new challenges on both sides of this trade-off, care was needed in anticipating how these closely related issues affected each other.

In scanning the horizon for future issues, those interviewed for the report saw several particularly troubling new problems. The emerging worldwide debate over global warming and sustainable development presented difficult challenges for energy and environmental policy makers. Such global issues transcended the old debates about the proper balance between energy and environment in the United States. Here the stakes were even higher, the costs and benefits even less certain. While acknowledging the growing concern about global climate change, *Future Issues* counseled all involved to take a long-term view and to build a body of the best available scientific information before making far-reaching public policy choices. The report reminded readers that global efforts to regulate climate change inevitably would involve new departures in international agreements, raising difficult issues of equity and authority among nations.

Sustainable development, which many observers closely associated with global warming, posed similar dilemmas for the future. The petroleum industry had a long-term interest in achieving sustainable development, and the natural gas industry had a growing role in energy markets in most discussions of sustainable futures. But, the report noted, "the concept of sustainable development is not amenable to precise definition," and the unspoken fear was that such nebulous issues had at times in the past been embodied in environmental regulations that were far from nebulous in their impact on the industry. Regulations hastily written and passed to deal with "crises" had too often become permanent parts of the regulatory landscape, resistant to subsequent revisions when better science and a fuller understanding of costs and benefits had become available.[8]

A reasonable balance on global warming or sustainable development or any other energy/environment trade-off could only be defined through the political process. This made the industry uneasy, since it feared that Big Oil might become a whipping boy in a global rush to do something about such emerging issues as global warming. The petroleum industry as a whole saw itself as a responsible participant in the pursuit of environmental quality; at great cost it had made striking improvements in its performance in this area since the 1960s. Many in the industry seemed increasingly frustrated that they were viewed with marked skepticism by environmentalists.

This sense of frustration found its way into *Future Issues* in discussion of the last major future issue identified: industry image. In the past the petroleum industry's public image had not been a significant concern of the National Petroleum Council. Its reports presented the facts in a detached manner that conveyed a sense of professionalism and objectivity. While obviously the voice of the industry, the NPC sought to avoid even the appearance of pleading the industry's case on the many controversial issues that came before it for study. This was an effective approach for presentation of materials to energy experts in government. But neither the council nor the industry as a whole had found an especially effective voice with which to address the general public.

The key was education. The public needed to learn more about the principles of science and economics as they applied to the industry's operations; the industry needed to obtain "a better understanding of public and consumer concerns." While acknowledging that the "oil and gas industry may never captivate the public," the report concluded that "better communication between industry members and the public can at least improve public understanding of the industry" and "help the public develop informed and, hopefully, supportive opinions about the industry." Such communications could not, however, successfully improve the industry's public image without going beyond traditional public relations that used images and advertising to change opinion. Instead, "performance by the industry on environment and other matters is viewed as the key to its future image." In short, the industry had to have concrete accomplishments to talk about before society would listen to it without skepticism.[9]

Performance on issues facing the industry would be shaped in the future by broad forces affecting all aspects of energy production and use. *Future Issues* identified several such "cross-cutting themes," including changes in markets and technology, foreign affairs and other international policies affecting energy and economics, and the achievement of greater communication and cooperation among "the oil and gas industry, the government, and various stakeholder." Changes in the market could be expected to have the greatest impact on future issues facing the petroleum industry, since market forces continued to be both unpredictable and far-reaching in their impact on energy supply and demand.[10]

The original letter of request from Secretary O'Leary had asked the NPC's advice on "the most constructive and realistic resolution of these issues with respect to the future vitality of both the industry and the economy." The council's report avoided the pitfalls of providing detailed solutions for specific future issues by focusing on the "question of process." In the report were eight general recommendations on industry and government actions needed "to position the nation for more effective resolution of critical issues it faces."[11]

Though general in scope and restrained in tone, these recommendations at least indirectly touched on every significant public policy issue facing the petroleum industry. Industry and government were advised to encourage responsible development of domestic resources as well as encourage development of the widest possible range of foreign sources; use sound science in legislative, regulatory, and judicial processes; require cost-benefit analyses for regulatory interventions; use goal-oriented regulatory mechanisms where regulatory intervention is necessary; and encourage science, economic, and energy education. In addition industry should improve and expand communication with stakeholders outside the industry, and government should improve coordination of policies affecting the oil and gas industry.[12]

Underneath the surface of each of these general recommendations were heated political debates over specific energy policies. From an industry perspective, for example, "responsible development of domestic resources" meant easier access to public lands, which to many included offshore sites in California and the Arctic National Wildlife Refuge. But by leaving such specific controversies largely unnamed, the report seemed to make a determined effort to heed its own previous call for efforts to build a more positive industry image. Avoiding direct confrontation, the report laid out general principles in language meant to build bridges, not burn them.

Soon after the publication of *Future Issues* in August, 1995, Secretary O'Leary asked the NPC for additional information on the report's final recommendation that government should improve coordination of its energy policies. In response the council prepared a supplement to *Future Issues* entitled *Issues for Interagency Consideration.* Using a poll of NPC membership, the supplemental report produced a prioritized list of the most important areas in need of "improved coordination" among government agencies. At the top of the list were three issues that had long concerned the petroleum industry: regulation of consumer fuel choice, the cumulative impact of regulations, and access to resources from federal lands. To aid the members in prioritizing the issues, the survey and the report provided a short summary of the need for greater government coordination on eighteen separate public policy issues, with examples of possible actions government could take toward improvements in the enumerated areas.

The act of listing such issues did not, of course, ensure that the various government agencies involved would take the actions recommended. But if Secretary O'Leary were inclined to push forward on these issues, then the NPC's supplemental report pointed the way toward meaningful change. Unfortunately, her resignation and three subsequent changes in DOE leadership over the next three years made the supplemental report into more of a wish list for the industry than an action plan for government reform. Old-timers at the NPC were all too familiar with the problems presented by the frequent turnover among top government energy officials. They could take some solace, however, in the knowledge that career energy specialists in the federal government provided a measure of continuity—and a ready audience for the council's report. The report had set an agenda for the future by defining areas where greater government coordination was most needed; at times small victories or preparation for future battles is all that is possible.

Future Issues served as a letter of introduction of sorts from the NPC to the new secretary of energy, Federico Peña. Little more than a year after its publication, Secretary Peña sought to go beyond the general concerns expressed in *Future Issues* to the identification of more specific proposals for future studies. In April, 1997, he attended a meeting of the NPC's Cochairs' Coordinating Committee and asked for opinions on the five issues most worthy of attention from the council and the Department of Energy. Responses collected from members of the NPC were used to compile a list of possible topics for future studies.

The major issues affecting the petroleum industry seldom changed abruptly, and the list of potential topics for studies submitted were variants of the perennial issues studied by the council as colored by conditions specific to the late 1990s. The DOE organized these lists, and similar lists generated from within the DOE, into a pamphlet entitled *Priority List of Potential, Focused Study Topics,* which was circulated to the NPC's membership at its December, 1997, general meeting.

In addressing the meeting, Secretary Peña made use of the list of potential study topics to discuss how the NPC had contributed to energy policy debates in the past and would continue to do so in the future. The list discussed in priority order the following potential studies: an update of the council's landmark study, *The Potential for Natural Gas in the United States* (1992); a follow-up study on the long-term viability of the U.S. refining system; examinations of government policies affecting access to onshore and offshore federal lands for oil and gas recovery; a study of cost-effective strategies for reducing greenhouse gas emissions; an analysis of the economic competitiveness of the U.S. oil and gas industry in the global economy; and a study of the possible "reinvention" of the National Environmental Policy Act. These important topics all had roots in the council's past work; they also had obvious relevance to major policy choices facing the nation in the future.[13]

In his remaining months in office Secretary Peña acted quickly, starting at the top of the list and moving downward. In May, 1998, the NPC received and accepted a request to reassess its 1992 study of natural gas in light of changing conditions. As the council launched this ambitious study, Secretary Peña requested that it undertake the second study on the list presented in December, 1997: examining the long-term economic viability of the U.S. petroleum refining industry. He then left office. His successor, Bill Richardson, did not continue on down the list of potential study topics presented earlier by Peña, but he did turn quickly to the NPC for advice on another pressing issue.

In September, 1998, Secretary Richardson approached the council to discuss the "appropriateness of the National Petroleum Council providing the Department of Energy with advice and counsel on how best to coordinate the oil and gas industry's role" in "developing a national plan for the protection of the critical infrastructure of the oil and gas industry."[14] As discussed in chapter 2, this was simply the latest chapter in the council's involvement in preparedness, but it encompassed difficult new dimensions. Preparedness could not, as in the past, be ensured primarily by mobilizing standing reserves of industry executives or by ensuring that the nation would have ample oil products in the event of war. With modern technology, preparedness required proactive, industry-led measures to limit the possibility of supplies disruption by terrorists bent on crippling the United States, not on waging outright war against it.

In organizing the critical infrastructure study the NPC turned to the chairman of Halliburton, Dick Cheney, to chair the committee. As the study moved forward, Cheney found new employment, first as a candidate for the vice presidency and then as vice president of the United States in the administration of George W. Bush. In an interesting turn of events for the NPC, the first report completed under the administration's newly appointed secretary of energy, Spencer Abraham, was the critical infrastructure report that Vice President Cheney had launched for the NPC before he reentered politics.

The report on cyberterrorism brings to mind the reminder in *Future Issues* that "unexpected new issues are likely to arise over time."[15] Few such issues will be completely new, given the NPC's long history of studying the petroleum industry. But as new variants of traditional concerns surface—or in the event that new conditions generate completely new concerns—the council will remain an important resource for government officials in need of authoritative information delivered in a timely, objective manner.

CONCLUSIONS

Whatever the future brings, the NPC will do as it has done since 1946, when it was created as a leap of faith by President Harry Truman and a group of oil executives and government officials. Having seen the benefits of cooperation in the mobilization of the petroleum industry during World War II, these leaders looked for a creative way to build a peacetime partnership of business and government. To do so they had to look beyond traditional institutions and attitudes, beyond the confrontations that had marked so much of the historical relationship between the oil industry and the federal government. They had to accept the risk of failure and to overcome the skepticism of those who felt that effective cooperation could not continue in the absence of the exigencies of war. In a spirit of experimentation they created a new type of industry advisory committee, the National Petroleum Council. For more than fifty years the council has remained a unique experiment in business-government cooperation.

The NPC's unusual standing among advisory committees reflected, in part, good choices made by its organizers. Self-financing gave the organization a healthy measure of independence, allowing it considerable leeway in responding to government officials' requests. The use of volunteers from industry to conduct council business enabled a small permanent NPC staff to manage operations and coordinate the work of far-flung networks of industry experts tapped to conduct council studies. A broad membership base gave the NPC the capacity to reach down into all segments of the petroleum industry for data, expertise, and cooperation.

The council's early members saw themselves as direct descendants of those who had served the national interest in World War II by coordinating petroleum industry activities. As decades passed and personal memories of the unifying experience of World War II inevitably faded, the council tapped its membership's impulse for public service to mobilize the petroleum industry's people and technical expertise in government service. At the heart of the successful cooperation between the NPC and government was the assumption that members would set aside their personal and corporate interests and pursue a broader national interest in their work on council reports (see appendix F).

The strong role of the NPC in advising government reflected the petroleum industry's vital importance to national security and its significance in foreign relations, economic prosperity, and environmental quality. Two world wars had shown decisively the centrality of petroleum products in modern warfare. In the cold war that followed World War II, oil played an increasingly important role in foreign policy. Since the domestic and world economies required large supplies of petroleum to prosper, their economic security was threatened by the growing dependence on oil imports from the developed nations. The worldwide demand for improved environmental quality and later for sustainable development placed major demands on the petroleum industry, since energy production and use had far-reaching impacts on the environment. For all of these reasons petroleum could not be considered just another industry by government officials, who understood the need for cooperation with the oil and gas industries. The National Petroleum Council provided a much-needed liaison between government and the petroleum industry that proved valuable to both parties.

After more than a half century of experience, a final source of the NPC's uniqueness is its longevity. Despite recurring bouts with antitrust considerations and anti-oil sentiments, the council has persevered year after year, decade after decade. The NPC has stayed the course, offering information and advice to presidents, secretaries of the interior, and energy secretaries since 1946 (see appendix C). In these years it has witnessed the beginning and end of the cold war in Europe, numerous shooting wars, the rise of OPEC after its creation in 1960, the environmental movement and the coming of the EPA in 1970, the energy crises of the 1970s, the DOE's birth in 1977, the 1970s boom in oil and the 1980s bust, low prices and high prices for oil, the regulation and deregulation of natural gas. Through all of this and more the NPC has studied and reported on an industry regularly transformed by the forces of technology, economics, and government regulation. Along the way the council has gained much experience in interpreting change over time, a broad long-term perspective on its industry, and considerable standing in both industry and government. The NPC serves as an institutional memory of sorts on energy policies; such is often of great value and always in short supply in public policy making.

Why has the council survived so long? In a capitalist system with a modern tradition of strong regulatory powers vested in government, it has provided an important service: the education of government officials about conditions in the marketplace. The NPC has helped them understand the impact of energy policies on the energy industries and the implications of public policy choices on the supply and demand for energy. One longtime aide for the U.S. Senate's Energy Committee summarized the value of NPC reports by noting that they "had legs in the marketplace." He and others in the relatively small world of federal government energy specialists came to rely heavily on the council's reports, finding them to be accurate, detailed, nonpartisan, and timely. Quite simply, on many critical issues the NPC provided government officials with useful information. Over time its consistent record in producing detailed reports on changing conditions within the petroleum industry earned the council a permanent place as a valuable part of the energy policy-making process.

The framing of the topics addressed by the NPC regularly changed to reflect current concerns, but the underlying issues remained constant. National security stayed at the top of the council's list of topics, but it took on different dimensions over the decades. Preparedness for the next shooting war was the most pressing concern of the NPC immediately after World War II, but preparedness gradually came to include other issues, from the response to nuclear attack, to the creation and operation of the Strategic Petroleum Reserve. Theoretical discussions of the proper usages of the SPR became all too real at the onset of the Persian Gulf War, when the NPC advised government officials on the best ways to use petroleum reserves to minimize disruptions of oil markets. Through its past reports on the creation and use of the reserves, the National Petroleum Council has earned a strong voice in any future debates about the SPR—and, indeed, in general discussions of the petroleum industry's role in the pursuit of national security, however broadly or narrowly defined. Recent concern about the threat to the petroleum industry's smooth operations posed by cyberterrorism well illustrates how technological advances produce new variants of old issues and how government officials turn to the NPC for assistance in understanding the implications of such changes.

A second major issue of continuing importance for the NPC has been the balance between energy policies and environmental policies. In reports from 1971 through the 1990s the council developed several common themes, including the need for balance in coordinating environmental policies and energy policies and the need to take into consideration the costs and benefits of new pollution control measures. The NPC's reports have consistently argued that command-and-control regulations are unnecessarily costly and that marketlike regulations that specify goals but leave more flexibility for industry to achieve them would prove more efficient in enhancing environmental quality in the long term.

Such reports have not, however, led to an overhaul of the nation's environmental laws. While many observers now concede that command-and-control regulations have carried a high cost, their contributions to improved air and water quality have made them popular politically. In a sense the petroleum industry has been a victim of its own success. Despite its frequent objections to command-and-control regulations, the industry has made the investments and technical changes needed to meet their stringent standards while continuing to deliver abundant supplies of relatively inexpensive energy. The existing system is perceived to be functioning well enough to be left alone, even if alternative approaches hold theoretical advantages.

Debate over reform of environmental regulations continues at the turn of the twenty-first century, encouraged in part by NPC reports and other industry voices. Such change no doubt will move more slowly than many in the petroleum industry prefer. In the intense political conflicts that undoubtedly will accompany any movement toward a new approach to environmental regulation, the council will have an important role to play as one voice of the petroleum industry on this critical set of issues. It also will be called upon to produce information and recommendations about global environmental issues coming to the fore in recent years, notably global warming and sustainable development.

The third set of issues that flows through the history of the NPC and on into its future involves the supply of domestic oil and gas and the debate over alternatives to imported oil. Throughout the postwar era the NPC remained one of the few petroleum-related organizations capable of containing the often divisive debate on international versus domestic oil. On several occasions the council published recommendations for government policy on imports.

U.S. Energy Outlook (1972), the council's pathbreaking study of the broad trends affecting past and future energy supply and demand, gave rise to often bitter debates within the industry over the prospects for expanding domestic production and the implications of import increases. When domestic production did not climb substantially despite the high oil prices of the 1970s, a consensus finally emerged that the nation should seek to find new and varied sources of imports outside of OPEC and that a hard look should be taken at alternatives to oil.

The council responded to this new consensus by producing a variety of detailed reports about the costs and technical problems involved in producing alternatives to imported crude oil. Included have been reports on enhanced oil recovery, arctic petroleum, unconventional gas supplies, and conservation. But the council's most detailed study on this general topic was published in 1992; *The Potential for Natural Gas in the United States* was a landmark report on the most significant alternative to domestic oil in our immediate future— natural gas.

The council's reports on all of these varied issues went forward amid a variety of tensions. The NPC certainly was not immune to the conflicts within its industry, particularly on the divisive issue of imports. Different parts of its membership were affected in different ways by this and other issues, and the council's study process often became a place to deliberate or at least debate such issues. On its broader studies of trends in energy, the council could expect tensions among representatives of inherently competitive industries. Political tensions often arose, particularly around reports that dealt with issues of great concern to the voting public, notably imports and the environment. On such issues the council's work often drew the criticism of interest groups with far different points of view.

Antitrust and conflict-of-interest laws regularly resurfaced as points of political contention during periods of heightened public awareness of energy-related issues. Another source of tension for the NPC was the division of authority among federal government agencies on issues of direct and indirect importance to its industry. This was particularly vexing on the issue of energy/environmental trade-offs, public policies which were generally the domain of separate governmental groups. All of these tensions registered within the NPC at one time or another. On several occasions the council seemed on the verge of dissolution. But it survived these near-death experiences and bounced back even stronger from them.

The NPC did so because its leaders avoided confrontations with government whenever possible and because its reports were too valuable to be lightly discarded. Admittedly, at times the council's membership labored mightily to produce reports that had little ultimate impact. But such cases were the exception, not the rule. Some reports, notably those on the SPR, played central roles in framing public policy debates on specific issues. Others, such as the 1993 report on the impact of the Clean Air Act amendments on refining and the report on the Oil Pollution Act of 1990, helped shape the implementation of regulations. Still others, notably the studies of synthetic fuels in the early 1950s, helped block the passage of public policies that the industry strongly opposed. In all cases the direct and indirect impacts of the council's reports on public policy were difficult to measure but impossible to ignore.

The impact of these reports was enhanced by their tone. In general the council's reports avoided aggressive lobbying. Like Sgt. Joe Friday of *Dragnet* fame, they were concerned with "just the facts." Never polemical and only rarely confrontational, the reports allowed their hard-won facts to speak for themselves. Data-dense and, when called for, technically sophisticated, these reports stated their recommendations in careful terms designed to gain full consideration from officials with varied political backgrounds.

To produce such reports, the study process stressed the need to define areas of agreement and resolve areas of disagreement. At times the search for common ground within the study process helped make the NPC a focal point of consensus-building within the industry. This was nowhere clearer than in the preparation of *The Potential for Natural Gas in the United States* (1992), which brought together people from all sectors of a long-segmented industry and helped them build a common understanding of the newly competitive natural gas industry. In this and other, less obvious cases the study process gave a common purpose to people from different companies and stakeholder groups and with different training and perspectives by encouraging them to learn more broadly about their industry. In the process many participants gained a broader understanding of their own jobs and their own companies and industries.

Such collaboration and cooperation have been particularly important in eras of rapid change, when traditional assumptions and methods of operation are called into question by new conditions in the industry. The future of the NPC will be shaped by its ability to continue to respond to and interpret change as it has in the past. Given more leeway by the loosening of government powers over energy markets in much of the world, competitive forces have pushed out in new directions, raising fundamental questions about the pace and direction of future change. As a new energy order pushes up against the remains of the traditional order, the National Petroleum Council finds itself well prepared by its history to assist government in understanding and responding to new conditions affecting energy markets.

The transformation of the marketplace in energy has gone forward rapidly in the recent past. The combination of the fall of communism, privatization of formerly nationalized energy companies, and deregulation within the United States has fostered a market revolution that has introduced increased competition in world energy markets. The U.S. government now faces a new array of national and international issues involving the impact of these changes on energy policy and national security. At the same time governments around the world are in search of information and understanding about the energy industry and their nations' place within it.[16] In such a situation the National Petroleum Council is in an excellent position to serve an expanded historical purpose.

The voice of the marketplace becomes even more important when market forces are given freer rein; good information for government becomes even more important when policy makers are reevaluating and redefining their roles. With its broad membership and its long experience, the NPC has a capacity to monitor and interpret the breakdown of traditional markets and the emergence of a more unified market for energy matched by few, if any, existing institutions in the public or private sector.

The rapid breakdown of traditional boundaries separating markets for various forms of energy is forcing business and government to search for a broader context in which to analyze the future prospects for different forms of energy and the overall supply and demand for energy from all sources. The NPC has almost thirty years' experience studying the place of petroleum within the broader category of energy. Since publication of the pioneering *U.S. Energy Outlook* in the early 1970s, the council has remained mindful of the broad issues of energy usage as they affect petroleum. In the last decade it has gained the experience of studying in great detail the competitive revolution within the natural gas industry. As the traditional lines dividing oil from gas and from electricity and other alternative fuels have continued to blur, the NPC is logically positioned by its history and organizational capabilities to report on the process of change and its implications for the energy industries, including petroleum.

Such changes are going forward on a global scale. Although the NPC remains an American institution with a mandate to advise U.S. government officials, its studies are of obvious value to officials and oil executives outside the country. Council reports on U.S. conditions are of interest to many world energy leaders, since U.S.-based multinational companies remain at the heart of the international industry and U.S. government policies continue to reverberate throughout the world due to the large size of the American market and the nation's role as the world's police force.

In addition, the long history of the NPC makes it one of the world's most experienced collectors of energy-related data. Those needing the same or similar information as context for decision making outside the United States might look at the NPC as both a source of data and a model for organizing and operating their own industry-sponsored advisory councils. Somewhere at some time in the near future an organization similar to the NPC likely will emerge at the international level. In the year 2002 it is not yet clear where such an organization might fit among existing international institutions. As in the years after World War II, that choice will be determined by creative industry and government leaders able to see beyond traditional institutions and attitudes and to envision a new way of doing things. When a world energy council of some sort is created, its leaders would do well to look hard at the NPC's history for guidance.

One lesson there for the taking is the value of cooperation between industry and government. In an age when market forces are on the ascent and government regulation is in retreat, the need for cooperation has increased. Governments around the world exercise the authority to define the legal and regulatory framework within which market forces are allowed to operate. They retain the power to go back toward nationalization and regulation if mounting public concerns over the results of freer energy market workings convince them to reverse course. In building long-term cooperative ties with these governments, the industry as a whole would do well to heed the example of the NPC. Throughout its history the council has earned the respect and trust of government policy makers by providing them with accurate information and responsible recommendations presented in a nonpartisan and nonconfrontational voice.

If the market revolution is to go forward in energy around the world, much will be asked of industry. With increased control over decisions affecting the supply of energy will come increased responsibilities for ensuring outcomes acceptable to the public and to government officials. Considerations of national security will not disappear, nor will efforts to protect the quality of the environment while ensuring adequate supplies of energy at affordable costs. Cooperation and consensus-building over the long term, not the short-term harvesting of economic advantages, will be needed to create a climate of public opinion favorable to freer markets. To create and sustain such a climate of opinion will require the petroleum industry to earn a public image as a responsible manager of a critical sector of the world's energy supply. In such an energy future the National Petroleum Council could play a substantial role, both as a source of information and recommendations on key issues and as a historical example of the benefits of cooperation.

APPENDIX A

Secretaries of the Interior and of Energy

INTERIOR (1946–77)

Julius A. Krug, 1946–49
Oscar L. Chapman, 1949–53
Douglas McKay, 1953–56
Fred A. Seaton, 1956–61
Stewart L. Udall, 1961–69
Walter Hickel, 1969–70
Rogers C. B. Morton, 1971–75
Stanley K. Hathaway, 1975
Thomas S. Kleppe, 1975–77
Cecil B. Andrus, 1977

ENERGY (1977–2001)

James R. Schlesinger, 1977–79
Charles W. Duncan, Jr., 1979–81
James B. Edwards, 1981–82
Donald Paul Hodel, 1982–85
John S. Herrington, 1985–89
James D. Watkins, 1989–93
Hazel R. O'Leary, 1993–97
Federico F. Peña, 1997–98
Bill Richardson, 1998–2001
Spencer Abraham, 2001–

APPENDIX B

National Petroleum Council Reports (by Subject)

EMERGENCY PLANNING AND PREPAREDNESS

Securing Oil and Natural Gas Infrastructures in the New Economy, 2001

Industry Assistance to Government—Methods for Providing Petroleum Industry Expertise during Emergencies, 1991

Short-Term Petroleum Outlook—An Examination of Issues and Projections, 1991

Emergency Preparedness for Interruption of Petroleum Imports into the United States, 1981

Emergency Preparedness for Interruption of Petroleum Imports into the United States (Final Report), 1974

Emergency Preparedness for Interruption of Petroleum into the United States—Interim Report, 1973

Emergency Preparedness for Interruption of Petroleum into the United States—Supplemental Interim Report, 1973

Emergency Preparedness for Interruption of Petroleum into the United States—Supplemental Interim Report Papers, 1973

Emergency Petroleum and Gas Administration procedures manuals (10 volumes), 1967

What Is the Emergency Petroleum and Gas Administration? 1966

Impact of Electric Power Outages on Petroleum Industry Facilities, 1966

Emergency Fuel Convertibility, 1965

Civil Defense and Emergency Planning for the Petroleum and Gas Industries, 1964

Petroleum and Gas in a National Emergency (An Analysis of Government Planning), 1964

National Emergency Oil and Gas Mobilization, 1959
Oil and Gas Emergency Defense Organization (Communication Facilities),
    1956
Security Principles for the Petroleum and Gas Industries, 1955
Disaster Planning for the Oil and Gas Industries, 1955
Oil and Gas Emergency Defense Organization, 1954
Form of Organization for a Government Petroleum Agency in Connection
    with Present Emergency, 1950
Organization Structure under the National Defense Production Act, 1950
National Petroleum Emergency, 1949
Military and Government Petroleum Requirements, 1949
Military and Government Petroleum Requirements, 1948
Military Aircraft Fuels Productive Capacity, 1947
Military and Government Petroleum Requirements, 1947
Petroleum Production and Crude Availability, 1947

ENERGY CONSERVATION

Potential for Energy Conservation in the United States: 1979–1985, 1975
Potential for Energy Conservation in the United States: 1974–1978, 1974
Trends in Petroleum Consuming Equipment, 1951

ENERGY OUTLOOK

Issues for Interagency Consideration—A Supplement to the NPC's Report:
    Future Issues—A View of U.S. Oil & Natural Gas to 2020, 1996
Future Issues—A View of U.S. Oil & Natural Gas to 2020, 1995
Factors Affecting U.S. Oil & Gas Outlook (Final Report), 1987
U.S. Oil & Gas Outlook (Interim Report), 1986
Short-Term U.S. Petroleum Outlook—A Reappraisal, 1974
U.S. Energy Outlook—A Summary Report of the National Petroleum Coun-
    cil, 1972
U.S. Energy Outlook—A Report of the National Petroleum Council's Com-
    mittee on U.S. Energy Outlook, 1972
Guide to National Petroleum Council Report on U.S. Energy Outlook, 1972
U.S. Energy Outlook—An Initial Appraisal (1971–1985), Volume I, 1971
U.S. Energy Outlook—An Initial Appraisal (1971–1985), Volume II, 1971
Short-Term Fuel Oil Outlook, 1970

ENVIRONMENTAL ISSUES

Environmental Conservation—The Oil and Gas Industries (Final Report), 1982
Environmental Conservation—The Oil and Gas Industries: An Overview
    (Interim Report), 1981
Environmental Conservation—The Oil and Gas Industries, Volume I, 1971
Environmental Conservation—The Oil and Gas Industries, Volume II, 1972
Current Key Issues Relating to Environmental Conservation—The Oil and
    Gas Industries, 1970

GOVERNMENT POLICY

The Oil Pollution Act of 1990—Issues and Solutions (Final Report), 1994
The Oil Pollution Act of 1990—An Interim Report, 1993
Law of the Sea—Particular Aspects Affecting the Petroleum Industry, 1973
Participation in the Water for Peace Program, 1966
Petroleum Policies for the United States, 1966
Impact of Oil Exports from the Soviet Bloc (Supplement), 1964
Impact of Oil Exports from the Soviet Bloc, Volume I, 1962
Impact of Oil Exports from the Soviet Bloc, Volume II, 1962
The National Petroleum Council: A Unique Experience in Government-
    Industry Cooperation—First Seven Years: 1946–1953, 1961
Shale Oil Policy, 1955
Petroleum Imports, 1955
Federal Lands Oil and Gas Policy, 1953
Government Oil and Gas Organization, 1953
A National Oil Policy for the United States, 1949
Advisory Activities—District I, 1949
Advisory Activities—District IV, 1949
Advisory Activities—District V, 1949
Voluntary Allocation Agreements, 1948
Advisory Activities—District I, 1948
Advisory Activities—District III, 1948
Advisory Activities—District V, 1948
Analyzation of the Report of Sixteen Nations, 1948
Government Royalty Oil Regulations, 1948
International Standards for Measurement of Liquid Petroleum Fuels, 1947
Federal Mineral Leasing Act, 1946

MATERIALS AND MANPOWER REQUIREMENTS

Materials and Manpower Requirements for U.S. Oil and Gas Exploration and Production—1979–1990, 1979

Availability of Materials, Manpower and Equipment for the Exploration, Drilling and Production of Oil—1974–1976, 1974

Skills and Occupations of People in the United States Oil and Gas Industries, 1969

Materials Requirements for Petroleum Exploration and Production, 1969

Critical Materials Requirements for Petroleum Refining, 1966

Chemical Manufacturing Facilities of the Petroleum and Natural Gas Industries, 1963

Materials Requirements for Oil and Gas Exploration, Drilling and Production, 1963

Petroleum and Gas Industries Manpower Requirements, 1963

Maintenance and Chemical Requirements for U.S. Petroleum Refineries and Natural Gasoline Plants, 1961

Petroleum Industry Use of the Radio Spectrum (Final Report), 1960

Petroleum Industry Use of the Radio Spectrum (Interim Report), 1959

Oil and Gas Industries Manpower (Final Report), 1956

Oil and Gas Industries Manpower (Interim Report), 1955

Use of Radio and Radar, 1955

Use of Radio and Radar, 1953

Oil Country Tubular Goods, 1952

Capital and Materials Requirements for Increasing Availability of Petroleum Products, 1951

Materials and Chemicals Requirements of the Oil and Gas Industries, 1951

Oil and Gas Industries Manpower, 1951

Quebracho Requirements of the Petroleum Industry, 1951

Transportation and Materials Requirements for Liquefied Petroleum Gas Availability, 1951

Petroleum Industry Manpower, 1950

Petroleum Industry Steel Requirements, 1950

Petroleum Industry Steel Requirements, 1949

Quebracho Requirements of the Petroleum Industry, 1949

Materials Requirements by the Oil and Gas Industry, 1948

Petroleum Industry Steel Requirements, 1948

Materials Requirements by the Oil and Gas Industry, 1946

NATURAL GAS

Meeting the Challenges of the Nation's Growing Natural Gas Demand, 1999
The Potential for Natural Gas in the United States, 1992

REFINING

U.S. Petroleum Refining—Assuring the Adequacy and Affordability of Cleaner
    Fuels, 2000
U.S. Petroleum Refining—Meeting Requirements for Cleaner Fuels and Refin-
    eries, 1993
Petroleum Refining in the 1990s—Meeting the Challenges of the Clean Air
    Act, 1991
U.S. Petroleum Refining, 1986
Refinery Flexibility (Final Report), 1980
Refinery Flexibility—An Interim Report, 1979
Factors Affecting U.S. Petroleum Refining—A Summary, 1973
Factors Affecting U.S. Petroleum Refining—Final Report, 1973
Factors Affecting U.S. Petroleum Refining—Impact of New Technology, 1973
United States Refinery Capacity, 1957
Petroleum Refining Capacity, 1949
Petroleum Refining Capacity, 1948
Petroleum Refining Capacity, 1947

RESEARCH

Research, Development, and Demonstration Needs of the Oil and Gas In-
    dustry, 1995
Integrating R&D Efforts, 1988
Impact of New Technology on the U.S. Petroleum Industry (1946–1965), 1967

RESOURCE DEVELOPMENT

Marginal Wells, 1994
Enhanced Oil Recovery, 1984

Third World Petroleum Development: A Statement of Principles, 1982
U.S. Arctic Oil & Gas, 1981
Unconventional Gas Sources (Final Report), 1980
Unconventional Gas Sources (Interim Report), 1979
Enhanced Oil Recovery: An Analysis of the Potential for Enhanced Oil Recovery of Known Fields in the United States—1976 to 2000, 1976
Ocean Petroleum Resources, 1975
Petroleum Resources Under the Ocean Floor—Supplemental Report, 1971
Future Petroleum Provinces in the United States—A Summary, 1970
Petroleum Resources Under the Ocean Floor (Final Report), 1969
Petroleum Resources Under the Ocean Floor (Interim Report), 1968
Factors affecting U.S. Exploration, Development and Production (1946–1965), 1967
Estimated Productive Capacities of Crude Oil, Natural Gas and Natural Gas Liquids in the United States (1965–1970), 1966
Proved Discoveries and Productive Capacity of Crude Oil, Natural Gas and Natural Gas Liquids in the United States, 1965
Proved Discoveries and Productive Capacity of Crude Oil, Natural Gas and Natural Gas Liquids in the United States, 1961
Availability of Liquefied Petroleum Gas, 1957
Petroleum Productive Capacity, 1957
Petroleum Productive Capacity, 1955
Oil and Gas Exploration, Drilling and Production Requirements, 1953
Petroleum Productive Capacity, 1953
Submerged Lands Productive Capacity, 1953
Synthetic Liquid Fuels Production Costs, 1953
Synthetic Liquid Fuels Production Costs, 1952
Oil and Gas Availability, 1952
Petroleum Productive Capacity, 1952
Petroleum Productive Capacity, 1951
Synthetic Liquid Fuels Production Costs, 1951
Liquefied Petroleum Gas, 1951
Synthetic Liquid Fuels Production Costs, 1950
Crude Petroleum Reserve Production Capacity, 1950
Federal Oil and Gas Leasing, 1950
Petroleum Products Supplies and Availability, 1948
Petroleum Production and Crude Availability, 1948
Liquefied Petroleum Gas, 1948

STATISTICS

U.S. Crude Oil Data, 1860–1944, 1970
U.S. Petroleum Imports, 1969
Bunker "C" Fuel Oil, 1952
Petroleum Imports, 1950
Mineral Industries Census, 1949
Temporary Statistical Advisory Committee, 1947

STORAGE

U.S. Petroleum Product Supply—Inventory Dynamics, 1998
Petroleum Storage & Transportation, 1989
Petroleum Inventories and Storage Capacity (Final Report), 1984
Petroleum Inventories and Storage Capacity (Interim Report), 1983
Petroleum Storage & Transportation Capacities, 1979
Petroleum Storage Capacity, 1974
U.S. Petroleum Inventories and Storage Capacity, 1970
Petroleum Storage Capacity, 1963
Petroleum Storage Facilities, 1960
Petroleum Storage Capacity, 1957
Underground Storage for Petroleum (Final Report), 1957
Underground Storage for Petroleum (Interim Report), 1956
Petroleum Storage Capacity, 1954
Underground Storage for Petroleum (Final Report), 1952
Petroleum Storage Capacity, 1952
Underground Storage for Petroleum (Interim Report), 1951
Petroleum Storage Capacity, 1950
Petroleum Storage Capacity, 1948

STRATEGIC PETROLEUM RESERVE

The Strategic Petroleum Reserve: A Report on the Capability to Distribute
    SPR Oil, 1984
Petroleum Storage for National Security, 1975

TRANSPORTATION

Petroleum Storage & Transportation, 1989
Petroleum Storage & Transportation Capacities, 1979
Capacity of Crude Oil Gathering Systems and Deep-Water Terminals, 1970
U.S. Petroleum and Gas Transportation Capacities, 1967
Oil and Gas Transportation Facilities, 1962
Petroleum Transportation, 1958
World Petroleum Tanker Construction (Final Report), 1957
World Petroleum Tanker Construction (Interim Report), 1956
Tank Truck Transportation, 1956
Tank Truck Transportation Census, 1952
Transportation and Materials Requirements for Liquefied Petroleum Gas
    Availability, 1951
Petroleum Transportation, 1950
Petroleum Barge Transportation, 1947
Illinois River Winter Transportation, 1947
Petroleum Pipeline Transportation, 1947
Petroleum Rail Transportation, 1947
Petroleum Tank Car Steel Requirements, 1947
Petroleum Tanker Transportation, 1947
Petroleum Transportation Facilities, 1947
Petroleum Truck Transportation, 1947
High Pressure Tank Cars for the Transportation of Liquefied Petroleum Gas,
    1946

APPENDIX C

National Petroleum Council Reports (by Year, 1946–2001)

1946
Federal Mineral Leasing Act
High Pressure Tank Cars for the Transportation of Liquefied Petroleum Gas
Materials Requirements by the Oil and Gas Industry

1947
Illinois River Winter Transportation
International Standards for Measurement of Liquid Petroleum Fuels
Military Aircraft Fuels Productive Capacity
Military and Government Petroleum Requirements
Petroleum Barge Transportation
Petroleum Pipeline Transportation
Petroleum Production and Crude Availability
Petroleum Rail Transportation
Petroleum Refining Capacity
Petroleum Tank Car Steel Requirements
Petroleum Tanker Transportation
Petroleum Transportation Facilities
Petroleum Truck Transportation
Temporary Statistical Advisory Committee

1948
Advisory Activities—District I
Advisory Activities—District III
Advisory Activities—District V
Analyzation of the Report of Sixteen Nations

Government Royalty Oil Regulations
Liquefied Petroleum Gas
Materials Requirements by the Oil and Gas Industry
Military and Government Petroleum Requirements
Petroleum Industry Steel Requirements
Petroleum Products Supplies and Availability
Petroleum Production and Crude Availability
Petroleum Refining Capacity
Petroleum Storage Capacity
Voluntary Allocation Agreements

1949
Advisory Activities—District I
Advisory Activities—District IV
Advisory Activities—District V
Military and Government Petroleum Requirements
Mineral Industries Census
A National Oil Policy for the United States
National Petroleum Emergency
Petroleum Industry Steel Requirements
Petroleum Refining Capacity
Quebracho Requirements of the Petroleum Industry

1950
Crude Petroleum Reserve Production Capacity
Federal Oil and Gas Leasing
Form of Organization for a Government Petroleum Agency in Connection
    with Present Emergency
Organization Structure Under the National Defense Production Act
Petroleum Imports
Petroleum Industry Manpower
Petroleum Industry Steel Requirements
Petroleum Storage Capacity
Petroleum Transportation
Synthetic Liquid Fuels Production Costs

1951
Capital and Materials Requirements for Increasing Availability of Petroleum
    Products

Liquefied Petroleum Gas
Materials and Chemicals Requirements of the Oil and Gas Industries
Oil and Gas Industries Manpower
Petroleum Productive Capacity
Quebracho Requirements of the Petroleum Industry
Synthetic Liquid Fuels Production Costs
Transportation and Materials Requirements for Liquefied Petroleum Gas Availability
Trends in Petroleum Consuming Equipment
Underground Storage for Petroleum (Interim Report)

1952
Bunker "C" Fuel Oil
Oil Country Tubular Goods
Oil and Gas Availability
Petroleum Productive Capacity
Petroleum Storage Capacity
Synthetic Liquid Fuels Production Costs
Tank Truck Transportation Census
Underground Storage for Petroleum (Final Report)

1953
Federal Lands Oil and Gas Policy
Government Oil and Gas Organization
Oil and Gas Exploration, Drilling and Production Requirements
Petroleum Productive Capacity
Submerged Lands Productive Capacity
Synthetic Liquid Fuels Production Costs
Use of Radio and Radar

1954
Oil and Gas Emergency Defense Organization
Petroleum Storage Capacity

1955
Disaster Planning for the Oil and Gas Industries
Oil and Gas Industries Manpower (Interim Report)
Petroleum Imports
Petroleum Productive Capacity

Security Principles for the Petroleum and Gas Industries
Shale Oil Policy
Use of Radio and Radar

1956
Oil and Gas Emergency Defense Organization (Communication Facilities)
Oil and Gas Industries Manpower (Final Report)
Tank Truck Transportation
Underground Storage for Petroleum (Interim Report)
World Petroleum Tanker Construction (Interim Report)

1957
Availability of Liquefied Petroleum Gas
Petroleum Productive Capacity
Petroleum Storage Capacity
Underground Storage for Petroleum (Final Report)
United States Refinery Capacity
World Petroleum Tanker Construction (Final Report)

1958
Petroleum Transportation

1959
National Emergency Oil and Gas Mobilization
Petroleum Industry Use of the Radio Spectrum (Interim Report)

1960
Petroleum Industry Use of the Radio Spectrum (Final Report)
Petroleum Storage Facilities

1961
Maintenance and Chemical Requirements for U.S. Petroleum Refineries and
    Natural Gasoline Plants
The National Petroleum Council: A Unique Experience in Government-
    Industry Cooperation—First Seven Years: 1946–1953
Proved Discoveries and Productive Capacity of Crude Oil, Natural Gas and
    Natural Gas Liquids in the United States

1962
Impact of Oil Exports from the Soviet Bloc, Volume I
Impact of Oil Exports from the Soviet Bloc, Volume II
Oil and Gas Transportation Facilities

1963
Chemical Manufacturing Facilities of the Petroleum and Natural Gas Indus-
    tries
Materials Requirements for Oil and Gas Exploration, Drilling and Production
Petroleum and Gas Industries Manpower Requirements
Petroleum Storage Capacity

1964
Civil Defense and Emergency Planning for the Petroleum and Gas Industries
Impact of Oil Exports from the Soviet Bloc (Supplement)
Petroleum and Gas in a National Emergency (An Analysis of Government
    Planning)

1965
Emergency Fuel Convertibility
Proved Discoveries and Productive Capacity of Crude Oil, Natural Gas and
    Natural Gas Liquids in the United States

1966
Critical Materials Requirements for Petroleum Refining
Estimated Productive Capacities of Crude Oil, Natural Gas and Natural Gas
    Liquids in the United States (1965–1970)
Impact of Electric Power Outages on Petroleum Industry Facilities
Participation in the Water for Peace Program
Petroleum Policies for the United States
What Is the Emergency Petroleum and Gas Administration?

1967
Emergency Petroleum and Gas Administration procedures manuals (10
volumes)
Factors Affecting U.S. Exploration, Development and Production (1946–1965)
Impact of New Technology on the U.S. Petroleum Industry (1946–1965)
U.S. Petroleum and Gas Transportation Capacities

1968
Petroleum Resources Under the Ocean Floor (Interim Report)

1969
Materials Requirements for Petroleum Exploration and Production
Petroleum Resources Under the Ocean Floor (Final Report)
Skills and Occupations of People in the United States Oil and Gas Industries
U.S. Petroleum Imports

1970
Capacity of Crude Oil Gathering Systems and Deep-Water Terminals
Current Key Issues Relating to Environmental Conservation—The Oil and
    Gas Industries
Future Petroleum Provinces in the United States—A Summary
Short-Term Fuel Oil Outlook
U.S. Crude Oil Data, 1860–1944
U.S. Petroleum Inventories and Storage Capacity

1971
Environmental Conservation—The Oil and Gas Industries, Volume I
Petroleum Resources Under the Ocean Floor—Supplemental Report
U.S. Energy Outlook—An Initial Appraisal (1971–1985), Volume I
U.S. Energy Outlook—An Initial Appraisal (1971–1985), Volume II

1972
Environmental Conservation—The Oil and Gas Industries, Volume II
Guide to National Petroleum Council Report on U.S. Energy Outlook
U.S. Energy Outlook—A Summary Report of the National Petroleum Council
U.S. Energy Outlook—A Report of the National Petroleum Council's Com-
    mittee on U.S. Energy Outlook

1973
Emergency Preparedness for Interruption of Petroleum into the
    United States—Interim Report
Emergency Preparedness for Interruption of Petroleum into the
    United States—Supplemental Interim Report
Emergency Preparedness for Interruption of Petroleum into the
    United States—Supplemental Interim Report Papers
Factors Affecting U.S. Petroleum Refining—A Summary

Factors Affecting U.S. Petroleum Refining—Final Report
Factors Affecting U.S. Petroleum Refining—Impact of New Technology
Law of the Sea—Particular Aspects affecting the Petroleum Industry

1974
Availability of Materials, Manpower and Equipment for the Exploration,
     Drilling and Production of Oil—1974–1976
Emergency Preparedness for the Interruption of Petroleum Imports into the
     United States (Final Report)
Petroleum Storage Capacity
Potential for Energy Conservation in the United States: 1974–1978
Short-Term U.S. Petroleum Outlook—A Reappraisal

1975
Ocean Petroleum Resources
Petroleum Storage for National Security
Potential for Energy Conservation in the United States: 1979–1985

1976
Enhanced Oil Recovery: An Analysis of the Potential for Enhanced Oil Re-
     covery of Known Fields in the United States—1976 to 2000

1979
Materials and Manpower Requirements for U.S. Oil and Gas
     Exploration and Production—1979–1990
Petroleum Storage & Transportation Capacities
Refinery Flexibility—An Interim Report
Unconventional Gas Sources (Interim Report)

1980
Refinery Flexibility (Final Report)
Unconventional Gas Sources (Final Report)

1981
Emergency Preparedness for Interruption of Petroleum Imports into the
     United States
Environmental Conservation—The Oil and Gas Industries: An Overview
     (Interim Report)
U.S. Arctic Oil & Gas

1982
Environmental Conservation—The Oil and Gas Industries (Final Report)
Third World Petroleum Development: A Statement of Principles

1983
Petroleum Inventories and Storage Capacity (Interim Report)

1984
Enhanced Oil Recovery
Petroleum Inventories and Storage Capacity (Final Report)
The Strategic Petroleum Reserve: A Report on the Capability to Distribute
    SPR Oil

1986
U.S. Oil & Gas Outlook (Interim Report)
U.S. Petroleum Refining

1987
Factors Affecting U.S. Oil & Gas Outlook (Final Report)

1988
Integrating R&D Efforts

1989
Petroleum Storage & Transportation

1991
Industry Assistance to Government—Methods for Providing Petroleum In-
    dustry Expertise during Emergencies
Petroleum Refining in the 1990s—Meeting the Challenges of the Clean Air Act
Short-Term Petroleum Outlook—An Examination of Issues and Projections

1992
The Potential for Natural Gas in the United States

1993
The Oil Pollution Act of 1990—An Interim Report
U.S. Petroleum Refining—Meeting Requirements for Cleaner Fuels and
    Refineries

1994
Marginal Wells
The Oil Pollution Act of 1990—Issues and Solutions (Final Report)

1995
Future Issues—A View of U.S. Oil & Natural Gas to 2020
Research, Development, and Demonstration Needs of the Oil and Gas
    Industry

1996
Issues for Interagency Consideration—A Supplement to the NPC's Report:
    Future Issues—A View of U.S. Oil & Natural Gas to 2020

1998
U.S. Petroleum Product Supply—Inventory Dynamics

1999
Meeting the Challenges of the Nation's Growing Natural Gas Demand

2000
U.S. Petroleum Refining—Assuring the Adequacy and Affordability of Cleaner
    Fuels

2001
Securing Oil and Natural Gas Infrastructures in the New Economy

APPENDIX D

National Petroleum Council Membership, June 18, 1946

Kenneth S. Adams
President
Phillips Petroleum Company

Holbrook T. Ashton
President
Western Petroleum Refiners
    Association

Thomas H. Barton
President
Lion Oil Company

Burt R. Bay
President
Northern Natural Gas Company

Roy W. Blair
President
National Oil Marketers Association

Jacob Blaustein
President
American Trading & Production
    Company

Paul G. Blazer
Chairman of the Board
Ashland Oil & Refining Company

William R. Boyd, Jr.
President
American Petroleum Institute

Reid Brazell
President and General Manager
Leonard Refineries, Inc.

J. S. Bridwell
Partner
Bridwell Oil Company

Russell B. Brown
General Counsel
Independent Petroleum Association
    of America

William F. Clinger
President
Pennsylvania Grade Crude Oil
    Association

Robert H. Colley
President
The Atlantic Refining Company

Howard A. Cowden
President
Consumers Cooperative
    Association

Stewart M. Crocker
President
Columbia Gas and Electric
    Company

Henry M. Dawes
President
The Pure Oil Company

Everett L. DeGolyer
Chairman of the Board
DeGolyer and MacNaughton

Otto Dewey Donnell
President
The Ohio Oil Company

Fayette B. Dow
General Counsel
National Petroleum Association

J. Frank Drake
President
Gulf Oil Corporation

Gordon Duke
Petroleum Executive
Southeastern Oil, Inc.

James H. Dunn
President
Natural Gasoline Association of
    America

James P. Dunnigan
Producers Refining Company, Inc.

Leroy M. Edwards
President
Southern California Gas Company

Richard Fenton
Executive Vice President
California Stripper Well Association

William H. Ferguson
Executive Vice President
Continental Oil Company

R. Gwin Follis
President
Standard Oil Company of
    California

Jacob France
Chairman of the Board
Mid-Continent Petroleum Corp.

Walter S. Hallanan
President
Plymouth Oil Company

D. P. Hamilton
President
Root Petroleum Company

Jake L. Hamon
Cox and Hamon

Burton A. Hardey
Partner
The Hardey Company

George A. Hill, Jr.
President
Houston Oil Company of Texas

Wallace T. Holliday
President
The Standard Oil Company
    (Ohio)

Eugene Holman
President
Standard Oil Company
    (New Jersey)

D. A. Hulcy
President
Lone Star Gas Company

William F. Humphrey
President
Tide Water Associated Oil
    Company

H. L. Hunt
President
Hunt Oil Company

A. Jacobsen
President
Amerada Petroleum Company

B. Brewster Jennings
President
Socony-Vacuum Oil Company,
    Inc.

Allen A. Jergins
President
San Joaquin Valley Oil Producers
    Association

Carl A. Johnson
President
Independent Refiners Association
    of California, Inc.

Charles S. Jones
President
Richfield Oil Corporation

W. Alton Jones
President
Cities Service Oil Company

Frank H. Lerch, Jr.
President
Consolidated Natural Gas
    Company

Ralph Lloyd
President
Western Oil & Gas Association

John M. Lovejoy
President
Seaboard Oil Company of Delaware

William G. Maguire
Chairman of the Board
Panhandle Eastern Pipe Line
    Company

B. L. Majewski
Vice President
Deep Rock Oil Company

Albert C. Mattei
President
Honolulu Oil Corporation

Harold M. McClure, Sr.
President
National Stripper Well Association

Norris C. McGowen
President
United Gas Pipe Line Company

Clyde G. Morrill
Executive Vice President
Independent Oil Men's Association
    of New England

S. B. Mosher
President and General Manager
Signal Oil and Gas Company

Henry D. Moyle
Vice President
Wasatch Oil Refining Company

Joseph L. Nolan
Manager, Oil Department
Farmers Union Central Exchange

I. A. O'Shaugnnessy
President
The Globe Oil and Refining
    Company

J. R. Parten
President
Premier Oil Refining Company
    of Texas

William T. Payne
President
American Association of Oil Well
    Drilling Contractors

J. Howard Pew
President
Sun Oil Company

Joseph E. Pogue
Vice President
Chase National Bank

Frank M. Porter
President
Mid Continent Oil & Gas
    Association

H. Jackson Porter
Independent Oil Producer
Houston, Texas

E. E. Pyles
Independent Oil Producer
Los Angeles, California

Edwin B. Reeser
President
Barnsdall Oil Company

Walter R. Reitz
President
Quaker State Oil Refining
    Company

Maurice H. Robineau
President
The Frontier Refining Company

William S. S. Rodgers
Chairman of the Board
The Texas Company

Charles F. Roeser
President
Roeser and Pendleton, Inc.

Arch H. Rowan
Chairman of the Board
Rowan Drilling Company

G. L. Rowsey
President
Gulf Coast Refiners Association

Richard S. Shannon
President
Pioneer Oil Corporation

Harry F. Sinclair
President
Sinclair Oil Corporation

William G. Skelly
President
Skelly Oil Company

Ferd J. Spang
President
Petroleum Equipment Suppliers
  Association

Reese H. Taylor
President
Union Oil Company of California

Hugh L. Thatcher
Chairman
National Council of Independent
  Petroleum Associations

R. G. A. Van der Woude
President
Shell Union Oil Corporation

W. W. Vandeveer
Allied Oil Corporation

Grady H. Vaughn
President
G. H. Vaughn Producing Company

Eric V. Weber
President
The Ohio Petroleum Marketers
  Association

William C. Whaley
President
Oil Producers Agency of California

Harry C. Wiess
President
Humble Oil & Refining Company

Robert E. Wilson
Chairman of the Board
Standard Oil Company (Indiana)

Ralph T. Zook
President
The Sloan and Zook Company

APPENDIX E

National Petroleum Council Membership, 2000–2001

Jacob Adams
President
Arctic Slope Regional Corporation

Robert O. Agbede
President and Chief Executive
    Officer
Advanced Technology Systems, Inc.

George A. Alcorn
President
Alcorn Exploration, Inc.

Benjamin B. Alexander
President
Dasco Energy Corporation

Conrad K. Allen
Vice President
National Association of Black
    Geologists and Geophysicists

Robert J. Allison, Jr.
Chairman and Chief Executive
    Officer

Anadarko Petroleum Corporation
Robert O. Anderson
Roswell, New Mexico

Philip F. Anschutz
President
The Anschutz Corporation

Gregory L. Armstrong
Chairman and Chief Executive
    Officer
Plains All American

Robert G. Armstrong President
Armstrong Energy Corporation

Ralph E. Bailey
Chairman and Chief Executive
    Officer
Xpronet, Inc.

D. Euan Baird
Chairman, President and
    Chief Executive Officer
Schlumberger Limited

William J. Barrett
Chairman and Chief Executive
    Officer
Barrett Resources Corporation

Gonzalo Barrientos
State Senator
Senate of the State of Texas

Michael L. Beatty
Michael L. Beatty & Associates

Riley P. Bechtel
Chairman and Chief Executive
    Officer
Bechtel Group, Inc.

David W. Biegler
President and Chief Operating
    Officer
TXU

M. Frank Bishop
Executive Director
National Association of State
    Energy Officials

Carl E. Bolch, Jr.
Chairman and Chief Executive
    Officer
Racetrac Petroleum, Inc.

John F. Bookout
Houston, Texas

Charles T. Bryan
President and Chief Executive
    Officer
DeGolyer and MacNaughton, Inc.

Carl Burhanan
President
Oasis Aviation, Inc.

Victor A. Burk
Managing Partner
Global Energy & Utilities
Arthur Andersen, L.L.P.

Frank M. Burke, Jr.
Chairman and Chief Executive
    Officer
Burke, Mayborn Company, Ltd.

Charles William Burton
Partner
Jones, Day, Reavis & Pogue

Karl R. Butler
President and Chief Executive
    Officer
ICC Energy Corporation

George Campbell, Jr.
President
The Cooper Union for the
    Advancement of Science and Art

Philip J. Carroll
Chairman and Chief Executive
    Officer
Fluor Corporation

R. D. Cash
Chairman and Chief Executive
    Officer
Questar Corporation

Robert B. Catell
Chairman and Chief Executive
    Officer
KeySpan

Clarence P. Cazalot, Jr.
President
Marathon Oil Company

Paul W. Chellgren
Chairman of the Board and Chief
    Exceutive Officer
Ashland, Inc.

Danny H. Conklin
Partner
Philcon Development Company

Luke R. Corbett
Chairman and Chief Executive
    Officer
Kerr-McGee Corporation

Michael B. Coulson
President
Coulson Oil Company

Gregory L. Craig
President
Cook Inlet Energy Supply

Hector J. Cuellar
Managing Director
Area/Industries Manager
Bank of America

William A. Custard
President and Chief Executive
    Officer
Dallas Production, Inc.

Robert Darbelnet
President and Chief Executive
    Officer
AAA

Claiborne P. Deming
President and Chief Executive
    Officer
Murphy Oil Corporation

Cortlandt S. Dietler
President and Chief Executive
    Officer
TransMontaigne Oil Company

David F. Dorn
Chairman Emeritus
Forest Oil Corporation

John G. Drosdick
Chairman, President, and
    Chief Executive Officer
Sunoco, Inc.

Archie W. Dunham
Chairman, President, and
    Chief Executive Officer
Conoco, Inc.

W. Byron Dunn
President and Chief Executive
    Officer
Lone Star Steel Company

Daniel C. Eckermann
President and Chief Executive
    Officer
LeTourneau, Inc.

James W. Emison
Chairman and Chief Executive
    Officer
Western Petroleum Company

Ronald A. Erickson
Chief Executive Officer
Holiday Companies

Sheldon R. Erikson
Chairman of the Board, President
    and Chief Executive Officer
Cooper Cameron Corporation

John G. Farbes
President
Big Lake Corporation

Thomas L. Fisher
Chairman, President, and
    Chief Executive Officer
Nicor, Inc.

William L. Fisher
Leonidas T. Barrow Chair in
    Mineral Resources
Department of Geological Sciences
University of Texas at Austin

James C. Flores
Chairman, President and Chief
    Executive Officer
Sable Minerals, Inc.

Douglas L. Foshee
Executive Vice President and Chief
    Financial Officer
Halliburton Company

Joe B. Foster
Nonexecutive Chairman
Newfield Exploration Company

Robert W. Fri
Director
The National Museum of Natural
    History
Smithsonian Institution

J. E. Gallegos
Attorney
Energy & Environmental Law
Gallegos Law Firm

Jean Gaulin
Chairman, President and Chief
    Executive Officer
Ultramar Diamond Shamrock
    Corporation

Murry S. Gerber
President and Chief Executive
    Officer
Equitable Resources

James A. Gibbs
President
Five States Energy Company

Rufus D. Gladney
Chairman
American Association of Blacks in
    Energy

Bruce C. Gottwald
Chairman of the Board
Ethyl Corporation

S. Diane Graham
Chairman and Chief Executive
    Officer
STRATCO, Inc.

Frederic C. Hamilton
Chairman
The Hamilton Companies

Christine Hansen
Executive Director
Interstate Oil and Gas
    Compact Commission

Michael F. Harness
President
Osyka Corporation

Angela E. Harrison
Chairman and Chief Executive
    Officer
WELSCO, Inc.

Timothy C. Headington
President/Owner
Headington Oil Company

John B. Hess
Chairman, President and
    Chief Executive Officer
Amerada Hess Corporation

Jack D. Hightower
Chairman of the Board, President,
    and Chief Executive Officer
Pure Resources, Inc.

Jerry V. Hoffman
Chairman, President, and Chief
    Executive Officer
Berry Petroleum Company

R. Earl Holding
President and Chief Executive
    Officer
Sinclair Oil Corporation

Roy M. Huffington
Chairman of the Board and
    Chief Executive Officer
Roy M. Huffington, Inc.

Ray L. Hunt
Chairman of the Board
Hunt Oil Company

James M. Hutchison
President
HUTCO, Inc.

Frank J. Iarossi
Chairman and Chief Executive
    Officer
American Bureau of Shipping &
Affiliated Companies

Eugene M. Isenberg
Chairman and Chief Executive
    Officer
Nabors Industries, Inc.

A. V. Jones, Jr.
Chairman
Van Operating, Ltd.

Jon Rex Jones
Chairman
EnerVest Management Company,
    L.C.

Jerry D. Jordan
President
Jordan Energy, Inc.

Fred C. Julander
President
Julander Energy Company

Bernard J. Kennedy
Chairman and Chief Executive
    Officer
National Fuel Gas Company

Richard D. Kinder
Chairman and Chief Executive
    Officer
Kinder Morgan Energy Partners, L.P.

Harold M. Korell
President and Chief Executive
    Officer
Southwestern Energy Company

Fred Krupp
Executive Director
Environmental Defense Fund

Susan M. Landon
Petroleum Geologist

Kenneth L. Lay
Chairman and Chief Executive
    Officer
Enron Corporation

Stephen D. Layton
President
E&B Natural Resources

Virginia B. Lazenby
Chairman and Chief Executive
    Officer
Bretagne G.P.

Lila Leathers
President and Chief Executive
    Officer
Leathers Oil Company

David L. Lemmon
President and Chief Executive
    Officer
Colonial Pipeline Company

David J. Lesar
Chairman of the Board, President,
    and Chief Executive Officer
Halliburton Company

John H. Lichtblau
Chairman and Chief Executive
    Officer
Petroleum Industry Research
    Foundation, Inc.

Daniel H. Lopez
President
New Mexico Institute of
    Mining and Technology

Thomas E. Love
Chairman and Chief Executive
     Officer
Love's Country Stores, Inc.

William D. McCabe
Vice President Energy Resources
ThermoEnergy Corporation

Ferrell P. McClean
Managing Director
J. P. Morgan Securities, Inc.

S. Todd Maclin
Managing Director and Global Oil
     & Gas Group Executive
J. P. Morgan Securities, Inc.

Cary M. Maguire
President
Maguire Oil Company

Robert A. Malone
Regional President for the Western
     United States
BP P.L.C.

Timothy M. Marquez
President and Chief Executive Officer
Venoco, Inc.

Frederick R. Mayer
Chairman
Captiva Resources, Inc.

F. H. Merelli
Chairman and Chief Executive
     Officer
Key Production Company, Inc.

C. John Miller
Chief Executive Officer
Miller Energy, Inc.

Steven L. Miller
Chairman, President, and Chief
     Executive Officer
Shell Oil Company

Claudie D. Minor, Jr.
President and Chief Executive
     Officer
Premier Energy Supply Corporation

George P. Mitchell
Chairman of the Board and
     Chief Executive Officer
Mitchell Energy and Development
     Corporation

Mark E. Monroe
President and Chief Executive
     Officer
Louis Dreyfus Natural Gas

Herman Morris, Jr.
President and Chief Executive
     Officer
Memphis Light, Gas & Water
     Division

Robert A. Mosbacher
Chairman
Mosbacher Energy Company

James J. Mulva
Chairman of the Board and
     Chief Executive Officer
Phillips Petroleum Company

John Thomas Munro
President
Munro Petroleum &
    Terminal Corporation

Mark B. Murphy
President
Strata Production Company

Gary L. Neale
Chairman, President and
    Chief Executive Officer
NiSource Inc.

J. Larry Nichols
Chairman of the Board, President,
    and Chief Executive Officer
Devon Energy Corporation

René O. Oliveira
State Representative
House of Representatives of the
    State of Texas

David J. O'Reilly
Chairman of the Board and
    Chief Executive Officer
ChevronTexaco Corporation

C. R. Palmer
Chairman of the Board, President,
    and Chief Executive Officer
Rowan Companies, Inc.

Mark G. Papa
Chairman and Chief Executive
    Officer
EOG Resources, Inc.

Paul H. Parker
Vice President
Center for Resource Management

Robert L. Parker, Sr.
Chairman of the Board
Parker Drilling Company

Emil Peña
President and Chief Executive
    Officer
Generation Power, Inc.

L. Frank Pitts
Owner
Pitts Energy Group

Richard B. Priory
Chairman, President and Chief
    Executive Officer
Duke Energy Corporation

Caroline Quinn
President
Farrar Oil Company

Edward B. Rasmuson
Former Chairman of the Board and
    Chief Executive Officer
National Bank of Alaska

Lee R. Raymond
Chairman, President, and
    Chief Executive Officer
Exxon Mobil Corporation

John G. Rice
President and Chief Executive Officer
GE Power Systems

Corbin J. Robertson, Jr.
President
Quintana Minerals Corporation

Robert E. Rose
Chairman, President, and
    Chief Executive Officer
Global Marine, Inc.

Henry A. Rosenberg, Jr.
Chairman of the Board
Crown Central Petroleum
    Corporation

A. R. Sanchez, Jr.
Chairman of the Board and
    Chief Executive Officer
Sanchez-O'Brien Oil and Gas
    Corporation

Robert Santistevan
Director
Southern Ute Indian Tribe
    Growth Fund

S. Scott Sewell
President
Delta Energy Management, Inc.

Bobby S. Shackouls
Chairman, President, and
    Chief Executive Officer
Burlington Resources, Inc.

Donald M. Simmons
Muskogee, Oklahoma

Matthew R. Simmons
President
Simmons and Company Interna-
    tional

Arlie M. Skov
President
Arlie M. Skov, Inc.

Arthur L. Smith
Chairman
John S. Herold, Inc.

Bruce A. Smith
Chairman, President, and
    Chief Executive Officer
Tesoro Petroleum Corporation

Joel V. Staff
Chairman and Chief Executive
    Officer
National-Oilwell, Inc.

Charles C. Stephenson, Jr.
Chairman of the Board
Vintage Petroleum, Inc.

James H. Stone
Chairman of the Board
Stone Energy Corporation

Carroll W. Suggs
Metairie, Louisiana

Patrick F. Taylor
Chairman and Chief Executive
    Officer
Taylor Energy Company

Richard E. Terry
Chairman and Chief Executive
  Officer
Peoples Energy Corporation

Gerald Torres
Associate Dean for Academic
  Affairs
University of Texas School of Law,
and Vice Provost,
University of Texas at Austin

H. A. True III
Partner
True Oil Company

Randy E. Velarde
President
The Plaza Group

Thurman Velarde
Administrator
Oil and Gas Administration
Jicarilla Apache Tribe

Philip K. Verleger, Jr.
PKVerleger, L.L.C.

Joseph C. Walter III
President
Walter Oil & Gas Corporation

L. O. Ward
Owner-President
Ward Petroleum Corporation

C. L. Watson
Chairman of the Board and
  Chief Executive Officer
Dynegy, Inc.

Michael E. Wiley
Chairman, President, and
  Chief Executive Officer
Baker Hughes, Inc.

Bruce W. Wilkinson
Chairman of the Board and
  Chief Executive Officer
McDermott International, Inc.

Mary Jane Wilson
President and Chief Executive
  Officer
WZI, Inc.

Irene S. Wischer
President and Chief Executive
  Officer
Panhandle Producing Company

Brion G. Wise
Chairman and Chief Executive
  Officer
Western Gas Resources, Inc.

William A. Wise
Chairman, President and
  Chief Executive Officer
El Paso Corporation

George M. Yates
President and Chief Executive
    Officer
Harvey E. Yates Company

John A. Yates
President
Yates Petroleum Corporation

Daniel H. Yergin
President
Cambridge Energy Research
    Associates

Henry Zarrow
Vice Chairman
Sooner Pipe & Supply Corporation

Biographies of National Petroleum Council Leaders

Walter S. Hallanan

JUNE 18, 1949, TO JULY 17, 1962

Walter Simms Hallanan, son of a country doctor, was born in Huntington, West Virginia, on April 28, 1890. He attended Morris-Harvey College. At the age of seventeen, he became a cub reporter on the *Huntington Herald.* Two years later he was managing editor of that newspaper, a position he held until 1913, when he became secretary to Gov. H. D. Hatfield of West Virginia.

In 1917, at the close of Governor Hatfield's term, he was appointed state tax commissioner. At the conclusion of his six-year tenure in that office, he became identified with the oil and gas industry.

In 1923, he and others organized Plymouth Oil Company in Charleston, West Virginia. He was elected the first president and served continuously in that capacity for thirty-seven years as Plymouth grew into one of the larger and more successful independent integrated oil companies in the country.

Walter Hallanan's interest in politics and public affairs did not cease with his entry into the oil business. He was elected to the West Virginia state senate in 1926, and in 1928 he was elected West Virginia's member of the Republican National Committee, a post he held until his death. He was chairman of the Committee on Arrangements for the Republican national conventions of 1948 and 1952, and he presided at the 1952 Republican national convention that nominated Dwight D. Eisenhower for president.

During World War II, Hallanan served on the Petroleum Industry War Council, and when its peacetime successor, the National Petroleum Council, was established in 1946, he was elected its first chairman. He was reelected to that post fifteen consecutive times, resigning on July 17, 1962, for health reasons before passing away on December 28, 1962, after a long illness.

R. Gwin Follis
JULY 17, 1962, TO JULY 28, 1964
(ACTING CHAIRMAN FROM JULY 17 TO
OCTOBER 4, 1962)
R. Gwin Follis joined Chevron in 1924 after earning a bachelor of science degree in physics and geology from Princeton University. He began his career with Chevron Corporation in the refining organization, eventually becoming general manager of the group in 1940. Follis was elected president and director of Chevron in 1945. In 1948, he was elected vice chairman of the board, and in 1950, he became chairman. Under his leadership, Chevron expanded from a predominantly western U.S.-based company to the ninth-largest U.S. corporation, based on total assets at the time, and company earnings more than doubled. For more than two decades, he was associated with the management of Chevron's widespread foreign activities and traveled in that capacity, particularly in the Middle East, where he worked in Saudi Arabia, Iran, and Bahrain.

Follis was one of the founders of the National Petroleum Council. He also served as a director of the American Petroleum Institute and was chairman of the National Industrial Conference Board.

Follis had a long history of civic and community service. He was instrumental in bringing the Avery Brundage Oriental art collection to San Francisco and was a trustee of the Asian Art Museum. In addition, he was a former director of the First National City Bank, Crocker National Bank, Stanford Research Institute, The Asia Foundation, The San Francisco Palace of Fine Arts League, and the San Francisco Opera Association. He was a trustee of Princeton University, American University of Beirut, the M. H. De Young Memorial Museum, Grace Cathedral, Children's Hospital, and the San Francisco Art Institute.

Jake L. Hamon
JULY 28, 1964, TO JULY 19, 1966
Jake Louis Hamon, Jr., was born in 1902,
in the town of Lawton, part of the Terri-
tory of Oklahoma. His father was one of
the first to obtain substantial oil leases in
the fast-developing field near Healdtown,
Oklahoma, and he achieved great success
as an oil entrepreneur and a builder of
railroads. When Jake, Sr., died in 1920,
however, his estate was insolvent and Jake,
Jr., became his family's sole support.

Hamon was seventeen years old when he went to work in the Ranger oil
field. Working on wells during the day, he spent his nights studying deeds
and leases and potential oil lands. At the age of eighteen he was already
selling and buying oil leases. Meanwhile, he was working his way up in the
Sturm Drilling Company; by 1924 he owned a quarter interest, which he
sold for funds to go into partnership with a veteran Oklahoma oilman,
Edwin B. Cox, in buying up a group of small producing wells in the Ranger
field. Cox and Hamon reworked the wells, substantially increasing production and giving the partnership enough capital to expand their leasing and
oil-hunting activities. The Cox-Hamon partnership lasted for more than
twenty years.

Eventually, Hamon went into business on his own. Drilling wells in Texas,
Oklahoma, Louisiana, Arkansas, and New Mexico, he became one of the
nation's most successful oil producers. While running a successful business,
he also held dozens of top-level positions in a variety of oil industry organizations, including the chairmanship of the American Petroleum Institute's board
of directors. During World War II, he was a member of the Petroleum Industry War Council, and in 1946 he was appointed as one of the original members of the National Petroleum Council, which grew out of the PIWC. From
1964 to 1966, he was chairman of the National Petroleum Council, and he
continued as a council member through 1981.

He devoted much time to civic activities in his adopted hometown of
Dallas. He was a member of the Athletic Commission and was a director of
the Dallas Civic Opera, Art Museum, Cotton Bowl, Chamber of Commerce,
Friends of the Public Library, and the Dallas Citizens Council. He died on
May 3, 1985.

James C. Donnell II
JULY 19, 1966, TO JULY 9, 1968
James C. Donnell II was born in Findlay, Ohio, on June 30, 1910. He attended the Findlay public schools and graduated from Princeton University with a bachelor of arts degree in 1932. After graduation Donnell began his permanent employment with Marathon Oil Company. He was elected a director in 1936 and a vice president the following year. In May, 1948, he was elected president of the company, a position he held until November, 1972, when he was elected chairman of the board. He retired as board chairman and chief executive officer on July 1, 1975.

Under Donnell's leadership, Marathon made its first significant moves into international petroleum exploration and production. The company also maintained its commitment to a strong foundation of petroleum reserves and facilities in the United States. Most notably, the company began exploration in Alaska that resulted in successful development of production along the Kenai Peninsula and in Cook Inlet. In addition, Donnell oversaw the establishment of Marathon's research organization and the Denver Research Center, fostered the company's early entry into corporate aviation, and greatly expanded the company's refining capability.

Donnell also took an active part in a number of industry organizations. He was first elected to the board of directors of the American Petroleum Institute in 1945 and to the executive committee in 1948. He received the institute's Gold Medal for distinguished achievement in 1977. He was also a member of the National Petroleum Council for more than twenty-seven years, as well as a member of various oil and gas associations.

In 1947, at age thirty-seven, he was elected chairman of the National Board of the YMCA. In 1955 he was named president of the National Council, and at the YMCA World Conference in Paris in that year, he was elected vice president of the World Alliance. After holding that position until 1965, he was elected president of the World Alliance of YMCAs and served in that capacity for a four-year term. He was also a trustee of Princeton University from 1965 to 1969.

Jack H. Abernathy
JULY 9, 1968, TO JULY 17, 1970
Jack Harvey Abernathy was born on June 10, 1911, in Shawnee, Oklahoma. He died on October 26, 1996. He attended the University of Oklahoma, where he received a bachelor of science degree as a member of the first graduating class in petroleum engineering in 1932. After graduation he spent the following fifty-six years of his life as an active participant in the oil and gas industry.

Abernathy was employed by Big Chief Drilling Company for thirty-seven years, first as vice president and later as president and chairman of the board. He also was a former chief engineer and production superintendent for Sunray Oil Company; chief engineer of the Oklahoma City Wilcox Pool Association; president, Seneca Oil Company; vice chairman, Entex, Inc., Houston, Texas; vice chairman, General Producing Company, Houston, Texas; and chairman and founder, Post Oak Oil Company. He was chairman of the board of Southwestern Bank and Trust Company until his death.

Abernathy believed in the petroleum industry and worked tirelessly on its behalf. A reflection of this belief was his involvement as a director of the following organizations: Mid-Continent Oil and Gas Association, National Petroleum Council, American Petroleum Institute, Independent Petroleum Association of America, Oklahoma Independent Petroleum Association, United States Chamber of Commerce, Oklahoma City Chamber of Commerce, Oklahoma State Chamber of Commerce, Oklahoma State Board of Registration for Professional Engineers, Governor's Council for Petroleum Development, and International Association of Drilling Contractors. Abernathy was recognized for his contributions to Oklahoma and the oil and gas industry with his induction into the Oklahoma Hall of Fame in 1971. He was further recognized for his contributions when he was named Oklahoma Petroleum Council Oil Man of the Year in 1978. He was a member of the All-American Wildcatters and also was inducted into the National Petroleum Hall of Fame.

E. Del Brockett

JULY 17, 1970, TO DECEMBER 31, 1971

E. Del Brockett was born in Itasca, Texas, on April 16, 1913, and grew up in Fort Worth. He graduated from Texas A&M College in 1934. He joined Gulf Oil Corporation as a "roustabout" in the McElroy area of West Texas in 1934. His Gulf Oil career was interrupted in 1940 by World War II, during which he saw service in the Pacific theater of operations. He returned to Gulf as an engineer and rose to the position of staff engineer in the production department at the Pittsburgh general office. Transferred to Caracas, Venezuela, late in 1952, he served first as assistant to the president of Mene Grande Oil Company (a wholly owned Gulf subsidiary) and later as district manager in eastern Venezuela.

Brockett returned to the United States in January of 1955 as vice president of Gulf Oil Corporation and Gulf Refining Company, in charge of the Houston production division. Two years later, he became administrative vice president for the production department in the Pittsburgh executive offices.

Brockett became president and chief executive officer of the British American Oil Company Limited (which has since become Gulf Oil Canada Limited) in April of 1958. He returned to Gulf in Pittsburgh as executive vice president on January 1, 1960. Shortly afterward, he was elected to the board and made a member of the executive committee.

He became president of Gulf Oil Corporation on October 25, 1960, and held this office until he became chairman of the board and chief executive officer in January, 1965. He continued in this capacity until his early retirement, at age fifty-eight, on December 31, 1971.

H. A. (Dave) True, Jr.
JANUARY 1, 1972, TO
SEPTEMBER 10, 1974
(ACTING CHAIRMAN FROM JANUARY 1
TO FEBRUARY 10, 1972)

Henry Alfonso (Dave) True, Jr., was born on June 12, 1915, in Cheyenne, Wyoming. He died on June 4, 1994. True received a bachelor of science degree in industrial engineering from Montana State College in 1937. After graduating, he started his career in the oil business with a job as a roustabout for the Texas Company. Over the course of his career, Dave True was oil producer, drilling contractor, rancher, and banker.

After working for a decade at the Texas Company, True worked in a variety of independent companies in and around Wyoming. He remained a partner in True Drilling Company until his death, and he also became involved with companies active in ranching, pipelines, oil services, banking, and geothermal drilling.

John E. Swearingen
SEPTEMBER 10, 1974, TO
DECEMBER 9, 1976

John E. Swearingen retired as chairman of the board of directors of Standard Oil Company (Indiana), now Amoco Corporation, in 1983, after forty-four years service. He became chairman in 1965, after having served as president since 1958, as chief executive officer since 1960, and as a director since 1952. Under his leadership, Amoco maintained its traditional strength in the domestic petroleum industry while also expanding aggressively into international production and chemicals.

In 1984, John E. Swearingen was elected chairman of the board of directors and chief executive officer of Continental Illinois Corporation. Mr. Swearingen retired as an officer of the corporation in 1987, and as a director in 1989.

A native of Columbia, South Carolina, Swearingen graduated in 1938 from the University of South Carolina with a bachelor of science degree in chemical engineering. He received his master of science degree in 1939 from Carnegie-Mellon University. He is a member of the National Academy of Engineering, the Business Hall of Fame, and a fellow of the American Institute of Chemical Engineers. He has been decorated by the governments of Egypt, Italy, and Iran.

Swearingen served as chairman of the National Petroleum Council in 1974 and 1975 and as chairman of the board of the American Petroleum Institute in 1978 and 1979. He has been a director of Organization Resources Counselors, Inc., McGraw Wildlife Foundation, Aon Corporation, Lockheed Corporation, Sara Lee Corporation, Gulfstream Aerospace Corporation, Chase Manhattan Corporation, First Chicago Corporation, and American National Bank and Trust Company of Chicago, and as a trustee of DePauw University.

He is a life trustee of Carnegie-Mellon University and Northwestern Memorial Hospital and a former chairman and member of the board of directors of the Boys and Girls Clubs of Chicago.

Collis P. Chandler, Jr.

DECEMBER 9, 1976 TO MARCH 8, 1979

Collis Paul Chandler, Jr., was born in Tulsa, Oklahoma, in 1926. After serving in the U.S. Navy during World War II, he graduated from Purdue University with a bachelor of science degree in mechanical engineering in 1948. Following graduation, he joined Sohio Petroleum Company, working in Louisiana and Kansas. In 1954, he founded the first of the Chandler Companies—Chandler-Simpson, Inc., in Denver, Colorado. Until his death, he chaired the Chandler Company and its subsidiaries, Chandler-Simpson, Inc., Chandler & Associates, Inc., and Chandler Drilling Corporation. His companies have drilled more than twelve hundred test wells, resulting in oil or gas discoveries or significant field extensions that number more than one hundred.

In addition to his own business interests, Chandler was active on behalf of the nation's petroleum industry. He was a past chairman of the National Petroleum Council (1976–79), having become a member in 1965. Chandler was also a past chairman and a charter member of the Natural Gas Supply Association. He also served as president of the Rocky Mountain Oil and Gas Association from 1965 to 1967 and became a member of its executive committee in 1962. Moreover, he was active in a number of other petroleum industry groups, including the Independent Petroleum Association of America, as a former director of the Gas Research Institute, the American Association of Professional Landmen, the Rocky Mountain Association of Geologists, and the Society of Petroleum Engineers of AIME.

Chandler built an impressive record of leadership in the American Petroleum Institute and the National Petroleum Council. He received the secretary of energy's Distinguished Service Medal in 1979, the American Petroleum Institute's highest award—the Gold Medal for Distinguished Achievement— in 1994, the Texas Mid-Continent Oil & Gas Association Independent of the Year Award; the Rocky Mountain Oil & Gas Association Life Membership Award; the American Association of Petroleum Landmen's Distinguished Service Award, and the Betty McWhorter Memorial Commendation of Honor from the Denver Desk & Derrick Club.

His business activities outside of the petroleum industry included membership on the board of directors of the Public Service Company of Colorado and the Colorado National Bank. Education was also a major interest of Chandler. He gave generously of his time and talents to his alma mater Purdue University, serving as a past president of the Purdue Alumni Association and as a member of its board of directors. He also served on the board of governors of the Purdue Foundation.

Charles H. Murphy, Jr.
MARCH 8, 1979, TO APRIL 16, 1981
Charles Murphy became head of the Murphy family enterprise (Murphy Oil Corporation) of necessity when he was twenty-one. He worked for five decades, save for a respite in the infantry in World War II, to build a regional producing operation into a multinational integrated oil company. In October, 1994, he retired as chairman of the board of Murphy Oil Corporation. He still serves as a board member.

Murphy served seventeen years on the Arkansas Board of Higher Education and ten years as a trustee of Hendrix College. He established the Murphy

Institute of Political Economy at Tulane, and he served as a trustee of the Ochsner Medical Institutions. He served six years as a director of the Smithsonian Institution. He received a citation for outstanding service in natural resource management from the National Wildlife Federation.

John F. Bookout
APRIL 16, 1981, TO MAY 19, 1983
Born in Shreveport, Louisiana, John F. Bookout graduated from the University of Texas with bachelor of science and master of arts degrees in geology. He also holds honorary degrees of doctor of science from Tulane University and doctor of law from Centenary College. He received the 1981 Distinguished Alumnus Award from the University of Texas and the 1985 Distinguished Graduate Award from the University of Texas Geology Foundation.

Bookout served as president and chief executive officer of Shell Oil Company from May, 1976, through June, 1988. He joined Shell Oil in 1950 as a geologist in the Tulsa, Oklahoma, area and served in positions of increasing responsibility throughout his career with Shell. He was a member of the supervisory board of Royal Dutch Petroleum Company and served on the board and executive committee of Shell Petroleum, Inc., from 1988 to 1993.

After retiring from Shell, Bookout served as chairman, president, and chief executive officer of Kelley Oil & Gas Corporation, an independent oil and gas producer.

Bookout is on the board of directors of McDermott International Inc.; J. Ray McDermott, S.A., Corporate Partners; and the Texas Medical Center. He is also chairman of the board of directors of Methodist Hospital System of Houston, a member of the advisory board for The Investment Company of America, and a member of the board of trustees for the United States Council for International Business. He is also a member of the Council on Foreign Relations, Inc., and the Conference Board. He is a lifetime member of the 1001 World Wildlife Fund and a past chairman of the American Petroleum Institute.

In 1990 he received the American Association of Petroleum Geologists' award for "excellence in Exploration Leadership" and the American Petroleum Institute's Gold Medal for Distinguished Achievement. He also received the 1979 Distinguished Service Award from the National Association of Secondary School Principals for his significant contributions and outstanding service to American education. He is a member of the Southern Regional Advisory Board for the Institute of International Education, Inc., the Chancellor's Council of the University of Texas, and the Council of Overseers for the Jesse H. Jones Graduate School of Administration of Rice University. He is an emeritus administrator of the board of administrators of Tulane University.

Bookout received various medals of honor for his service in the Army Air Force during World War II.

Robert A. Mosbacher, Sr.
MAY 19, 1983, TO MAY 22, 1985
Robert Adam Mosbacher, Sr., was born to a family of New York investors on March 11, 1927. He was reared in White Plains, attended Choate as a schoolboy, and received a bachelor of science degree in business administration at Washington & Lee University in 1947. He now resides in Houston, Texas.

In his business career, he served as chairman of Mosbacher Energy Company and Mosbacher Power Company. He was a director of Texas Commerce Bancshares, Enron Corporation, and New York Life Insurance Company. He also served on the board of the American Petroleum Institute and as chairman of the Mid-Continent Oil and Gas Association.

Active in Texas and national politics, he served as secretary of commerce from 1989 to 1992 in the administration of President George Bush.

Ralph E. Bailey
MAY 22, 1985, TO FEBRUARY 24, 1987
Born March 23, 1924, in Indiana, Ralph E. Bailey earned a mechanical engineering degree from Purdue University. He is chairman of the board of American Bailey Corporation, a privately owned investment company. He also served as chairman and chief executive officer of United Meridian Corporation, a public holding company engaged in making equity investments in the oil and gas industry.

Bailey joined Consolidation Coal Company, a wholly owned Conoco subsidiary, in 1965. He was named president in 1974, chief executive officer in 1975, and chairman in 1976. He was named a vice chairman and director of Conoco in 1975 before being named president of the company in 1977, deputy chairman in 1978, and chairman and chief executive officer of Conoco in 1979. He has also served as vice chairman of the board of E. I. du Pont de Nemours and Company.

His directorships include General Signal Corporation, Rowan Companies, Inc., Clean Diesel Technologies Inc., the American Petroleum Institute, the American Mining Congress, the National Forest Foundation, the World Rehabilitation Fund, Inc., and the International Executive Service Corps.

He is a member of the advisory council of J. P. Morgan and Company, Inc., and Morgan Guaranty Trust Company of New York, as well as the president's council of Purdue University.

Edwin L. Cox
FEBRUARY 24, 1987, TO
APRIL 18, 1989
Edwin Lochridge Cox was born October 20, 1921, in Mena, Arkansas. He graduated from Ardmore High School, Ardmore, Oklahoma, in 1938, attended Southern Methodist University from 1938 to 1940, received a bachelor of business administration degree from the University of Texas in 1942, and earned industrial administrator and master of

business administration degrees from Harvard Business School in 1943 and 1946. He was in the U.S. Navy from 1943 to 1946 and was honorably discharged with the rank of lieutenant, USNR.

Cox has built his own independent company, Edwin L. Cox Company (oil and gas, venture capital), which is based in Dallas, Texas.

He is active in the affairs of the Library of Congress, where he has served as vice chairman of James Madison Council and chairman of James Madison Council Steering Committee. Cox is a member of the Library of Congress Trust Fund; the National Gallery of Art; Southern Methodist University, where he has been a member of Trustees Council; the University of Texas M. D. Anderson Cancer Center, where he is a life member of the board of visitors; and the Hoover Institution on War, Revolution & Peace at Stanford University, where he serves on the board of governors.

Lodwrick M. Cook

APRIL 18, 1989, TO JUNE 5, 1991

Lodwrick (Lod) Monroe Cook was born in Castor, Louisiana, on June 17, 1928, and raised in Grand Cane, Louisiana. He received bachelor of science degrees in mathematics and petroleum engineering at Louisiana State University in 1950 and 1955, the latter coming after a tour of duty in the U.S. Army. Later, while working, he finished an evening MBA program at Southern Methodist University.

He began his career with ARCO in 1956 as an engineer trainee. He went on to hold management positions in labor relations, refining/marketing, planning, supply, and transportation. Elected a corporate vice president in 1970, he advanced through the executive positions of senior vice president, executive vice president, and chief operating officer–products. While president of ARCO Transportation Company, he served as chairman of the owners' committee of the Trans Alaska Pipeline System.

Cook has been a member of ARCO's board of directors since 1980. He became president and chief executive officer in October, 1985, and chairman of the board of directors and chief executive officer in January, 1986, retiring as chief executive officer on June 30, 1994. He retired as ARCO's chairman on June 30, 1995, and became chairman emeritus.

Cook's interests outside the company focus upon education, youth, and minority programs. He has had a long association with Junior Achievement and served on the national JA board of directors, of which he also was a past chairman; he now serves on the local Southern California board of governors and is director emeritus of National Junior Achievement. His other national and international volunteer work includes serving as a trustee of the George Bush Presidential Library Foundation, member of the board of advisors of the Carter Center of Emory University, director of the LSU Alumni Association, and member of the chancellor's court of benefactors of Oxford University. His California community involvements include serving as chairman of RLA (Rebuild Los Angeles), chairman of the Ronald Reagan Presidential Foundation, and member of the Library Foundation of Los Angeles of which he is founder chairman. In November, 1994, upon appointment by Her Majesty the Queen, Cook was invested by the Prince of Wales with the insignia of Honorary Knight Commander of the Most Excellent Order of the British Empire (KB) for his contribution to Anglo-American relations and support for philanthropic projects around the world.

His business interests include the Business Council, Los Angeles World Affairs Council, and American Petroleum Institute. He is a member of the board of directors of Castle & Cooke, Inc., J. Ray McDermott, S.A., Bank One Louisiana, Greenwich Capital Partners, and South Park Sports Center. He is also a member of the Investment Advisory Committee of Aurora Capital Partners, L.P.

Ray L. Hunt
JUNE 5, 1991, TO JULY 27, 1994
Ray L. Hunt is a Dallas businessman whose association with Hunt Oil Company began in 1958 as a summer employee in the oil fields. He was educated at Southern Methodist University and received a degree in economics in June of 1965. Hunt now serves as chairman of the board, president, and chief executive officer of Hunt Consolidated, Inc., and chairman of the board and CEO of Hunt Oil Company.

Additionally, he serves as a member of the board of directors of Dresser Industries, Inc., Pepsico, Electronic Data Systems Corporation, the Security

Capital Group, ErgoScience, Inc., and the advisory board of Texas Commerce Bank.

Hunt is active in civic affairs in Dallas. From 1987 to 1992 he served as chairman of the board of trustees of Southern Methodist University. He also served for three years as a director of the Dallas Chamber of Commerce and for ten years as a trustee of the Dallas Museum of Art. Hunt currently serves on the board of trustees of the Center for Strategic and International Studies in Washington, D.C., and on the board of directors of both the Texas Research League and the Southwestern Legal Foundation. He is the current chairman of the Texas Medical Resource (a not-for-profit organization whose members consist of the eight largest hospitals in Dallas plus the University of Texas Southwestern Medical Center) and is a member of the executive committee of the Southwestern Medical Foundation in Dallas.

Within the oil and gas industry, Hunt has also been active, as immediate past chairman of the National Petroleum Council in Washington, D.C., and as a member of the board of directors and public policy committee of the American Petroleum Institute. Hunt is a past chairman of the Dallas Wildcat Committee and, in 1988, he was elected an All-American Wildcatter by the national organization of the same name. Hunt is also a past president of the Dallas Petroleum Club.

H. Laurance Fuller
JULY 27, 1994, TO JUNE 21, 1996
H. Laurance Fuller served as chairman of the board and chief executive officer of Amoco Corporation from 1991 to 1998. Joining Amoco in 1961, Fuller had assignments in engineering, law, refining, marketing and supply. After serving a year as executive vice president for Amoco Oil Company, Fuller was named president of the petroleum refining, marketing, and transportation subsidiary in 1978. He was named executive vice president of Amoco Corporation in 1981 and president in 1983.

Fuller received a bachelor of science degree in chemical engineering from Cornell University and a law degree from DePaul University, and he attended the Advanced Management Program at the Harvard Business School.

He served on the board of directors of the Chase Manhattan Corporation, the Chase Manhattan Bank, N.A., Abbott Laboratories, the American Petroleum Institute, Motorola, Catalyst, and the Rehabilitation Institute of Chicago. He is a trustee of Northwestern University, a member of the university council of Cornell University, chairman and trustee of the Chicago Orchestral Association, and a member of the civic committee of the Commercial Club of Chicago.

Dennis R. Hendrix
JUNE 21, 1996, TO JUNE 30, 1997
Dennis Hendrix was born January 8, 1940. He is a graduate of the University of Tennessee, earned a master's degree in business administration from Georgia State University, and is a certified public accountant. After serving as president and chief executive officer of United Foods, Inc., in Memphis (1968–73), he was associated with Touche Ross & Company and Arthur Andersen & Company.

He began his energy industry career in 1973 as assistant to the president of Texas Gas Resources Corporation, Owensboro, Kentucky. Hendrix was elected executive vice president in 1975, president and chief operating officer the following year, chief executive officer in 1978, and board chairman in 1983. Following Texas Gas Resources' acquisition by CSX Corporation in 1984, Hendrix served as vice chairman and a director of CSX and later as executive vice president and a director of the Halliburton Company, Dallas.

Hendrix was chief executive officer of PanEnergy from November, 1990, until April, 1995, when he relinquished that position as part of a management succession plan. Prior to joining PanEnergy, from 1986 until 1989 Hendrix was president and chief executive officer of Texas Eastern Corporation, which he joined as president and a member of the board of directors in 1985.

Hendrix is a director of the Greater Houston Partnership, having served as its chairman for 1995, and he is chairman of the board of M. D. Anderson Cancer Center Outreach Corporation. He is a board member of the Robert A. Welch Foundation, the Texas Medical Center, Baylor College of Medicine, the Children's Assessment Center Foundation, and the Museum of Fine Arts. He is director and former national chairman of Junior Achievement, Inc., and he chaired the 1993 United Way of the Texas Gulf Coast campaign.

He served as a chairman of the Interstate Natural Gas Association of America during 1994. In addition, he is chairman of the board of TEPPCO Partners, L.P., and a board member of TECO Energy, Inc., of Tampa, Florida, and Texas Commerce Bancshares.

Joe B. Foster
JULY 1, 1997, TO DECEMBER 15, 1999
Joe B. Foster was born July 25, 1934, in Arp, Texas. He attended Texas A&M University and graduated in 1957 with a bachelor of science degree in petroleum engineering and a bachelor of business administration degree in general business.

He is the founder and chairman of Newfield. He served with the additional titles of president and chief executive officer from 1989 until he retired from those positions in January, 2000. Prior to founding Newfield, Foster served in various leadership roles with Tenneco, Inc., and its subsidiaries for thirty-one years. He served as chairman of the board of Tenneco Oil Company and chairman of the board of the Tenneco Gas Pipeline Group and was director of Tenneco, Inc.

Most recently, Joe Foster served as the interim chairman, president, and chief executive officer of Baker Hughes Incorporated. Foster also serves on the boards of directors of New Jersey Resources and McDermott International.

Archie W. Dunham
DECEMBER 15, 1999, TO JUNE 16, 2001
Archie W. Dunham was born in 1938, and he earned a bachelor's degree in geological engineering and a master's degree in business administration from the University of Oklahoma.

Dunham is chairman of the board, president, and chief executive officer of Conoco, Inc. He joined Conoco in 1966 as an associate engineer in Houston. For seven years he worked in various positions within the natural gas and gas products department and the corporate new project development group. In 1973, he became manager of the gas products division, followed by an appointment to Harvard University's Management Development Program.

He was elected executive vice president of Douglas Oil Company, a Conoco subsidiary in California, in 1976 and became president of the subsidiary in 1979. He returned to Houston in 1981 as vice president of logistics and downstream planning. In 1983, he was named vice president of transportation, natural gas and gas products. After participating in Stanford University's Senior Executive Management Program, he became executive vice president of petroleum products, North America, in 1985 and was elected to Conoco's board of directors.

In 1987, Dunham transferred to E. I. du Pont de Nemours and Company (Conoco's parent company at the time) as group vice president of the chemicals and pigments sector, in Wilmington, Delaware. He became a senior vice president for DuPont's polymer products business in 1989. While in Wilmington, he was chairman of DuPont's Environmental Leadership Council. Dunham served as an executive vice president of DuPont and a member of DuPont's office of the chief executive from 1996 to 1998.

Archie Dunham returned to Houston in 1992 as Conoco's executive vice president, Exploration Production. He held that position until becoming President and chief executive officer in January 1996. He became chairman of the board in August, 1999.

William A. Wise
JUNE 6, 2001–
William A. Wise earned a bachelor of arts degree from Vanderbilt University, and he received his law degree from the University of Colorado School of Law.

Wise is the chairman of the board of directors, president, and chief executive officer of El Paso Corporation. He has been with the company since 1970, becoming counsel, senior counsel, and principal counsel of the El Paso Company in 1980. He became vice president and assistant general counsel of that company in May, 1982, and general counsel and senior vice president in August, 1983. In January, 1984, he became senior vice president of El Paso Natural Gas Company, and in May 1987 he became executive vice president. Wise became president and chief operating officer in April, 1989, chief executive officer in January, 1990, and chairman in January, 1994, and he assumed the title of chairman, president, and chief executive officer of El Paso Energy Corporation in April, 1996.

Notes

CHAPTER I

1. NPC, *The National Petroleum Council: A Unique Experience in Government-Industry Cooperation: The First Seven Years, 1946–1953* (Washington, D.C., 1961).
2. Richard H. K. Vietor, *Energy Policy in America since 1945: A Study of Business-Government Relations* (New York: Cambridge University Press, 1984), 27, 39; Robert L. Bradley, Jr., *Oil, Gas, and Government: The U.S. Experience,* 2 vols. (New York: Rowman & Littlefield, 1996), 1:234–48. The standard history of the petroleum industry's organization during World War II remains John W. Frey and H. Chandler Ide, eds., *A History of the Petroleum Administration for War* (Washington, D.C.: GPO, 1946).
3. Harry S Truman to Julius A. Krug, May 3, 1946, reproduced in NPC, *National Petroleum Council: A Unique Experience,* 36–37.
4. Chandler Ide, "Ralph K. Davies," in *Ralph K. Davies: As We Knew Him, Biographical Recollections of R. K. D. as Man and Businessman, Contributed by Associates, Friends and Family* (San Francisco: Privately printed, 1976), 14–21.
5. NPC, *National Petroleum Council: A Unique Experience,* 38–39.
6. Ibid., 43.
7. Harold F. Williamson et al., *The American Petroleum Industry: The Age of Energy, 1899–1959* (Evanston, Ill.: Northwestern University Press, 1963), 689–95.
8. The Justice Department briefly redocketed the case in 1946, but then it was modified into separate actions against smaller groups. See Vietor, *Energy Policy in America,* 34–35.
9. See Clark's letter of May 27, 1946, quoted in NPC, *National Petroleum Council: A Unique Experience,* 41.
10. Ibid., 42.
11. Ralph K. Davies, Remarks, June 21, 1946, in NPC, *National Petroleum Council: A Unique Experience,* Appendix B, 5.
12. Vietor, *Energy Policy in America,* 37–40; NPC, *National Petroleum Council: A Unique Experience,* 49.
13. NPC, *National Petroleum Council: A Unique Experience,* 50; Davies, Remarks, June 21, 1946, and J. A. Krug, Remarks, National Petroleum Council, June 21, 1946, both in NPC, *National Petroleum Council: A Unique Experience,* Appendix B, 1–5.
14. Quoted in NPC, *National Petroleum Council: A Unique Experience,* 50–51.
15. After becoming chairman of the NPC, Hallanan served as chair of the Republican National Convention that nominated Dwight Eisenhower for president in 1952.

16. Memorial Resolution for Walter S. Hallanan, Minutes of the NPC, Mar. 22, 1963, pp. 7–12. (All NPC documents and correspondence are located in the Washington, D.C., offices of the NPC [designated "NPC Archives"] unless otherwise specified.)

17. Aside from Hallanan, who served as chairman, the members of the organizing committee were: Paul G. Blazer (chairman of the board, Ashland Oil & Refining Company); J. Frank Drake (president, Gulf Oil Corporation); B. A. Hardy (Shreveport, La.); George A. Hill Jr. (president, Houston Oil Company of Texas); Eugene Holman (president, Standard Oil Company [New Jersey]); W. Alton Jones (president, Cities Service Company); B. L. Majewski (vice president, Deep Rock Oil Corporation); A. C. Mattei (president, Honolulu Oil Corporation); Howard Pew (president, Sun Oil Company); Joseph E. Pogue (vice president, Chase National Bank); A. Jacobsen (president, Amerada Petroleum Corporation); B. Brewster Jennings (president, Socony-Vacuum Oil Company, Inc.); Frank M. Porter (president, Mid-Continent Oil and Gas Association); Charles F. Roeser (president, Roeser and Pendleton, Inc.); and Robert E. Wilson (chairman of the board, Standard Oil Company [Indiana]).

18. NPC, *National Petroleum Council: A Unique Experience*, 51–52. The original members of the Agenda Committee were Hines H. Baker (Humble Oil & Refining Company); William R. Boyd Jr. (American Petroleum Institute); Gordon Duke (Southeastern Oil Companies); W. H. Ferguson; R. G. Follis (Standard Oil of California); Walter S. Hallanan (Plymouth Oil Company); B. A. Hardey (The Hardey Co.); George A. Hill Jr. (committee chairman, Houston Oil Company of Texas); A. Jacobsen (Amerada Petroleum Corporation); J. Howard Marshall (Ashland Oil & Refining Company); and A. C. Mattei (Honolulu Oil Co.).

19. NPC, *National Petroleum Council: A Unique Experience*, 52–54.

20. Members present numbered six, members absent five; see Minutes of the Meeting of the Agenda Committee of the National Petroleum Council (hereafter referred to as Agenda Committee Minutes), Sept. 26, 1946, pp. 1–2, File 1410. A copy of these minutes, compiled chronologically, is among the documents of NPC Archives.

21. NPC, *High Pressure Tank Cars for the Transportation of Liquefied Petroleum Gas* (Washington, D.C., 1946).

22. NPC, *Materials Requirements by the Oil and Gas Industry* (Washington, D.C., June, Nov. 1946).

23. Ralph K. Davies, acting director, Oil and Gas Division (OGD), to Walter S. Hallanan, temporary chairman, NPC, Sept. 26, 1946; Agenda Committee Minutes, Sept. 26, 1946, Dec. 10, 1946; George A. Hill, Jr., chairman, Agenda Committee, to Hallanan (still addressed as temporary chairman, NPC), Jan. 8, 1947; Report of the Agenda Committee to the National Petroleum Council, Jan. 13, 1947, all in NPC Archives.

24. Agenda Committee Minutes, Dec. 10, 1946; NPC, *Military Aircraft Fuels Productive Capacity* (Washington, D.C.: Apr., July, Sept., 1947).

25. The report of that meeting's decisions was dated Jan. 13, 1947.

26. Davies to Hallanan, Sept. 26, 1946; Hill to Hallanan, Jan. 8, 1947; Report of the Agenda Committee to the NPC, Jan. 13, 1947.

27. Report of the Agenda Committee to the NPC, Jan. 20, 1947, p. 3.

28. Ibid.

29. Max W. Ball, director, OGD, to Hallanan, Jan. 14, 1946.

30. Report of the Agenda Committee to the NPC, Jan. 20, 1947, pp. 2–3.

31. Ball to Hallanan, Jan. 14, 1946; Report of the Agenda Committee to the NPC, Jan. 20, 1947, p. 4.

32. Ball to Hallanan, Jan. 14, 1946; Report of the Agenda Committee to the NPC, Jan. 20, 1947, p. 5.

33. Memorial Resolution for Walter S. Hallanan, Minutes of the NPC, Mar. 22, 1963, pp. 7–12. (A copy of these minutes of the meetings of the NPC as a whole are on file in chronological order at the offices of the NPC in Washington, D.C.)

34. Minutes of the NPC, Jan. 21, 1947, p. 1.

35. Minutes of the NPC, Apr. 15, 1948, p. 4; Minutes, Meeting of the NPC, Oct. 21, 1948, p. 8.

36. Minutes of the NPC, Jan. 21, 1947, p. 12.

37. Ibid., p. 13.

38. Record of Agenda Committee Interim Actions on Requests from the Department of the Interior, July 29, 1948; Krug to Hallanan, July 3, 1948, in Report of the Agenda Committee, July 12, 1948.

39. Quoted in Krug to Hallanan, Jan. 7, 1948.

40. Krug to Hallanan, Jan. 7, 1948.

41. Minutes of the NPC, Apr. 15, 1948; Minutes of the NPC, Jan. 13, 1949, pp. 34–35.

42. Report of the NPC Committee on Proposed Petroleum Policy Council, Jan. 26, 1950, p. 11; Ball to Hallanan, Jan. 21, 1948; Hill to Hallanan, Jan. 2, 1948.

43. Minutes of the NPC, Jan. 22, 1948, pp. 16–19.

44. Report of District Five Regional Advisory Committee to the NPC, in Minutes of the NPC, Jan. 21, 1948.

45. Minutes of the NPC, Apr. 15, 1948, pp. 21–22.

46. Report of the NPC Committee on Proposed Petroleum Policy Council, Jan. 26, 1950, pp. 3–4.

47. Minutes of the NPC, Apr. 15, 1948, pp. 21–22.

48. Report of the Agenda Committee, Apr. 25, 1950; Oscar L. Chapman, secretary of the interior, to Hallanan, Jan. 17, 1950.

49. Vietor points out that a natural gas council established under the Defense Production Act was required to adhere to the Department of Justice's (DOJ) suggestions on structure and that the National Bituminous Coal Council, founded in 1948 by Secretary Krug, was dissolved when Chapman refused to provide an exemption from the DOJ rules. See Vietor, *Energy Policy in America,* 42–43.

50. Department of the Interior, Information Service, "Directive to the National Petroleum Council," June 4, 1951; Chapman to McGrath, June 6, 1951; and Hallanan to Chapman, June 8, 1951, all in 1010 Interior Directive 1951 file; "History of Correspondence between the Department of Justice and Department of Interior Relating to the NPC," no date, DOJ Criteria/NPC (COC-Proposed Revision in Structure, 1957–1958) file, both in NPC Archives.

51. "History of Correspondence between the Department of Justice and Department of Interior Relating to the NPC," no date.

52. Ibid.; Memorandum: "Statements of Officials of the Department of Justice Relating to the DOJ's 'Criteria' for Advisory Committees," DOJ/NPC General #1 file, no date, NPC Archives.

53. "History of Correspondence between the Department of Justice and Department of Interior Relating to the NPC," no date; V. M. Brown to J. M. Brown, H.R. 7390 (Amended), June 14, 1957; Hallanan to Brown, June 21, 1957, and Brown to Hallanan, July 10, 1957, both in DOJ/NPC General #1 file, NPC Archives.

54. Fred Seaton to Hallanan, Dec. 9, 1957, DOJ/NPC General #1 file; IRR Bulletin No. 129, Jan. 17, 1958, DOJ Criteria/NPC (NPC-Proposed Revision in Structure 1957–58) file, both in NPC Archives.

55. Hallanan to Seaton, Dec. 16, 1957, and Brown to Hallanan, Apr. 11, 1958, both in DOJ Criteria/NPC (NPC-Proposed Revision in Structure 1957–58) file; President,

Waverly Oil Works Company, to Hallanan, Dec. 19, 1957, DOJ/NPC General #1 file, both in NPC Archives.

56. The committee members' company affiliations were: Hines Baker (Humble Oil); Russell Brown (Independent Petroleum Association of America); Jake Hamon (independent, Dallas); W. Alton Jones (Cities Service); J. Howard Marshall (Signal Oil and Gas Company); J. R. Parten (Woodley Petroleum Company); and J. E. Warren (First National City Bank of New York).

57. "Directive to the National Petroleum Council," no date; Brown to Baker and Marshall, Apr. 9, 1958, both in DOJ Criteria/NPC (NPC-Proposed Revision in Structure, 1957–58) file, NPC Archives.

58. Minutes of the NPC, Jan. 27, 1959; Baker to Jacobsen, Jan. 12, 1959, Agenda Committee file, 1959, NPC Archives.

59. The White House, Memorandum: "Preventing Conflicts of Interest on the Part of Advisers and Consultants to the Government," Feb. 9, 1962, 1010 President Memo re Conflicts 1962 file; "Is NPC Headed for the Shelf?" *Oil & Gas Journal,* July 23, 1962, Clippings File, both in NPC Archives.

60. "Is NPC Headed for the Shelf?" *Oil & Gas Journal,* July 23, 1962; "Conflict of Interest Threat to NPC Scored," *Oil Daily,* July 17, 1962, Clippings File, NPC Archives.

61. The White House, Memorandum: "Preventing Conflicts of Interest on the Part of Advisers and Consultants to the Government," Feb. 9, 1962; John Kelly to R. G. Follis, Standard Oil of California, Aug. 14, 1962, 1010 Interior-Justice Correspondence 1962 file, NPC Archives.62. Executive Order 11007, Prescribing Regulations for the Formation and Use of Advisory Committees, Feb. 26, 1962; Minutes of the Special Committee to Review the By-Laws of the NPC, Mar. 21, 1963, 1010 Committee to Review the By-Laws of the NPC 3/21/63 file, NPC Archives.

63. NPC Press Release, July 18, 1962, 1940 Press Releases 1957–1963 file, NPC Archives.

64. Minutes of the NPC, Oct. 4, 1962.

65. Minutes of the NPC, Mar. 22, 1963.

66. Minutes of the NPC, Mar. 19, 1964, July 28, 1965.

67. Minutes of the NPC, July 28, 1965.

68. "Answers to Interrogatories Directed to Defendants Frank Zarb and the Federal Energy Administration," *Metcalf v. National Petroleum Council,* June 9, 1975, 1100 Metcalf et al. vs. NPC et al. (Suit 1975) file, NPC Archives.

69. "Advisory Committees, Highlights of Congressional Hearings Conducted by the U.S. Senate Subcommittee on Intergovernmental Relations, Committee on Government Operations, Pertaining to the NPC, July 13, 1971," 1100 Metcalf et al. vs. NPC et al. (Suit 1975) file, NPC Archives.

70. Ibid.

71. Henry J. Steck, "Private Influence on Environmental Policy: The Case of the National Industrial Control Council," and Jerry W. Markam, "The Federal Advisory Committee Act," both reprinted in U.S. Congress, Operations, *Energy Advisory Committees,* 94th Cong., 1st sess., pp. 192–284.

72. Steck, "Private Influence on Environmental Policy," 194–201.

73. Department of Interior News Release, "National Petroleum Council Membership Broadened," Jan. 6, 1975; "Advisory Committees, Highlights of the Oversight Hearings before the Subcommittee on Budgeting, Management and Expenditures of the Committee on Government Operations, U.S. Senate, Pertaining to the National Petroleum Council," Dec. 13, 1973, both in NPC Archives; James B. Sullivan, *Public Participation on Federal Energy Advisory Committees* (Washington, D.C.: National Council for the Public Assessment of Technology, 1976), 1–5.

74. Joseph A. Pratt, "The Department of Energy," in *Encyclopedia of American Institutions,* ed. Donald Whitnah (Westport, Conn.: Greenwood Press, 1984).

74. Those attending were Collis P. Chandler, Jr., chairman, NPC; Charles H. Murphy, Jr., vice chairman, NPC; Jack H. Abernathy, Big Chief Drilling Company; Robert O. Anderson, Atlantic Richfield Company; H. J. Haynes, Standard Oil Company of California; Jerry McAfee, Gulf Oil Corporation; Randall Meyer, Exxon Company; C. John Miller, Miller Brothers; Kenneth E. Montague, General Crude Oil Company; Charles E. Spahr, Standard Oil Company (Ohio); and John E. Swearingen, Standard Oil Company (Indiana). Invited but not attending were Harold E. Berg, Getty Oil Company; John A. Carver, Jr., University of Denver; R. L. O'Shields, Panhandle Eastern Pipe Line Company; and Elvis J. Stahr, National Audubon Society.

75. "Plan of Action for Meeting with James R. Schlesinger," Dec. 15, 1977, NPC Archives; Collis Chandler, interview by Joseph A. Pratt, Aug. 29, 1996, Denver, Colo.

76. "DOE Gives NPC New Charter, Cuts Membership to 100," *Platt's Oilgram News,* Jan. 26, 1979, p. 4, Clippings File, NPC Archives; James Schlesinger, interview by Joseph A. Pratt, Sept. 11, 1998, Arlington, Va.

77. Transcript, Jan. 23, 1991, pp. 75–78, 1200 Proceedings Jan. 23, 1991, Meeting file, NPC Archives.

78. "Report to the Secretary of Energy, Findings/Recommendations of the National Petroleum Council's Ad Hoc Committee on Structure and Procedures," Feb. 11, 1992, copy in NPC Archives.

79. Committee members were Ray L. Hunt, chairman, NPC; Collis P. Chandler, Jr., Chandler & Associates, Inc.; Kenneth T. Derr, Chevron Corporation; John R. Hall, Ashland Oil, Inc.; Robert McClements, Jr., Sun Company, Inc.; Frank A. McPherson, Kerr-McGee Corporation; Marshall Nichols, executive director, NPC; Frank H. Richardson, Shell Oil Company; James H. Ross, BP America, Inc.; William D. Stevens, Exxon Company, U.S.A.; and Lodwrick M. Cook, Atlantic Richfield Company (the latter served in an advisory capacity).

80. "Report to the Secretary of Energy, Findings/Recommendations of the National Petroleum Council's Ad Hoc Committee on Structure and Procedures," Feb. 11, 1992.

81. On the thinking behind these changes, see Ray H. Hunt to Collis Chandler et al., June 6, 1991, and Aug. 20, 1991, Finance Committee Files, NPC Archives.

CHAPTER 2

1. Max W. Ball, director, OGD, to Walter Hallanan, temporary chairman, NPC, Jan. 14, 1947, NPC Archives.

2. NPC, *Illinois River Winter Transportation* (Washington, D.C., 1947); *Materials Requirements by the Oil and Gas Industry* (Washington, D.C., Jan., Oct., 1947); *Military Aircraft Fuels Productive Capacity* (Washington, D.C., Apr., July, Sept., 1947); *Military and Government Petroleum Requirements* (Washington, D.C., June, July, Aug., Oct., Nov., 1947).

3. NPC, *Petroleum Tanker Transportation* (Washington, D.C., June, Nov., 1947); Report of the Agenda Committee, Jan. 13, 1947, p. 2.

4. Report of Agenda Committee, Jan. 13, 1947, p. 2.

5. See, for example, NPC, *Military and Government Petroleum Requirements* (Washington, D.C., Jan., Feb., Mar., Apr., June, July, Aug., Oct., 1948).

6. NPC, Preamble, *National Petroleum Emergency* (Washington, D.C., 1949), 65–66.

7. Charles Primoff, *Industry-Government Relationships in Emergency Petroleum and Gas Planning and Operations from Pre-World War II to the Present,* Student Research Report No. 131 (Washington, D.C.: Industrial College of the Armed Services, 1969), 67–69.

8. Bruce K. Brown, *Oil Men in Washington: An Informal Account of the Organization and Activities of the Petroleum Administration for Defense during the Korean War, 1950–1952* (Washington, D.C.: Evanil Press, 1965), 19–29; Primoff, *Industry-Government Relationships,* 69–70.

9. Primoff, *Industry-Government Relationships,* 70–73; for a detailed personal history of the PAD, see Brown, *Oil Men in Washington.*

10. Primoff, *Industry-Government Relationships,* 71–73; Brown, *Oil Men in Washington,* 57–71.

11. *Report of the National Petroleum Council's Committee on Government Oil and Gas Organization* (Washington, D.C., Dec. 3, 1953), 7–10.

12. Col. Ted E. Enter, director, Continuity of Industry Division, Office of Defense Mobilization, Minutes of the NPC, Mar. 23, 1954, p. 14; James Winfrey, interview by Joseph A. Pratt, Sept. 16, 1996, Houston, Tex. The Office of Defense Mobilization (ODM) created an Industrial Defense Committee, which included the Department of the Interior. The committee advised the ODM on policies, plans, and programs to reduce and overcome the effects on industry of a nuclear attack.

13. H. A. Stewart, acting deputy administrator, Petroleum Administration for Defense, to Walter S. Hallanan, Mar. 22, 1954, printed in NPC, *Report of the National Petroleum Council's Committee on Oil and Gas Emergency Defense Organization* (Washington, D.C., July 15, 1954); Minutes of the NPC, Mar. 23, 1954, p. 13.

14. NPC, *Report of the National Petroleum Council's Committee on Oil and Gas Emergency Defense Organization* (July 15, 1954).

15. Ibid.

16. NPC, *Disaster Planning for the Oil and Gas Industries* (Washington, D.C., May 5, 1955).

17. Minutes of the NPC, May 5, 1955, pp. 9–13.

18. NPC, *National Emergency Oil and Gas Mobilization* (Washington, D.C., 1959), 5–6; Primoff, *Industry-Government Relationships,* 129–31.

19. NPC, *National Emergency Oil and Gas Mobilization* (1959), 5–6.

20. National Petroleum Administration, *What Is the Emergency Petroleum and Gas Administration?* (Washington, D.C.: GPO, 1966), 5–7.

21. Ibid., 12–13.

22. The work of the NPC was mirrored by that of the Emergency Advisory Committee for Natural Gas. It prepared an emergency operations manual for the natural gas transmission industry and also a procedural manual for the gas divisions of the EPGA. See National Petroleum Council, *What Is the Emergency Petroleum and Gas Administration?* (1966), 12; Primoff, *Industry-Government Relationships,* 146.

23. NPC, *Voluntary Allocation Agreements* (Washington, D.C., Jan., Apr., 1948); Primoff, *Industry-Government Relationships,* 62–63, 100; Minutes of the NPC, Apr. 15, 1948, pp. 7–8.

24. Yergin, *The Prize,* 469–70.

25. Primoff, *Industry-Government Relationships,* 87–88.

26. Ibid., 106–108.

27. Ibid., 109–25.

28. Minutes of the NPC, Dec. 14, 1956, pp. 41–45.

29. Hugh A. Stewart, director, Office of Oil and Gas, Department of the Interior, Minutes of the NPC, Sept. 28, 1956, p. 9.

30. Primoff, *Industry-Government Relationships,* 114.

31. Ibid., 114–15.

32. Yergin, *The Prize,* 556–57.

33. The final report, *Emergency Preparedness for the Interruption of Petroleum Imports into the United States* (1974), and several interim reports produced earlier will be discussed in chap. 4.

34. NPC, *Industry Assistance to Government: Methods for Providing Petroleum Industry Expertise during Emergencies* (Washington, D.C., Jan., 1991); "Oil Industry Advises Government What to Do in Supply Emergency," *National Petroleum News* (Mar., 1991): 23–24; "A Furor over Stockpiling Oil," *Business Week,* Mar. 14, 1983, p. 26; John Guy, deputy executive director, NPC, interview by Joseph A. Pratt, Nov. 13, 1996, Washington, D.C.

35. NPC, *Securing Oil and Natural Gas Infrastructures in the New Economy* (Washington, D.C., June, 2001), 1.

36. Ibid., A-1.

37. Ibid., 11.

38. Ibid., 6.

39. Ibid., 7.

CHAPTER 3

1. Two of the most useful accounts of post–World War II energy policies are Vietor, *Energy Policy in America,* and Craufurd D. Goodwin, ed., *Energy Policy in Perspective: Today's Problems, Yesterday's Solutions* (Washington, D.C.: The Brookings Institution, 1981).

2. After publishing *U.S. Energy Outlook: An Initial Appraisal, 1971–1985,* in July, 1971, the NPC issued its final report, *U.S. Energy Outlook,* in December, 1972. In the next two years it released a series of ten reports by the task groups involved in the study: *Coal Availability, Energy Demand, Fuels for Electricity, Gas Demand, Gas Transportation, New Energy Forms, Oil Shale Availability, Nuclear Energy Availability, Oil and Gas Availability,* and *Water Availability.*

3. Petroleum Industry War Council, *A Petroleum Policy for the United States,* Oct. 24, 1945 (Washington, D.C., 1945), 3.

4. Agenda Committee Minutes, Dec. 10, 1946, p. 3.

5. Ibid., p. 4.

6. Eugene V. Rostow, *A National Policy for the Oil Industry* (New Haven: Yale University Press, 1948).

7. Vietor, *Energy Policy in America,* Goodwin, *Energy Policy in Perspective,* and Gerald Nash, *U.S. Oil Policy, 1890–1964* (Pittsburgh: University of Pittsburgh Press, 1968) discuss public policy toward oil in this era.

8. Max Ball to Walter Hallanan, June 15, 1948, File 1420, Agenda Committee, 1948, NPC Archives.

9. Minutes of first meeting of NPC Committee on Oil Policy, July 28, 1948, pp. 1–2.

10. Agenda Committee Minutes, Feb. 3, 1965, p. 6.

11. Minutes of first meeting of NPC Committee on Oil Policy, July 28, 1948, p. 2.

12. NPC, *A National Oil Policy for the United States* (Washington, D.C., 1949), 19.

13. Ibid., 2–19.
14. Ibid., 20.
15. Krug, as quoted in Goodwin, *Energy Policy in Perspective,* 99.
16. Quotations in the text come from an "unsent memorandum" quoted in Goodwin, *Energy Policy in Perspective,* 99–100.
17. U.S. Bureau of Mines, *Annual Report of the Secretary of Interior, 1949* (Washington, D.C., 1950), 143.
18. Richard H. K. Vietor, "The Synthetic Liquid Fuels Program: Energy Politics in the Truman Era," *Business History Review* (spring, 1980): 1–34; Vietor, *Energy Policy in America,* 44–63.
19. The various NPC reports on synthetic fuels were published as pamphlets between 1950 and 1955. These included the following, all of which were published by the NPC in Washington, D.C.: *Synthetic Liquid Fuels Production Costs* (1950), *Synthetic Liquid Fuels Production Costs* (May, July, Oct., 1951), *Synthetic Liquid Fuels Production Costs* (Jan., July, 1952), *Synthetic Liquid Fuels Production Costs* (1953), and *Shale Oil Policy* (1955).
20. Vietor, "Synthetic Liquid Fuels Program," 317.
21. NPC, *Synthetic Liquid Fuels Production Costs* (1953), 7.
22. John M. Kelly, assistant secretary of the interior, to Jake Hamon, chairman, NPC, Jan. 12, 1964, copy in Agenda Committee Minutes, 1965.
23. Agenda Committee Minutes, Feb. 3, 1965, p. 7.
24. Minutes of Meeting of Drafting Subcommittee of the NPC's Committee on National Oil Policy, Oct. 4, 5, 1965.
25. NPC, *Petroleum Policies for the United States* (Washington, D.C., 1966), 2.
26. Ibid., 4.
27. Goodwin, *Energy Policy in Perspective,* 405–406.
28. Douglas R. Bohi and Milton Russell, *Limiting Oil Imports: An Economic History and Analysis* (Baltimore: Johns Hopkins University Press, 1978). See also Robert L. Bradley, Jr., *The Mirage of Oil Protection* (New York: University Press of America, 1989), 46–70.
29. Cabinet Task Force on Import Control, *The Oil Import Question* (Washington, D.C.: GPO, 1970); Goodwin, *Energy Policy in Perspective,* 478.
30. Agenda Committee Minutes, Jan. 20, 1970, p. 10.
31. Ibid., p. 15.
32. NPC, *U.S. Energy Outlook* (Washington, D.C., 1972), 325.
33. John McLean, chairman of the Committee on U.S. Energy Outlook, report to NPC, July 15, 1971, Minutes of the NPC.
34. Ibid.
35. NPC, *U.S. Energy Outlook: An Initial Appraisal, 1971–1985,* 2 vols. (Washington, D.C., 1971), 1:1.
36. Ibid., 1:3.
37. Ibid., 1:25.
38. NPC, *U.S. Energy Outlook: A Summary Report of the National Petroleum Council* (Washington, D.C., 1972), 17–18.
39. Ibid., 1.
40. Richard Gonzalez to H. A. True, Nov. 20, 1972, Correspondence-Main Committee, Folder 6015, NPC Archives.
41. Notes from Main Committee Meeting, Apr. 6, 1972, Correspondence-Main Committee, Folder 6015, NPC Archives.
42. Ibid.

43. Ibid.
44. NPC, *U.S. Energy Outlook: A Summary Report*, p. 3.
45. Ibid., pp. 319–24.
46. "Historic NPC Study Lays Out U.S. Energy Options," *Oil & Gas Journal*, Dec. 12, 1972; "NPC Calls on Administration to Establish Industry Incentives," *World Oil*, Feb. 1, 1973, copies of both in Clippings File, NPC Archives.
47. Goodwin, *Energy Policy in Perspective*, 420–21.
48. Federal Energy Administration, *Project Independence: A Summary* (Washington, D.C., 1974), preface.
49. Rogers Morton to H. A. True, July 23, 1973, in NPC, *Energy Conservation in the United States: Short-Term Potential, an Interim Report of the National Petroleum Council* (Washington, D.C., 1974), 74.
50. Agenda Committee Minutes, July 23, 1973, pp. 24, 30.
51. "Report of the NPC Committee on Energy Conservation," Minutes of the NPC, Aug. 6, 1975.
52. The NPC reports on conservation are as follows: *Energy Conservation in the United States: Short-Term Potential, 1974–1978* (Interim Report) (Washington, D.C., Mar. 29, 1974); *Potential for Energy Conservation in the United States: 1974–1978* (Washington, D.C., Sept., 1974); Industrial, Residential/Commercial, Transportation, and Electric Utility Task Group Reports; and *Potential for Energy Conservation in the United States: 1979–1985* (Washington, D.C., Aug. 6, 1975).
53. NPC, *Potential for Energy Conservation, 1974–1978*, 3.
54. Agenda Committee Minutes, Aug. 5, 1975, p. 2.
55. Ibid., pp. 3–7, 20–21.
56. Ibid., pp. 5–6.

CHAPTER 4

1. The most thorough account of the SPR's history is Bruce Andre Beaubouef's "The Strategic Petroleum Reserve: U.S. Energy Security, Oil Politics, and Petroleum Reserves Policies in the Twentieth Century," Ph.D. diss., University of Houston, Aug., 1997. We thank him for his assistance on this chapter.
2. H. A. Stewart to Walter S. Hallanan, May 8, 1951, in "National Petroleum Council," Papers of Oscar Chapman, Box 98, Harry S. Truman Library, Independence, Mo.
3. NPC, *Underground Storage for Petroleum* (Washington, D.C., 1952), 1–8; Rodger L. Simons, "Underground Storage Proved Practical" and "Feasibility of Underground Storage Studied by NPC Committee," *World Petroleum* (July, 1952): 38–40; George C. Grow, Jr., "Survey of Underground Storage Facilities in the United States," in *Drilling and Production Practice: 1970* (Washington, D.C.: API, 1971), 267–78.
4. Walter J. Mead and Phillip E. Sorensen, "A National Defense Petroleum Reserve Alternative to Oil Import Quotas," *Land Economics* 47 (Aug., 1971): 211–24.
5. U.S. Congress, Senate Committee on Interior and Insular Affairs, *Strategic Petroleum Reserves*, 93rd Cong., 1st sess., May 30 and July 26, 1973 (Washington, D.C.: GPO, 1973), 2–16, 84–93, 101–106, 414, 422, 427.
6. NPC, *Emergency Preparedness for Interruption of Petroleum Imports into the United States: An Interim Report* (Washington, D.C.: July, 1973), 1–14.
7. Wakefield's letter requesting a new NPC study is reprinted in NPC, *Emergency Preparedness for Interruption of Petroleum Imports into the United States: A Supplemental Interim Report of the NPC* (Washington, D.C.: Nov. 15, 1973), 45.

8. Ibid., 5–9.

9. In December the council's Emergency Preparedness Committee published *Emergency Preparedness for Interruption of Petroleum Imports into the United States: Supplemental Papers to the Interim Report of Nov. 15, 1973* (Washington, D.C., 1973).

10. NPC, *Emergency Preparedness for Interruption of Petroleum Imports into the United States: A Report of the National Petroleum Council* (Washington, D.C., 1974), 7, 87–90.

11. NPC, *Emergency Preparedness: Interim Report* (Washington, D.C., 1973), 2.

12. Neil de Marchi, "The Ford Administration: Energy as a Political Good," in Goodwin, *Energy Policy in Perspective,* 482–87; Thomas H. Tietenberg, *Energy Planning and Policy: The Political Economy of Project Independence* (Lexington, Mass.: Lexington Books, 1976), 88–92.

13. NPC, Committee on Emergency Preparedness, *Petroleum Storage for National Security* (Washington, D.C., 1975), 119–20.

14. Agenda Committee Minutes, Jan. 28, 1975, pp. 15–20.

15. NPC, *Petroleum Storage for National Security,* 121–22.

16. Ibid., i–ii, 1, 7–8, 19, 21–23, 104, 107–108.

17. Ibid., ii.

18. Ibid.

19. Ibid., 107–12; see also, Edward Krapels, *Oil Crisis Management* (Baltimore: Johns Hopkins University Press, 1980).

20. NPC, *Petroleum Storage for National Security,* 1–8.

21. Ibid., i. Throughout this section on the SPR the authors have drawn on insights from John H. Guy, deputy executive director of the NPC, who was active in all of the SPR studies. See Guy interview by Pratt, Nov. 13, 1996.

22. U.S. Congress, *Energy Policy and Conservation Act of 1975* (hereafter cited as *EPCA*), Public Law 94-163, *Statutes at Large* 89 (Dec. 22, 1975), 89 Stat. 871-969 (Washington, D.C.: GPO, 1977); "Senate Considers Strategic Energy Reserves," *CQWR,* July 5, 1975, pp. 1437–38; "Senate Action: Energy Reserves," *CQWR,* July 12, 1975, p. 1503; "Final Energy Bill Faces Uncertain Fate," *CQWR,* Dec. 13, 1975, pp. 2689–93.

23. JRB Associates, Inc., *Final Report: Feasibility Study for Requiring Storage of Crude Oil, Residual Fuel Oil and/or Refined Petroleum Products by Industry,* submitted to the Federal Energy Administration (FEA) Dec. 2, 1976 (McLean, Va., 1976), 1–2; "Senate Action: Energy Reserves," *CQWR,* July 12, 1975, p. 1503; Frank Zarb, former FEA administrator, telephone interview by Bruce Andre Beaubouef, Jan. 28, 1997.

24. SPR Office/FEA, *Strategic Petroleum Reserve Plan,* Dec. 15, 1976 (Washington, D.C.: GPO, 1977), 7–11, 14, 15–16, 20, 23, 38–42, 45–66, 93–94, 67–104, 179, 195; SPR Office, DOE, *Strategic Petroleum Reserve Annual Report,* Feb. 15, 1996 (Washington, D.C., 1996), 18, 55.

25. SPR Office/FEA, *Strategic Petroleum Reserve Plan,* Dec. 15, 1976 (Washington, D.C.: GPO, 1977), 145, 146, 151–59; JRB Associates, Inc., *Final Report,* 1–2, 3, 2–5, 6, 2–8, 9, 2–42; "Second Thoughts on Oil Stockpiles," *Business Week,* Dec. 5, 1977, 36; U.S. Government Accounting Office, *Factors Influencing the Size of the U.S. Strategic Petroleum Reserve,* ID-79-8, June 15, 1979 (Washington, D.C., 1979), 18–22.

26. New England Federal Regional Council, "A Report on Emergency Petroleum Storage in New England" (Oct., 1976), in U.S. Congress, Senate, *Review of the Strategic Petroleum Reserve Plan,* 131–230.

27. SPR Office/FEA, *Strategic Petroleum Reserve Plan,* 16–17, 105–43.

28. SPR Office, DOE, "Impacts of Regulation on the Strategic Petroleum Reserve: A Selective Analysis," in U.S. Congress, House, *Strategic Petroleum Reserves: Oil Supply and Construction Problems,* hearing before the Subcommittee on Energy and Power, Committee on Interstate and Foreign Commerce, 96th Cong., 2nd sess., Sept. 10, 1979 (Washington, D.C.: GPO, 1980), 79–95; Ann Pelham, "Energy Department Trying to Work Out Problems of Costly Storage Program," *CQWR,* Feb. 3, 1979, pp. 204–205; W. A. Bachman, "Problems Plague U.S. Crude Storage Program," *Oil & Gas Journal,* Aug. 6, 1979, pp. 49–53; Robert G. Lawson, "Strategic Petroleum Reserve Construction Ends First Phase," *Oil & Gas Journal,* July 21, 1980, pp. 47–53.

29. NPC, Committee on Emergency Preparedness, *Emergency Preparedness for Interruption of Petroleum Imports into the United States* (Washington, D.C., Apr., 1981), A-1, 1–16, 99–134.

30. Ibid., 1–4.

31. Ibid., 11.

32. Ibid., 36–42.

33. Ibid., 10, 26.

34. Ibid., 10, 97, 98.

35. Ibid., 11.

36. Sheila Tefft, "U.S. Oil Reserve: Can It Really Deliver?" *Chicago Tribune,* May 6, 1984, sec. 7, pp. 1, 2; Andy Pasztor, "Persian Gulf Attacks Stir Debate on Distributing U.S. Oil Reserves," *Wall Street Journal,* May 24, 1984, sec. 2, p. 235.

37. Richard Johns, "Crude Stocks: Building Up a Panic Buffer," *Financial Times,* appearing in the *Houston Chronicle,* May 28, 1984, sec. 2, p. 2.

38. William E. Clayton, Jr., "Hodel Sees No Threat of Severe Oil Cutoff," *Houston Chronicle,* Mar. 25, 1984, sec. 1, p. 1; Jim Landers, "War's Intricacy Confounds Use of Oil Stockpile," *Dallas Morning News,* June 5, 1984, sec. D, pp. 15–16.

39. NPC, *The Strategic Petroleum Reserve: A Report on the Capability to Distribute SPR Oil* (Washington, D.C., Dec., 1984), A-1.

40. Ibid., 5–9.

41. Guy interview by Pratt, Nov. 13, 1996.

42. U.S. Congress, Senate, Committee on Energy and Natural Resources, *World Oil Outlook,* 101st Cong., 2nd sess., Mar. 26, 1990 (Washington, D.C.: GPO, 1990), 78–103; James R. Schlesinger, "Inherent Difficulties in Producer-Consumer Cooperation," *Energy Journal* 12, no. 2 (1991): 9, 10–15; Dilip Hiro, *Desert Shield to Desert Storm: The Second Gulf War* (London: HarperCollins, 1992); Lester H. Brune, *America and the Iraqi Crisis, 1990–1992: Origins and Aftermath* (Claremont, Calif.: Regina Books, 1993); Lawrence Freedman and Efraim Karsh, *The Gulf Conflict, 1990–1991: Diplomacy and War in the New World Order* (Princeton, N.J.: Princeton University Press, 1993); and Kevin Don Hutchison, *Operation Desert Shield/Desert Storm: Chronology and Fact Book* (Westport, Conn.: Greenwood Press, 1995).

43. NPC, *Industry Assistance to Government,* A-1.

44. NPC, *Short-Term Petroleum Outlook: An Examination of Issues and Projections* (Washington, D.C., Jan., 1991), A-1, 1–10.

45. Ibid., 6, 40.

46. Ibid., 6, 43.

47. Ibid., 7.

48. Ibid.

49. Ibid., 7–8.

50. "DOE Issues Sales Notice for Strategic Reserve Drawdown," *DOE News*, Jan. 17, 1991, p. 2; "President Directs Drawdown of Strategic Reserve," *DOE News*, Jan. 16, 1991, pp. 1, 2.

51. "DOE Receives Bids from 26 Companies to Purchase Strategic Reserve Oil," *DOE News*, Jan. 28, 1991, p. 1 ("The response"); "DOE Selects 13 Firms Offering Best Prices for Crude Oil from Strategic Reserve Sale," *DOE News*, Jan. 30, 1991, pp. 1–3; "First Oil Shipped from the Strategic Petroleum Reserve," *DOE News*, Feb. 5, 1991, pp. 1, 2; "Energy Department Completes First Emergency Sale of 17.3 Million Barrels of Strategic Reserve Crude Oil," *DOE News*, Apr. 3, 1991, p. 2.

52. Michael Davis, "Debate Rages Above, But All Is Quiet Below," *Houston Chronicle*, Sept. 23, 2000, pp. 1-D, 3-D.

CHAPTER 5

1. NPC, *Current Key Issues Relating to Environmental Conservation—The Oil and Gas Industries-Interim Report* (Washington, D.C., 1970), Appendix A.

2. Transcript, NPC Agenda Committee, Apr. 16, 1969, pp. 40–43.

3. Ibid., pp. 40–43.

4. Ibid., pp. 43–52.

5. Ibid., pp. 50–54; Report, NPC Agenda Committee, Apr. 16, 1969, Proceedings Agenda Committee Apr. 16, 1969, file, NPC Archives.

6. Progress Report, Committee on Environmental Conservation—The Oil and Gas Industries, Jan. 21, 1970, 6970 Progress Reports file, NPC Archives.

7. NPC, *Current Key Issues Relating to Environmental Conservation—Interim Report*, June 22, 1970, pp. 1–5.

8. Ibid., pp. 11–27.

9. NPC, *Environmental Conservation—The Oil and Gas Industries*, 2 vols. (Washington, D.C., 1971), 1:16–18.

10. Ibid.

11. Ibid., 1:18–20.

12. Ibid., 1:20–22; Report of the Committee on Environmental Conservation—The Oil and Gas Industries, Feb. 10, 1972, NPC Minutes, in Minutes of Council Meetings, 1966–73, NPC Archives.

13. NPC, *U.S. Energy Outlook: A Summary Report of the National Petroleum Council* (Washington, D.C., 1972), 77–78.

14. NPC, *Environmental Conservation—The Oil and Gas Industries* (Washington, D.C., 1982), 465–68.

15. Ibid.

16. Ibid.; NPC, *U.S. Petroleum Refining—Meeting the Requirements for Cleaner Fuels and Refineries* (Washington, D.C., 1993).

17. Transcript, Agenda Committee Meeting, May 23, 1980, pp. 71–75.

18. Ibid., pp. 75–84.

19. Minutes of the coordinating subcommittee, Committee on Environmental Conservation, Sept. 10, 1980, 6971 C.S.C. Minutes—Environment file, NPC Archives.

20. Transcript of Meeting, Committee on Environmental Conservation, Sept. 23, 1980, pp. 1–16.

21. Ibid., p. 116.

22. Transcript of Meeting, Committee on Environmental Conservation, Mar. 9, 1982, pp. 14–15.

23. NPC, *Environmental Conservation—The Oil and Gas Industries* (1982), 1–2.

24. Ibid.. 3–4.

25. Ibid.

26. Ibid., 5–7.

27. NPC, *Environmental Conservation—The Oil and Gas Industries* (1971), 1:16–18.

28. NPC, *Environmental Conservation—The Oil and Gas Industries* (1982), 8.

29. Ibid., 8–9.

30. Ibid., 8–9, 466–70.

31. Ibid., 9–10.

32. Ibid., 10–11.

33. NPC, *The Oil Pollution Act of 1990—An Interim Report* (Washington, D.C., 1993), 1–2.

34. Ibid., 1–2.

35. Ibid., 11–21. On Oct. 18, 1991, President George Bush signed Executive Order No. 12777. It delegated jurisdiction over non-transportation-related offshore facilities and certain aspects of transportation-related pipelines that linked offshore production platforms to onshore facilities to the secretary of the interior, who delegated them to the Minerals Management Service (MMS).

36. NPC, *The Oil Pollution Act of 1990—An Interim Report* (1993), 18–23.

37. Ibid., 18–23.

38. Ibid., 9.

39. Transcript, Meeting of NPC Committee on the Oil Pollution Act, Nov. 3, 1993, pp. 5–19, OPA MC Transcripts file, NPC Archives.

40. Ibid., pp. 5–23, 26–53.

41. Minutes, Subcommittee of NPC on Oil Pollution Act of 1990, Nov. 10–11, 1993, OPA Subcommittee, Book 1, NPC Archives.

42. NPC, *The Oil Pollution Act of 1990—An Interim Report* (1993), 1–4, 11–26.

43. Ibid., 6–7, 38–42.

44. Ibid., 6–7.

45. Transcript, Meeting of NPC Committee on the Oil Pollution Act, Dec. 1, 1993, pp. 39–43, OPA MC Transcripts file, NPC Archives.

46. Ibid., pp. 47–60, 68–73.

47. Ibid., pp. 78–82.

48. Minutes, Subcommittee of NPC on Oil Pollution Act of 1990, Mar. 23, 1994, OPA Subcommittee, Book 1, NPC Archives.

49. NPC, *The Oil Pollution Act of 1990—Issues and Solutions* (Washington, D.C., 1994), 67–80.

50. Ibid., 80–89.

51. Since its inception in 1946 the NPC had undertaken the following studies of petroleum refining: *Petroleum Refining Capacity* (1947), *Petroleum Refining Capacity* (1948), *Petroleum Refining Capacity* (1949), *U.S. Refining Capacity* (1957), *Critical Materials Requirements for Petroleum Refining* (1966), *Factors Affecting U.S. Petroleum Refining* (1973), *Refinery Flexibility* (1980), *U.S. Petroleum Refining* (1986), *Petroleum Refining in the 1990s—Meeting the Challenges of the Clean Air Act* (1991), and *U.S. Petroleum Refining—Meeting Requirements for Cleaner Fuels and Refineries* (1993).

52. NPC, *U.S. Petroleum Refining—Meeting Requirements for Cleaner Fuels and Refineries,* 1:9–12.

53. Ibid., 1:9–15.

54. Ibid., 1:4–5.

55. Transcript, Agenda Committee Meeting, July 18, 1990, pp. 51–54, 60–62.
56. Ibid., pp. 50–53, 62–63.
57. Ibid., pp. 50–57.
58. Ibid., pp. 53–73.
59. Preliminary Draft of Scope Paper, NPC Committee on Refining, Proposed Study, Scope, Organization, and Timetable, Study: The U.S. Refining Sector in the 1990s, Sept. 14, 1990, NPC Refining Study, Coordinating Subcommittee, Book 1, NPC Archives.
60. Ibid.
61. Minutes, Coordinating Subcommittee, NPC Committee on Refining, Dec. 3, 1990, NPC Refining Study, Coordinating Subcommittee, Book 1, NPC Archives.
62. Ibid.; NPC, *Petroleum Refining in the 1990s—Meeting the Challenges of the Clean Air Act* (Washington, D.C., 1991), C:55–56; Bill Finger, interview by Joseph A. Pratt, Sept. 13, 1996, Friendswood, Tex.
63. Minutes, Coordinating Subcommittee, NPC Committee on Refining, Dec. 3, 1990.
64. Minutes, Coordinating Subcommittee, NPC Committee on Refining, Feb. 25, 1991.
65. Ibid.
66. Memorandum, Nichols to Cook, "NPC 1991 and 1992 Budget Estimates," 1991 Finance Book, NPC Archives.
67. Minutes, Coordinating Subcommittee, NPC Committee on Refining, Mar. 27, 1991.
68. NPC, *Petroleum Refining in the 1990s—Meeting the Challenges of the Clean Air Act,* 1–5.
69. Ibid.; NPC, *U.S. Petroleum Refining—Meeting Requirements for Cleaner Fuels and Refineries,* 2:54–55.
70. NPC, *Petroleum Refining in the 1990s—Meeting the Challenges of the Clean Air Act,* 7–8.
71. Minutes, Coordinating Subcommittee, NPC Committee on Refining, Apr. 18, 1991.
72. Minutes, Coordinating Subcommittee, NPC Committee on Refining, June 26, 1991.
73. Ibid.; Memorandum, NPC Flash Number 1 (for week ending June 7, 1991), Nichols to Hunt, June 7, 1991; Memorandum, NPC Flash Number 5 (for week ending July 5, 1991), Nichols to Hunt, July 5, 1991; Memorandum, NPC Flash Number 14 (for week ending Sept. 6, 1991), Nichols to Hunt, Sept. 6, 1991; Memorandum, NPC Flash Number 16 (for week ending Sept. 20, 1991), Nichols to Hunt, Sept. 24, 1991, all in 1100 Chairman Hunt Flash Memos file, NPC Archives.
74. Study on the U.S. Refining Sector in the 1990s, Progress Report to the NPC, Apr. 9, 1992, NPC Refining Study, Coordinating Subcommittee, Book 2, NPC Archives.
75. Minutes, Coordinating Subcommittee, NPC Committee on Refining, May 19, 1992, July 9, 1992, and Aug. 19, 1992, NPC Refining Study, Coordinating Subcommittee, Book 2; Memorandum, NPC Flash Number 48 (for July 6–17, 1992), Nichols to Hunt, July 17, 1992, 1100 Chairman Hunt Flash Memos file, NPC Archives.
76. Minutes, Coordinating Subcommittee, NPC Committee on Refining, Oct. 21–22, 1992.
77. Memorandum, NPC Flash Number 49 (for July 20–31, 1992), Guy to Hunt, Aug. 3, 1992, 1100 Chairman Hunt Flash Memos file, NPC Archives.
78. Letter, Hunt to Hazel O'Leary, Aug. 30, 1993, in NPC, *U.S. Petroleum Refining—Meeting Requirements for Cleaner Fuels and Refineries,* 1-A.
79. Ibid.
80. Ibid.
81. NPC, *U.S. Petroleum Refining: Assuring the Adequacy and Affordability of Cleaner Fuels* (Washington, D.C., 2000), 1-A.

82. Ibid., 3-A.
83. Ibid., 2-A.
84. Ibid., 1-A.
85. Ibid., 3-A.
86. Ibid., 2.

CHAPTER 6

1. NPC, *National Oil Policy for the United States,* 14–15. For overviews of the natural gas industry's history, see Christopher J. Castaneda, *Invisible Fuel: Manufactured and Natural Gas in America, 1880–2000* (New York: Twayne Publishers, 1999); and Arlon R. Tussing and Bob Tippee, eds., *The Natural Gas Industry: Evolution, Structure, and Economics,* 2nd ed. (Tulsa: PennWell Books, 1995). Two perspectives of natural gas regulation are presented in M. Elizabeth Sanders, *The Regulation of Natural Gas: Policy and Politics, 1938–1978* (Philadelphia: Temple University Press, 1981); and Bradley, *Oil, Gas, and Government.* For the Phillips case, see *Phillips Petroleum Co.* v. *Wisconsin,* 347 US. 672 (1954).
2. NPC, *Petroleum Policies for the United States,* 1, 6; Agenda Committee Minutes, Feb. 3, 1966, 1420 Proceedings Agenda Meeting 2/3/66 file, NPC Archives.
3. Agenda Committee Minutes, Jan. 20, 1970, 1420 Proceedings Agenda Committee Meeting file, NPC Archives.
4. Ibid.
5. NPC, *U.S. Energy Outlook: A Summary Report of the National Petroleum Council* (Washington, D.C., 1972), 85–106.
6. Ibid., 3–6, 42–43.
7. Ibid., 6–8.
8. Ibid., 7.
9. Vietor, *Energy Policy in America,* 272–78.
10. Jack W. Carlson to Swearingen, Mar. 17, 1975, attached to Agenda Committee Minutes, Mar. 18, 1975, 1420 Agenda Committee FY 75 file, NPC Archives.
11. Agenda Committee Minutes, Mar. 18, 1975.
12. Vietor, *Energy Policy in America,* 282–83; NPC, *Factors affecting U.S. Oil & Gas Outlook* (Washington, D.C., 1987), 58.
13. NPC, *Factors affecting U.S. Oil & Gas Outlook,* 58–60.
14. Ibid., 59–60.
15. NPC, *Unconventional Gas Sources, Executive Summary,* (Washington, D.C., 1980), 1-A–3-A.
16. Ibid., 25–26; NPC, *The Potential for Natural Gas in the United States,* 6 vols. (Washington, D.C., 1992), 2:97–100.
17. NPC, *Unconventional Gas Sources, Executive Summary,* 1–9; NPC, *Unconventional Gas Sources,* 5 vols. (Washington, D.C., 1980), 1:188–90.
18. NPC, *Unconventional Gas Sources, Executive Summary,* 25–32.
19. NPC, *The Potential for Natural Gas in the United States,* 2:11–12, 97–100.
20. NPC, *Factors Affecting U.S. Oil & Gas Outlook,* 1-A.
21. Transcript, Agenda Committee Meeting, Oct. 15, 1985, 1420 Agenda Committee, Oct. 15, 1985, file, NPC Archives.
22. NPC, *U.S. Oil & Gas Outlook (Interim Report)* (Washington, D.C.: Author, 1986), 5–6, 1-C, 2-C.

23. Ibid., 1–2, 20–24.
24. Ibid., 20–24.
25. NPC, *Factors Affecting U.S. Oil & Gas Outlook,* 167, 175–77.
26. Ibid., 175–77.
27. Ibid., 167–79.
28. Ibid., 173–75.
29. Ibid., 117–26.
30. Ibid., 117–26, 175.
31. In 1992 a Natural Gas Council was formed, but this was not an advisory committee under FACA. Initially the Natural Gas Council included eighteen industry executives from all segments of the industry and the presidents of the American Gas Association, Natural Gas Supply Association, Interstate Natural Gas Association of America, and Gas Research Institute. See "Natural Gas Council Announces Goals," *American Gas* (Sept., 1992): 36.
32. "DOE Boosts Natural Gas Membership on the National Petroleum Council," *DOE News,* May 11, 1990, p. 1.
33. James Watkins to Cook, June 25, 1990, in NPC, *The Potential for Natural Gas in the United States,* 1:1-A.
34. Transcript, Agenda Committee Meeting, July 18, 1990, pp. 18–24.
35. Ibid., pp. 30–34.
36. Ibid., pp. 36–49.
37. Larry Smith, interview by Joseph A. Pratt, Sept. 4, 1996, Houston, Tex.
38. Transcript, Meeting of the NPC, Jan. 23, 1991, pp. 65–69, 1200 Proceedings of 97th Meeting 1/23/91 file, NPC Archives.
39. Memorandum, "Potential for Expanding Natural Gas Production, Distribution and Use," Nov. 1, 1990, 2376 Coordinating Subcommittee file, NPC Archives.
40. Ibid.
41. Ibid.
42. Ibid.; Memorandum, "Potential for Expanding Natural Gas Production, Distribution, and Use," Jan. 23, 1991, Coordinating Subcommittee, Natural Gas, Book 1, General, NPC Archives.
43. Minutes, Coordinating Subcommittee, Natural Gas, Jan. 21 and 22, 1991, 2376 Minutes/Transcripts Coordinating Subcommittee—Natural Gas file, NPC Archives.
44. Minutes, Coordinating Subcommittee, Natural Gas, Feb. 13, 1991.
45. Minutes, Coordinating Subcommittee, Natural Gas, May 22, 1991.
46. Minutes, Coordinating Subcommittee, Natural Gas, July 17, 1991; Memorandum, NPC Flash Number 2 (for week ending June 14, 1991), Nichols to Hunt, June 14, 1991; Memorandum, NPC Flash Number 8 (for week ending July 26, 1991), Nichols to Hunt, July 26, 1991, both memoranda in 1100 Chairman Hunt Flash Memos file, NPC Archives.
47. Memorandum, NPC Flash Number 14 (for week ending Sept. 6, 1991), Nichols to Hunt, Sept. 6, 1991; Memorandum, NPC Flash Number 15 (for week ending Sept. 13, 1991), Nichols to Hunt, Sept. 13, 1991, both in 1100 Chairman Hunt Flash Memos file, NPC Archives.
48. Memorandum, NPC Flash Number 18 (for week ending Oct. 4, 1991), Nichols to Hunt, Oct. 7, 1991; Memorandum, NPC Flash Number 16 (for week ending Sept. 20, 1991), Nichols to Hunt, Sept. 24, 1991, both in 1100 Chairman Hunt Flash Memos file, NPC Archives.

49. Memorandum, NPC Flash Number 9 (for week ending Aug. 2, 1991), Nichols to Hunt, Aug. 2, 1991, 1100 Chairman Hunt Flash Memos file, NPC Archives.

50. Memorandum, Nichols to Coordinating Subcommittee and Task Groups of the Committee on Natural Gas, Aug. 9, 1991, 2376 Beaver Creek, Oct. 14, 1991, Mgt. file, NPC Archives.

51. Memorandum and attachments, L. L. Smith, Oct. 14, 1991, 2376 Beaver Creek, Oct. 14, 1991, Mgt. file, NPC Archives.

52. Memorandum, NPC Flash Number 19 (for Oct. 7–18, 1991), Nichols to Hunt, Oct. 18, 1991, 1100 Chairman Hunt Flash Memos file, NPC Archives.

53. Memorandum, NPC Flash Number 22 (for week ending Nov. 8, 1991), Nichols to Hunt, Nov. 11, 1991; Memorandum, NPC Flash Number 24 (for week ending Nov. 22, 1991), Nichols to Hunt, Nov. 22, 1991; Memorandum, NPC Flash Number 26 (for week ending Dec. 6, 1991), Nichols to Hunt, Dec. 9, 1991, all in 1100 Chairman Hunt Flash Memos file, NPC Archives.

54. Memorandum, NPC Flash Number 24 (for week ending Nov. 22, 1991), Nichols to Hunt, Nov. 22, 1991, 1100 Chairman Hunt Flash Memos file, NPC Archives.

55. Memorandum, NPC Flash Number 23 (for week ending Nov. 15, 1991), Nichols to Hunt, Nov. 15, 1991, 1100 Chairman Hunt Flash Memos file, NPC Archives.

56. Memorandum, NPC Flash Number 25 (for week ending Nov. 29, 1991), Nichols to Hunt, Nov. 29, 1991, 1100 Chairman Hunt Flash Memos file, NPC Archives.

57. Memorandum, NPC Flash Number 19 (for Oct. 7–18, 1991), Nichols to Hunt, Oct. 18, 1991.

58. Memorandum, NPC Flash Number 26 (for week ending Dec. 6, 1991), Nichols to Hunt, Dec. 9, 1991.

59. The Strawman and Scarecrow cases became reference case one and reference case two. In reference case one, a higher demand scenario, it was assumed that the price of a barrel of oil rises to $28 ($1990s) in 2010 and the natural gas equivalent is $3.50/MMBTU. In reference case two, a lower demand scenario, oil rises to $20 a barrel ($1990s) in 2010 and the natural gas equivalent is $2.50/MMBTU.

60. Memorandum, NPC Flash Number 27 (for Dec. 9–20, 1991), Nichols to Hunt, Dec. 20, 1991; Memorandum, NPC Flash Number 28 (for Jan. 1–10, 1992), Nichols to Hunt, Dec. 20, 1991, both in 1100 Chairman Hunt Flash Memos file, NPC Archives.

61. Memorandum, NPC Flash Number 33 (for Feb. 10–21, 1992), Nichols to Hunt, Feb. 24, 1992; Memorandum, NPC Flash Number 34 (for week ending Feb. 28, 1992), Nichols to Hunt, Mar. 2, 1992, both in 1100 Chairman Hunt Flash Memos file, NPC Archives.

62. Memorandum, NPC Flash Number 36 (for week ending Mar. 13, 1992), Guy to Hunt, Mar. 16, 1992; Memorandum, NPC Flash Number 33 (for Feb. 10–21, 1992), Nichols to Hunt, Feb. 24, 1992, both in 1100 Chairman Hunt Flash Memos file, NPC Archives.

63. Memorandum, NPC Flash Number 38 (for Mar. 30–Apr. 10, 1992), Nichols to Hunt, Apr. 14, 1992; Memorandum, NPC Flash Number 44 (for week ending May 29, 1992), Nichols to Hunt, June 1, 1992; Memorandum, NPC Flash Number 39 (for week ending Apr. 17, 1992), Nichols to Hunt, Apr. 23, 1992, all in 1100 Chairman Hunt Flash Memos file, NPC Archives.

64. Memorandum, NPC Flash Number 42 (for May 4–15, 1992), Nichols to Hunt, May 15, 1992, 1100 Chairman Hunt Flash Memos file, NPC Archives; NPC, *The Potential for Natural Gas in the United States,* 1:127.

65. Memorandum, NPC Flash Number 48 (for July 6–17, 1992), Nichols to Hunt, July 17, 1992.

66. Memorandum, NPC Flash Number 49 (for July 20–31, 1992), Guy to Hunt, Aug. 3, 1992.

67. Ibid.

68. Memorandum, NPC Flash Number 46 (for week ending June 19, 1992), Nichols to Hunt, June 19, 1992, 1100 Chairman Hunt Flash Memos file, NPC Archives.

69. Hunt to Watkins, Dec. 17, 1992, in NPC, *The Potential for Natural Gas in the United States,* vol. 1, n.p.

70. NPC, *The Potential for Natural Gas in the United States,* 1:1–5.

71. Ibid., 1:4–6.

72. Ibid.

73. Ibid., 1:8, 2:231–51.

74. NPC, *The Potential for Natural Gas in the United States,* 1:8–9, 71–89.

75. Ibid., 1:6–7.

76. Ibid., 1:9–10, 107–17.

77. Transcript, Press Conference, Dec. 17, 1992, pp. 1–9, 1200 Proceedings 12/17/92 Meeting file, NPC Archives.

78. NPC, *The Potential for Natural Gas in the United States,* 1:10–14.

79. Ibid., 1:14–15.

80. NPC, *The Potential for Natural Gas in the United States,* 1:14–15, 3:83–114, 3:139–45.

81. Ibid., 1:15–16, 112–14.

82. Ibid., 1:15–16, 5:30–31.

83. Ibid., 1:16–17.

84. Ibid., 1:17–18.

85. Ibid., 1:17–18, 122–27.

86. Ibid., 1:18–19, 129–49.

87. Ibid., 1:20–21, 151–62.

88. Ibid., 1:19–20, 119–27.

89. Ibid., 1:20, 119–27.

90. Ibid., 1:21.

91. Ibid., 1:21–22, 161–67.

92. Ibid., 1:22–24, 161–67, 187–90; Transcript, Meeting of NPC, Dec. 17, 1992, pp. 53–55, 1200 12/17/92 Meeting Transcript file, NPC Archives.

93. NPC, *The Potential for Natural Gas in the United States,* 1:22–23.

94. NPC, *Meeting the Challenges of the Nation's Growing Natural Gas Demand,* 3 vols. (Washington, D.C., 1999), 1:A-1.

95. Ibid., 1:3.

96. Ibid., 1:A-2.

97. Ibid., 1:5–7.

98. Ibid., 1:7–24.

99. Ibid., 1:53.

100. Ibid., 1:25–30.

CHAPTER 7

1. NPC, *Future Issues: A View of U.S. Oil & Natural Gas to 2020* (Washington, D.C., 1995), 1.

2. Ibid., 17.

3. Ibid., 17–21.

4. Ibid., 20–22.
5. Ibid., 23–26.
6. Ibid., 26–32.
7. Ibid., 28.
8. Ibid., 3–32.
9. Ibid., 32–33.
10. Ibid., 33–34.
11. Ibid., 35.
12. Ibid., 5–6, 35–38.
13. Department of Energy, *Priority List of Potential, Focused Study Topics for the National Petroleum Council* (Washington, D.C., 1997).
14. Bill Richardson to Joe B. Foster, Sept. 1, 1998, NPC Archives.
15. NPC, *Future Issues,* 35.
16. For a provocative discussion of such changes in the 1990s see Daniel Yergin and Joseph Stanislaw, *The Commanding Heights: The Battle between Government and the Marketplace That Is Remaking the Modern World* (New York: Simon & Schuster, 1988).

Index

ISBN 1-58544-185-6

90000